The Transgender Guidebook:

Keys to a Successful Transition

Anne L. Boedecker, PhD

The Transgender Guidebook: Keys to a Successful Transition

ISBN-13: 978-1461006206
ISBN-10: 1461006201

Book cover design: Lisa Swanson
Illustrations: Andrew Stearns

In Memory of:

Jennifer C.
(1958 - 2008)

Louis H.
(1967 - 2005)

Acknowledgments

Welcome! If you are reading this you are probably either:

a) questioning your gender identity or thinking about transitioning,
b) somewhere along the way on your own gender transformation,
c) trying to understand (and hopefully support) someone who is,
d) working in a field that cares for or caters to transgender people, or
e) just plain curious about what's involved in changing genders.

In any case, if you continue reading you are in for a fascinating ride. Just in picking up this book you have made the decision to step outside the box. You have some inkling that gender is more complex than most of us ever imagined, and are willing to consider that it is not a fixed binary attribute of human beings. Congratulations!

I am immensely grateful for the opportunity I have had to journey with the many transgender clients and friends I have known over the past 15 years. It has been a meaningful and deeply rewarding experience. To watch someone blossom from a scared, confused or conflicted person into a happy self-assured man or woman is a great joy. I cannot of course name the clients I have guided through their transitions. I just hope they know how much I appreciate their trust and confidence. I am deeply indebted to all of them. I am honored to be a part of their lives.

I am also deeply indebted to my writing coach, Leanne McCall Tigert. She has been a mentor, guide, gentle taskmaster, and witness to my growing pains as a writer.

Several other authors have provided me with support and guidance. Anne-Marie Bennett has been a steadfast cheerleader from the beginning and gave me helpful advice about self-publishing. Arlene Istar Lev has also been an inspiration and a tremendous support. Reid Vanderburgh provided valuable insights and feedback on sections of the book.

I am grateful to the community of therapists, physicians, researchers, and other members of the World Professional Association for Transgender Health. They are a uniquely dedicated and caring group of professionals.

This book would not be possible without the support of the many friends - too many to list - who have cheered me on. I would like to especially acknowledge the support of my comrades at the Unitarian Universalist Church of Manchester, NH. Special thanks go to John Angelo for his patient proofreading and Lisa Swanson for her book cover design.

I'd also like to acknowledge the time and talent of a wonderful young artist, Andrew Stearns, who provided the illustrations.

And last but not least I am deeply grateful for the unwavering support of my husband, Bevan C. Tulk. His faith in me sustained me whenever mine wavered.

Table of Contents

Prologue

PART ONE: PREPARATION

PART TWO: INITIATION

PART THREE: SEPARATION

PART FOUR: TRANSFORMATION

Prologue

I received a call in the summer of 1998 that changed my work from a profession into a true calling. It was from the Executive Director of the New Hampshire Psychological Association, with a referral request. "I just got off the phone with someone who's looking for a gender therapist, and with your background and interests I thought of you." I didn't know at the time what a gender specialist was, but after hearing more about the situation I agreed to meet with the person and see if I could help. My only external qualifications were a degree in Human Development, licensure as a clinical psychologist, courses and workshops on Human Sexuality, and experience working with sexual minorities. I had always been aware that there were some people who were born with a different sense of their gender identity than what one would expect, and I had always been open and accepting of gay, lesbian and bisexual clients. It turns out that my real qualifications were an open mind (and heart), a preference for non-dualistic thinking, and a genuine appreciation for the complexity and diversity of human experience.

When I saw "Chris" in the waiting room I had a moment of confusion. I thought the referral was a female wishing to transition to a male gender role, and the person in front of me already looked like a man! He had a deep voice, large frame, and facial hair. This was my first introduction to the complexity of gender variance. Chris was indeed assigned a female gender at birth, but at adolescence had the beginnings of masculine secondary sex characteristics. He had identified as lesbian for many years, but found that didn't really fit. He was here to figure out who he was, and how to become whole.

Chris brought with him a stack of material he had been able to find on transsexuals, including the Harry Benjamin International Gender Dysphoria Association Standards of Care. We agreed that we would look into this together, and began a therapeutic relationship that lasted until his death from a heart attack in 2005. He referred friends with similar issues, who referred friends, and word got out that there was someone willing and able to help people wanting to transition. By September of 2002 I had enough transgender referrals to start a support group for female-identified trans-gender people, which has run continuously ever since.

Since then I have counseled many transgender clients and family members, befriended others, read volumes, attended workshops and conferences, testified in support of Transgender Rights bills, and given talks and workshops to a variety of groups. My clients' ages have ranged from seven to 72, and have included MtF (male-to-female), FtM (female-to-male), intersex, and androgynous individuals. My clients have come from all over New Hampshire, as well as Massachusetts, Maine and Vermont. I have journeyed with many through the transition process to a successful com-pletion of their gender transformation.

I decided to write this book when I found myself wishing I had something to hand to clients that gave practical advice about transitioning. I couldn't find the kind of book I wanted them to have. I realized that I had accumu-lated a lot of information and experience from my work, and could probably write it myself. It's been an ambitious undertaking, but I've had a lot of encouragement. I hope you find it useful. As they say in AA: Take what you need and leave the rest.

Caveats and Disclaimers

First and Foremost: This book is not a substitute for medical advice and/or guidance by a gender specialist. I am a Licensed Psychologist, and a gender specialist by training and experience. I am not a medical doctor. If you are looking to transition physically, you must seek out a qualified therapist and a supportive physician. (For more on how to find them, see Chapter Six.)

Second: This book is also not a substitute for doing your own research. The information in this book is drawn from several sources:
    a) books and articles written primarily by and for professionals,
    b) web sites and books written primarily by and for transsexuals,
    c) my personal and professional experience with the many trans gender individuals I have had the good fortune to meet.

It is not possible to read everything written on the subject, or keep abreast of all the recent developments that could be relevant for you. My experience is limited to transgender clients in northern New England. I live and practice in an area that is predominantly white and fairly rural. I have not had the opportunity to work with many transgender men or women of color. Legal issues vary from state to state, and are constantly changing. By the time this book goes to print, much of what I've written about legal gender changes will be out-of-date.

Third:, I am a cisgendered woman, which means that my gender identity matches the body I was born into and the gender assigned to me at birth. I have always considered myself somewhat gender-variant, or gender-defiant, as I call it. I was very much a tomboy growing up, and had no use for dolls or dresses. I did my best to break every gender-based rule possible. But I have never experienced the profound gender dysphoria and distress that most transgender persons do, or the discrimination that affects anyone with an atypical gender presentation. I cannot tell you from personal experience what it's like to transition. On the other hand, I have lots of experience developing a feminine gender presentation that didn't come totally naturally.

Fourth: This book cannot tell you if you are a "real" transsexual or not, or whether you can or should transition. Defining who you are and how you want to present to the world is a very individual decision. Nobody can tell you who/what you are. There are as many transgender identities as there are people who feel they don't fit the mold of their assigned gender. Nor should anyone tell you that you should or should not transition. I don't assume that everyone with gender dysphoria needs or wants to make a complete social or physical change. Hopefully this book can answer some questions for you about gender identity and the transition process, and make your path clearer to you.

Fifth: English, like most languages, is a gendered language. There's been a lot of heated discussion about terminology and the use of gendered pronouns. I have attempted to be both as specific as possible and as respectful as possible in my use of language. There's no easy way to get around using he/him/his and she/her/hers, and I may refer to someone at times using their assigned gender in reference to his or her experience before beginning transition. If I use acronyms such as MtF and FtM, please understand that I am using them to refer to people going through a particular process, not someone's basic identity. I will use transgender people, or transmen and transwomen, as inclusive of transgender, trans-sexual, and gender nonconforming individuals. I would like to acknowledge and include every gender identity variation but to do so in each sentence would become too cumbersone. Also, the terminology acceptable today may offend someone tomorrow. I have a glossary of common terms at the end of Chapter Two that gives the definitions I will be using. I have tried to keep these up-to-date, knowing that other writers may be using these terms differently.

Sixth: I will use examples from my experience with clients, family, and friends, as well as stories I have heard or read. To protect confidentiality and privacy, I will use pseudonyms, and will change identifying characteristics that are not relevant to the discussion. Some stories may be a composite of different peoples' experience. I have also informed clients that I am writing a book, and have asked permission to share stories wherever possible.

Seventh: This book is geared to adults and mature adolescents who are exploring their gender identity. There is a wonderful book by Stephanie Brill and Rachel Pepper called *The Transgender Child*. If you are concerned about a child or early adolescent with gender issues, their book is the best place to start. There are also organizations listed in the Resources section that deal specifically with transgender youth and their families.

Eighth: This book is incomplete. There's a saying attributed to Paul Valery: An artist never really finishes his work; he merely abandons it. There's much more I could write, but it's time for me to send this out into the world. I do, however, plan two sequels: *The Transgender Workbook for the Male to Female Transition* and *The Transgender Workbook for the Female to Male Transition*. These will be spiral bound and/or available as e-books. For more information, visit: www.sitbyme.com. You can also follow my blog at thetransgenderguidebook.wordpress.com.

PART ONE

PREPARATION

The Transgender Guidebook

Chapter One

The Hero's Journey

A personal myth delineates an identity, illuminating the values of an individual life. The personal myth is not a legend or fairy tale, but a sacred story that embodies personal truth.[1]

Dan P. McAdams

Everyone who starts to question their gender identity and/or consider changing their gender presentation is embarking on a Hero's Journey. The metaphor of a journey is often used to describe transitioning. But a Hero's Journey is a mythic theme that serves as a more helpful framework for a gender transformation. Anyone undertaking the transition from one gender to another is a true Hero. (By Hero I mean Hero *or* Heroine.) Many of you reading this will balk or even cringe at this notion. I've had many clients protest when people tell them they're "so brave" to do what they're doing. "I'm not brave - I'm scared shitless! I'm just doing what I have to do!" That is exactly what a Hero says! Most heroes are Reluctant Heroes, called to do something they just have to do.

---

[1] Dan P. McAdams, *The Stories We Live By: Personal Myths and the Making of the Self,* Guilford Press, 1993

The essence of a Hero's Journey is that the hero must leave his/her familiar world and venture into unknown territory in search of something more valuable than safety and security - his/her True Self. Through the trials and tribulations of this journey the hero is transformed, and returns a different and better person. There are many ups and downs and twists and turns on the way, and always a cast of characters who help (and sometimes hinder) the heroine's efforts. Christopher Vogler describes in detail the elements of a Hero's Journey in the book *The Writer's Journey*.[2] He draws from the work of Carl Jung, Joseph Campbell and others who have traced the common themes in myths, legends and stories from ancient times to modern movie scripts. (*Star Wars* is a classic Hero's Journey movie, and so is the *Wizard of Oz*). I see these themes in the stories I hear daily. There is the Ordinary World (before even considering transition), the Call to Change, Refusing the Call (sometimes many times), Meetings with Mentors, Threshold Guardians and Allies, Crossing Thresholds, the Ordeal (arduous tasks and tests), the Reward (wholeness), and the Return to a new life. There are themes of death and rebirth. Transitioning has all of these elements, and more.

This is not meant to romanticize the transition process. It's no walk in the park, and it isn't always done gracefully. But we are guided and shaped by the narratives in our lives. You have probably seen or heard stories about transgender people as victims, as deviants, as poor pathetic souls. For the most part Hollywood has portrayed transsexual characters as either tragic victims or cross-dressing psychopathic killers. Both of these images perpetuate fear and loathing of transgender people. The only mainstream media portrayal of a transgender person that comes close to the Hero's Journey is *TransAmerica*. It is far better to embrace a Hero's Journey than to cast ourselves as victims, outcasts, or losers. My goal is to use this metaphor to guide, inspire, and at times challenge you on your way.

Here is a summary of the stages of the Hero's Journey, with corresponding stages in the transgender transition process.

---

[2] Christopher Vogler, The Writer's Journey: Mythic Structure for Writers, Third Edition, Michael Wiese Productions, 2007

The Hero's Journey

Stages of a Hero's Journey

Ordinary World	Playing the part you were assigned at birth, trying to be the man/woman you were supposed to be
Call to Change	That inner voice that keeps saying that the role doesn't fit, something has to change
Refusing the Call	Ignoring, denying, dismissing, drowning out that inner voice; refusing to change
Crisis/Catalyst	An event or experience that makes you realize you can no longer ignore or deny your needs
Meeting the Mentor	Finding someone who can help you face your conflicts and find the courage to change
Crossing the Threshold	Coming out as transgender, to yourself first and then to significant people in your life
The Transformation	Changing your appearance, learning the new role, starting the physical changes
Trials & Tribulations	The ordeals of transitioning; risks and rewards
Wrestling with Demons	Coming to terms with your own inner fears, conflicts, and internalized transphobia
Allies and Challengers	Coping with opposition from others, losing friends or family; gaining new friends
The Final Threshold	Legal name change, living in new role full-time, coming out at work and/or school
Passing the Tests	Looking in the mirror and liking what you see; being seen by others how you want to be seen

The Final Ordeal	Gender Reassignment Surgery and/or legal gender change
Rebirth and Return	Being out in the world as your new Self, beginning your new life

Beginning Your Heroic Story

I find it distressing that gender narratives, even transgender narratives, have become so standardized. My generation deliberately challenged conventional gender role stereotypes for both men and women. Do you remember unisex bell-bottom jeans, men in dashikis, hippie beads? I still have a picture of myself with my college boyfriend - both wearing overalls, flannel shirts and hiking boots, our hair equally long and unkempt. We were trying to make a statement with unisex clothing and hair styles: that neither gender should be restricted in their interests, activities or behavior. Yet now parents are finding out the gender of their new baby in the womb so they can color-code the nursery. Past the preschool toy aisle there is still a sharp division into "girl toys" and "boy toys". There are some positive signs - more gender-neutral names, more latitude in boys' and girls' behaviors. There is perhaps greater understanding that not all girls want to play with dolls, and not all boys want trucks. More opportunities have certainly opened up for girls in sports and other activities, and some for boys in art, dance, and theatre. Children grow up seeing more male nurses and female doctors, and the occasional female police officer or male elementary school teacher. Superheroes for girls are now as popular as those for boys. *Karate Kid 3* is a girl. This makes it more possible for girls and boys growing up to fashion their own stories, with themselves as heroes. We need a rainbow of superheroes for kids to emulate!

Just as there is more than one way to grow up male or female, there is more than one way to grow up transgender. Yet many people who struggle with their gender identity latch onto one of the stories they hear and present it as their own. "I'm a woman trapped in a man's body" is not the only transgender narrative. The medical profession has contributed to this, unfortunately, by trying to define a typical story of growing up transgender in order to determine who is a "primary" or "real" transsexual (and therefore a candidate for cross-gender treatment). In the early days of the first gender clinics there were only a handful of stories to go by. People desiring hormones and surgery read those same stories, and tried to make theirs fit the mold. This further skewed the criteria for treatment, since the researchers only heard those stories. They used to believe that all male-to-female transsexuals wanted to be with men, and they actually encouraged them to leave their wives.

This standardization of the transsexual narrative is reinforced by the multitude of autobiographical accounts available on-line. Reading those often contributes to a rewriting of personal history - either consciously, in order to convince a therapist, or unconsciously. Janis Walworth surveyed 36 male-to-female transsexuals after they had completed gender reassignment surgery, and found that 25% had lied to or misled their therapists in order to obtain approval for surgery.[3]

The focus on hormones and surgery also contributed to squeezing transgender people into two narrowly-defined boxes: male-to-female transsexual and female-to-male transsexual. You had to want surgery to be a "true" transsexual, and were called "pre-op", "post-op", or "non-op". Even Harry Benjamin, the godfather of transsexual treatment, believed that all transsexuals hated their penis - if someone derived any pleasure from his anatomy he was seen as a transvestite and therefore not eligible for hormones or surgery.

The transgender community has been challenging the restrictive criteria for hormones and surgery. There's no better way to challenge the status quo than with *true* transgender narratives. We not only express ourselves through stories, we define ourselves through them. Before you knew there was an alternative to the boy-or-girl narrative of growing up you had no way of explaining or even naming your internal experience. Many clients have

---

[3] Janis R. Walworth "Sex Reassignment Surgery in Male-to-Female Transsexuals: Client Satisfaction in Relation to Selection Criteria" in *Gender Blending*, ed. by Bonnie Bullough, Vern L. Bullough & James Elias, Prometheus Books, 1997

told me about the difference that just hearing the word transgender or transsexual made for them.

> The unfolding drama of life is revealed more by the telling than by the actual events themselves. Stories are not merely "chronicles", like a secretary's minutes of a meeting, written to report exactly what transpired and at what time. Stories are less about facts and more about meanings. ... Stories help us organize our thoughts, providing a narrative for human intentions and interpersonal events that is readily remembered and told. In some instances, stories may also mend us when we are broken, heal us when we are sick, and even move us toward psychological fulfillment and maturity.[4]

The mental health field has been slow to truly listen to transgender narratives. Psychotherapists tend to see people and problems through the lens of the theory that dominated their training. This can limit their ability to see gender dysphoria for what it is. "Donald" cross-dressed throughout a 30-year marriage, purging his wardrobe and swearing he would never do it again every time his wife found out. His wife dragged him into therapy periodically, hoping to find someone to fix his "problem." Thirty years ago they were told that his cross-dressing was because of an over-identification with a dominant mother. This was the common psychoanalytical interpretation at the time. (The dominant mother, weak father story was also used to try to explain homosexuality.) Long-term therapy would get to the root of the problem! Donald didn't stay long enough to find out. Then twenty years ago they went back, and were told that it was "just" a compulsive habit. With the right behavioral modification program he should be able to stop. That didn't work either. Ten years ago he came to see me. His wife didn't appreciate it when I told them that Donald was expressing a valid part of him/herself. It took him a while to accept that too. We explored the options available to him at that point in his life. He found some relief for his gender dysphoria with hormone treatment, but was unfortunately never able to fully express his feminine self. I often wonder what progress

---

[4] Dan P. McAdams, *The Stories We Live B: Personal Myths and the Making of the Self,* Guilford Press, 1993, p. 31

he/she would have been able to make if the previous therapists had been better informed, or at least more open-minded.

Another narrative that you will probably come across is the theory of *autogynephilia* put forth by Ray Blanchard in 1989.[5] (Even the name sounds nasty, doesn't it?) This was further promoted by Michael Bailey in a book called *The Man Who Would Be Queen*, published in 2003.[6] What's particularly distressing about this narrative is that some transgender writers have embraced it. Blanchard defined autogynephilia as "a man's paraphilic tendency to be aroused by the thought or image of himself as a woman". This theory is that the male-to-female transsexual has a sexual disorder that compels "him" to become a woman . (A paraphilia is a sexual fetish disorder.) Now it's true that dressing up in women's clothes, especially certain textures, can be erotic, for men *and* for women. For some cross-dressers that is their primary motivation. (That's called transvestic fetishism, another nasty term that ought to be abolished as a disorder.) And the thought of becoming the woman (or man) you've always wanted to be can bring out sexual feelings that aren't present in "guy (or girl) mode". One transwoman just told me that since she started taking estrogen she's been feeling more sexually alive than ever before. But for most transgender folks it's not about sex at all. To reduce gender dysphoria to a sexual need is absurd. So is the notion that transsexuals are really homosexuals who can't admit to it, and want to change their gender just to be with the partner they desire and appear heterosexual. I've seen just as many transsexuals *become* gay or lesbian as become heterosexual.

Another explanation for gender dysphoria that you may hear about is that it's caused by sexual abuse. It certainly sounds reasonable that children who are sexually abused might want to change their gender to get away from the abuse or from the feelings associated with memories of abuse.

---

[5] Blanchard, R. (1989). The concept of autogynephilia and the typology of male gender dysphoria. Journal of Nervous and Mental Disease, 177, 616-23. with introduction by M. H. Wyndzen. Retrievable from:
http://www.GenderPsychology.org/autogynephilia/male_gender_dysphoria/
[6] J. Michael Bailey *The Man Who Would Be Queen*, Joseph Henry Press, 2003

The problem is that it rarely happens that way. Yes, there are some transgender men and women who were abused as children, and some may be reacting to that abuse. But I've worked with many sexual abuse survivors in my 30 years as a psychotherapist, and not one chose to deny their gender. (That's another theory that was also used to try to explain homosexuality, without success.)

The common problem with these theories is that they see the need to present as the 'opposite sex' as sick, and look for an explanation for it in some underlying psychological disorder. If someone doesn't want to be a "well-adjusted" man or woman, as he or she was "meant" to be, there must be something wrong! (They used to say that about women who weren't happy being exclusively housewives and mothers.) These theories are not only inadequate for explaining the transgender experience, they contribute to feelings of shame and self-loathing. You are not sick or wrong for questioning your gender identity. And you don't need to fit your story into anyone else's mold.

The new *Standards of Care for the Health of Transsexual, Transgender, and Gender Nonconforming People* recognizes the diversity of trangender experience. The new guidelines take into consideration differing identities and individual goals. They make clear what many have been saying: "The expression of gender characteristics, including identities, that are not stereotypically associated with one's assigned sex at birth is a common and culturally-diverse human phenomenon [that] should not be judged as inherently pathological or negative." [7]

My challenge to you then is to tell *your* Story, *your* Truth. It might be helpful for you to write out (or draw, paint, or collage) your story. The questions at the end of this section are a way for you to start. They can also help you clarify what doesn't fit about being the way you are "supposed" to be.

---

[7] The World Professional Association for Transgender Health, *Standards of Care for the Health of Transexxual, Transgender, and Gender Nonconforming People*, Version 7, 2011

Heeding the Call

Every transsexual I know reports struggling with questions about his/her identity from an early age, often as young as five. A few tried to say something to a parent at some point, but were shut down, sometimes with the back of a hand. Now that transgender children have gotten sympathetic media attention, more parents are paying attention to kids who insist that they are "really a boy (or girl)". Oprah and Barbara Walters did a wonderful service for transgender people of all ages when they interviewed children who identified as the "opposite sex". If children that young feel that way, people are more likely to believe it's a real condition, something you're born with. I've seen a number of transgender children with supportive parents; they are blessed to have that support, but they still have their own challenges growing up transgender. And unfortunately supportive parents are still the exception rather than the rule. Self-identifying openly at a young age is still the exception rather than the norm.

If you're like most transgender folks, you've kept your feelings secret for a long time. You may have silenced your own questioning, and gone about trying to prove that you can be a man, often in extreme ways, in order to cure your gender dysphoria. Or you may have tried to find a compromise, being as masculine as you can get away with in a female body. You may have identified as a Lesbian or gay man, thinking that if you were attracted to the "same sex" you must be gay. If you are a male-to-female transsexual, you may have cross-dressed in private for many years. Not understanding why, you felt ashamed, fought the urges, and "purged" your feminine wardrobe many times. You have tried to fit in.

You have also probably tried to ignore that voice inside that said "Hey, I'm not really a girl (or boy)!" You've dismissed it as absurd. You may have prayed at night to wake up in the morning having a different body, but eventually you gave up. You did your best to get those thoughts, feelings, desires out of your mind. You probably thought you were sick or crazy or perverted, and may have been told as much.

Ignoring these internal conflicts takes a tremendous toll on one's health and sanity. Alcohol and drugs silence them, temporarily, but at a cost. Avoidance and denial take a lot of mental/emotional energy. Keeping a secret, feeling ashamed, always being on guard to not let the feminine or masculine self slip out, is exhausting and anxiety-producing. Over-compensating can be dangerous; going into the Army will not make a man out of someone who really isn't. (And those ugly tattoos are hard to get rid of!) Nor will getting married and having children - that just creates anoth-er set of problems. Hiding out as a butch lesbian can bring some refuge. but it's not an answer either. How can you be intimate in a relationship when you can't be honest and be yourself?

There comes a time for everyone when something tips the balance, and these questions can no longer be ignored. Sometimes there is an external catalyst, such as being caught by a spouse. Often it's someone else's story that you come across and recognize immediately as a mirror of your own. "Kendall" knew a lot of transmen, but couldn't identify as one until he met "Kyle", who was just as sensitive and artistic as he was. For middle-aged trans-folks, it's often a medical crisis that prompts a look at the life they *haven't* been living. All too often, it's a build-up of internal turmoil that just becomes unbearable. There is often literally a do-or-die moment that prompts seeking out help. "My doctor said I should call you", "Heather" said on the phone. "I had a loaded shotgun under my chin last week." The call to change often comes when you've simply run out of other options; the coping mechanisms you've been using to avoid the issue no longer work. "Jamie" came in for help after a heart attack had forced him to stop drinking and smoking and he found himself shopping for women's clothes for himself.

However it comes, there comes a time to heed the call to change. Some-thing isn't quite right, and you know it. You have been thrust into a full-blown identity crisis. You know things will never be the same again.

Like all identity crises, this creates a tremendous amount of anxiety and distress. It's unsettling and disorienting to question something as basic as one's gender. It shakes the foundation of your life, especially your relation-ships with others. Panic attacks are common, as well as insomnia, difficulty concentrating, and bouts of depression. You'll be tempted to run away and hide again, burying yourself in work, or another relationship. It's also tempting to try to resolve the crisis as quickly as possible, latching onto the first transgender identity that you find. This is especially true if you plug into an on-line transgender community, where there is often pressure to conform to a one-size-fits-all identity and show that you're a "real" transsexual. I have heard of clients being told they didn't belong on an on-line forum because they didn't want to "go all the way." Or that they weren't "trans enough". Ladies and gentle men, this is not a competition!

Please do not rush to judgment! There are as many transgender identities as there are people who are gender-variant. The true call here is to find out who *you* are. And it can't be done overnight. Arlene Istar Lev calls this a process of emergence. "This process of developing an authentic self for transgendered people means they must move through an experience of *emergence* - of realizing, discovering, identifying, or naming their gender identities."[8]

Here are the stages of emergence that she has observed in the many transgender clients she has seen:

1) **Awareness**: "the coming into consciousness of the internal sense of being different and the realization that indeed one may be different." (p.235) She describes this as an emergency stage, as it can be a time of acute distress.

2) **Seeking information/reaching out**: this is the time of coming out to oneself and reaching out for information. "Amassing information is essential to the client emerging as transgendered and is the first step in the development of a fully integrated identity." (p.242)

---

[8] Arlene Istar Lev, *Transgender Emergence: Therapeutic Guidelines for Working with Gender-Variant People and Their Families*, Haworth Press, 2004, p.229

3) **Disclosure to significant others**: this is the coming out process, and figuring how when, where and how to tell family and friends. It can be the most fearful, painful and difficult stage, but it can also bring great relief.

4) **Exploring identity and transition**: this stage involves "the exploration of roles, clothing, and mannerisms in ways that are exciting but can also be frightening" (p.254) This is the stage for trying on transgender identities and finding what feels right.

5) **Exploring transition and possible body modification**: this is the time for settling into one's own transgender identity, and deciding what body modifications are possible and desirable. This involves decisions about hormones, dressing in role, and possible surgeries.

6) **Integration**: this is the time when the new identity comes together and is worn proudly and with confidence. This is also the time to come to terms with issue and problems that transitioning has not solved.

Each stage of any journey has its promise and its pitfalls, and potential for success or failure. The success of each stage builds on the positive outcomes of the one before. My concern at this point is with the awareness stage, as it can be so overwhelming, in either a positive or negative way, that clients are often tempted to try to jump ahead. It can be terrifying to realize that you belong to a group that is so stigmatized and so mistreated by society. It can also be a great relief to recognize oneself in a label, and see all the pieces of the puzzle making sense for the first time. (I have been surprised at times at how happy clients can be when I tell them that I think they have Attention Deficit Disorder, for example. They've been told or led to believe that they're lazy, stupid, and/or incompetent.)

Whether the reaction is one of panic or elation, or both, it can be tempting to jump on transitioning to the other side of the gender continuum as the cure, and the sooner the better! In identity development theory this is called "foreclosure", when an individual makes a firm commitment to an identity or ideology prematurely. A path prematurely chosen can lead to disastrous outcomes. Ari Lev specifically emphasizes: "The awareness stage is not the time to make decisions about transitioning."[9]

The antidote to foreclosure is openness to experience. *Your* experience of *your* self in the world. You can and should look at other people's experiences to inform your exploration, but you need to look inside for your answers. Take the time to find out more about transgender identities, chart your own course, and prepare yourself for the journey into "no-man's land".

Beginning Your Narrative

Here is a list of questions to get you started thinking about your experiences growing up. Take some time to write out your own his/herstory.

What are your earliest memories regarding gender differences? Do you remember figuring out what the difference between boys and girls was supposed to be? How did you feel about that discovery?

What were you told about the differences between boys and girls? What were you told about how you were supposed to be because you were a boy or girl? (Boys don't cry, girls don't say things like that....) How did you react?

What is your earliest memory of questioning your assigned gender? What were your thoughts about it? Did you try to tell anyone? If so, how did they react?

What were your favorite TV shows and movies as a child? Favorite fairy tale? Book or book series? Who did you identify with most? Who were your heroes?

---

[9] *Trangender Emergence*, p.239

What were your favorite toys and activities as a child? Who did you play with most, boys or girls? What/who did you secretly long to play with? Who/what did you really want to dress up as for Halloween?

Were you teased or bullied for not fitting the stereotype for your assigned gender? What names were you called? How did that feel?

Who/what did you want to be when you grew up? What did you tell people when they asked? How was that received?

Was there anything you envied about the "opposite sex" growing up?

What was puberty like for you? How did you feel about your body changing? What did you have the most trouble with?

How do you feel about the sexual parts of your anatomy (penis, testicles, vagina, breasts)? Have you ever wanted to get rid of them? Wished they were different?

What were your earliest sexual and/or romantic fantasies? Who did you want to be with, and who did you want to be, in those fantasies? Did you have any secret crushes?

Who did you date in high school (if anyone), and why? Were you happy with that? Were you sexually active? If so, did that feel right?

How have you tried to cope with being gender-variant? What have you done to try to resolve, suppress, avoid, or deny any conflicts you felt about your gender? How have these worked for you?

What have you tried to do to fit in with your assigned gender role? Have you done anything to try to "prove you're a man" (or woman). Did you do anything you thought would "make a man (or woman) out of you"? How have those experiences worked out?

What have you done to allow yourself to express your preferred gender identity? Have you been "cross-dressing" in private? Have you gone out "dressed"? Engaged in any other activities (such as theatre, sports, etc.) that allowed you to express your feminine or masculine self?

How do you feel when you are dressed in the clothes you like? Do you like how it makes you look? Do you just like the feel of the fabric? Is it sexually arousing? Do you dress primarily for comfort and relaxation?

What were you told about being gay or lesbian growing up? What were the attitudes of the people around you, and how were those conveyed? Were you called queer or gay? How did you feel about that?

Did you know anything about transgender people growing up? What images did you come across? Transvestite stereotypes? Jerry Springer?

Do you know anyone now who's transgender? What stories have you heard or read? What are your sources of information about transgender life?

What are your own thoughts, feelings, prejudices about gay, lesbian, bisexual or transgender people? Do you ever find yourself not wanting to associate with, or be associated with, others in the community? Who are you uncomfortable with? Can you identify where those prejudices came from?

What is it about being transgender that fits for you? What does it explain? What questions does it answer for you?

What are your wishes, hopes, desires for the future? What (or who) stops you from pursuing those? What are your fears? How do you assume others in your life would react if you changed?

What is it about becoming a man or a woman that appeals to you? What do you expect to gain from changing your gender presentation?

If you were to wake up tomorrow and all your problems were solved, what would your life be like? What would you look like?

References and Resources

Dan P. McAdams, *The Stories We Live By: Personal Myths and the Making of the Self*, Guilford Press, 1993

Arlene Istar Lev, *Transgender Emergence: Therapeutic Guidelines for Working with Gender-Variant People and Their Families*, Haworth Press, 2004

Susan Stryker, *Transgender History*, Seal Press, 2008

Joseph Campbell, *The Hero with a Thousand Faces*, New World Library, 2008

Chapter Two

No-Man's Land: The Aerial View

I had crossed the line. I was free; but there was no one to welcome me to the land of freedom. I was a stranger in a strange land.

Harriet Tubman

So what does "transgender" mean? Is a transsexual the same as a transvestite? Aren't cross-dressers gay? What does it mean to have a "sex change"? Do women ever change to become men? How does someone tell if they're transgender? Is there a test you can take to find out? What causes it?

If you're confused or unsure about these and other questions, you're not alone. Even professionals can't agree on all the definitions. At the end of the book (Appendix A) you'll find a list of common terms, with current definitions. If this is all new to you, you might want to review that first. It's not easy to grasp some of the ideas I'm going to present. So let me start at the beginning.

We're going to be talking primarily about *gender* in this book. *Sex* is an activity, and *sexual orientation* is about who we want to do that activity with. *Gender* is one aspect of who we are. *Gender identity* is our internal sense of who we are - man, woman, or other. Gender and gender identity are more complex than most of us ever imagined. So let's talk about what goes into making us biologically a man or a woman. That in itself is a complicated process! Here is a simplified description:

In the beginning, there's an egg and a sperm with genetic markers for male and female. When they collide they create an embryo, with (usually) either XX (female) or XY(male). Both male and female embryos start out morphologically similar - that is, they look the same. They both have Wolffian (male) and Mullerian (female) ducts. The SRY gene, located on the Y chromosome, initiates a series of events that results in a baby who comes out looking like a girl or a boy (most of the time). First, an undifferentiated gonad begins to develop into an ovary or testis. The testes produce testosterone, the male hormone, and something called the Anti-Mullerian Hormone. This preserves the Wolffian ducts, and inhibits the development of the Mullerian duct. If the Mullerian duct is not inhibited, it develops into the oviduct, uterus, cervix, and vagina. In other words, the "natural" course of the embryo is to develop into a female. It's the presence of testosterone and AMH, at the right times and in the right amount, which creates the male anatomy. As the ovaries or testes develop, they secrete estrogen or testosterone. These hormones continue the development of the male and female sex organs. The hormones also have an effect on the developing brain, at later stages of prenatal and postnatal development. The result is that male and female brains have some structural differences. And the brain is the source of our *gender identity*, as well as sexual preference and perhaps some other sex-typed characteristics.

So what is it then that makes someone male or female? Is it possible to say for certain what makes the defining difference between men and women? Is it based on:

Chromosomes?

Genetic testing can reveal if someone is XX or XY. But there are a number of genetic variations, such as Turner's (XO) and Klinefelter's (XXY) Syndrome that result in atypical gender presentations. The Olympic Committee used to use genetic testing to verify gender for sports, but stopped after finding that too many of the athletes had atypical genetic profiles.[10]

Gonadal sex?

The presence of ovaries or testes is one of the major differences between men and women, but it is possible to be born with both, or neither. And there are non-functioning ovaries and testes in some men and women.

Reproductive organs?

Studies have shown that removing these does not change one's gender. Ask any woman post-hysterectomy! And there are men born without a penis, women born without a vagina. Our ability to procreate in particular ways does not define us as a man or a woman.

Anatomical differences?

There's too much variation in body shape, size and structure of genitals, and size of breasts to make this the determining factor. There are men with gynecomastia (enlarged breasts) that are larger than some women's breasts. And the difference between clitoromegaly (enlarged clitoris) and a micro-penis is minimal.

---

[10] Myron Genel, MD "Gender Verification No More?" Medscape Women's Health 5(3), 2000.

Hormones?

Men and women both have testosterone and estrogen in their bodies. Which one is more dominant can make a difference in how people feel, but hormones alone don't make the man (or woman). There are also conditions, such as Androgen Insensitivity Syndrome, where hormones are not metabolized properly, resulting in atypical gender presentations.

Sex of rearing /assigned gender?

One of the saddest debacles of 20th century medicine was an attempt to raise a boy as a girl. After a botched circumcision cut off his penis, David Reimer's parents took him to see Dr. John Money, a prominent sexologist. He convinced them to subject David to genital reconstruction and raise him as a girl. This was supposed to prove that gender is a product of how we're raised. It failed miserably. By age 14 David refused to continue with this experiment, and eventually transitioned back to living as a male.[11]

Gender identity?

Gender identity is the psychological self-identification, or the inner awareness of belonging to one gender or the other. This is a person's innate, internal experience of themselves as a boy or girl, man or woman (or other). It is considered to be "hard-wired" in the brain.

The answer is that no one biological marker defines gender. For most people, all of these different aspects of gender line up on one side of the continuum of male to female. For many people, one or more of these is somewhere other than at one end or the other. When this shows up as physical abnormalities, it's called an intersex condition. There are over 100 different intersex conditions; it's estimated that one out of every 100 infants is affected. Some of these show up at birth, some at puberty, and

---

[11] John Colapinto *As Nature Made Him: The Boy Who was Raised as a Girl*, Harper Collins, 2000

some go unnoticed until discovered in an autopsy.[12]

The treatment of intersex conditions is a subject for another book. Traditionally, infants born with ambiguous genitalia were surgically altered to appear female, and raised as girls. This was based on the assumption that gender identity was influenced more by nurture than nature. This has since been proven wrong. There are stories of "girls" trying to fit in, knowing something was wrong, being told they were crazy, and given massive doses of estrogen in adolescence to make them develop. One "woman" showed signs of color-blindness and male-pattern baldness and was finally tested and discovered to be a genetic male. "She" had to transition back to his true gender identity as a man.

Transsexuals experience one of the least obvious conditions - the mismatch between their own internal sense of who they are and their external appearance. Children learn to tell who's a boy and who's a girl starting around three or four years old. Most transsexuals report that they felt something was wrong by the age of five. What they were told they were did not match their own image of themselves. Some even insisted that they were *not* a girl (or boy), and were told in no uncertain terms that they were wrong (or crazy). Most try to accept the gender role they're assigned, and keep the conflict and confusion bottled up inside. But the 'gender dysphoria' - the sense of not fitting in one's assigned gender and the resulting distress - doesn't go away.

Many transsexuals wonder if they're physically intersexed, or wish they had something definite and biological that they could point to as causing their distress about their assigned gender. Some of the clients I see do have an intersexed condition. One woman, raised as a male, came to see me after she'd been diagnosed with Klinefelter's Syndrome, and found to have very little estrogen or testosterone in her system. She was never definite about her gender identity, but eventually chose estrogen and a female gender

---

[12] Blackless, Melanie, Anthony Charuvastra, Amanda Derryck, Anne Fausto-Sterling, Karl Lauzanne, and Ellen Lee. "How sexually dimorphic are we? Review and synthesis". *American Journal of Human Biology* 12:151-166, 2000

presentation. If you have those concerns, do some research and consult your physician. Genetic testing could clear up the confusion for you, or at least give you a place to start.

Not having an obvious physical intersex condition, however, does not mean that your "condition" is not real. Chances are the way you feel is biologically-based. Scientists are still working on pinpointing the origins of both sexual orientation and gender identity. Preliminary studies show gender differences in the brain related to transsexuality.[13] There is so much we don't know yet about the brain, but we're learning more and more every day. Until we know more, we validate the transgender experience through transgender narrative.

Binary Gender Paradigm

MALE	FEMALE
Born with penis and testes	Born with vagina, etc.
↓	↓
BOY	GIRL
Masculine behavior	Feminine behavior
↓	↓
MAN	WOMAN
↓	↓
Attracted to women	Attracted to men

---

[13] Jiang-Ning Zhou, Michel A. Hofman, Louis J. G. Gooren & Dick F. Swaab: "A sex difference in the human brain and its relation to transsexuality", *Nature* 378, 68 - 70

So let's compare two different paradigms or models of looking at gender. The first diagram is the *Binary Gender Paradigm*. In this way of looking at things, boys are born with a penis and testicles, become masculine, dress like boys, and are interested in girls when puberty hits. Boys become men, secure in their masculinity. Girls are born with a vagina, become feminine, dress like girls and are interested in boys. Girls become women, secure in their femininity. This is the heteronormative model. If you believe whole-heartedly in this model, and don't want to change that view, you can put this book away now. Because life, and gender, is not that simple.

Our second diagram (on page 26) is called *Dimensions of Sex/Gender*. In this view, there are different aspects of gender to consider, and each one is a continuum:

Biological Sex (for lack of a better term) ranges from typically male (having a penis and testicles, producing testosterone) to typically female (having a vagina, ovaries, etc.). Intersexed conditions fall somewhere in the middle of the continuum, depending on what's affected, and to what extent.

Gender Identity refers to our psychological sense of self. It can range from boy/man to girl/woman. Those who identify as both or neither may consider themselves transgender, androgynous, or bigendered, or simply "trans". Someone transitioning from one side to the other may consider him/herself transgender or transsexual.

Gender Expression is about how we present ourselves to others. A masculine gender presentation typically includes such things as short hair, clothes found in the men's department, a certain way of walking and talking, etc. A feminine presentation would include styled hair, make-up, jewelry, clothes from the women's department, etc. An androgynous presentation aims at a gender-neutral appearance, with clothes that could be worn by either men or women, a plain hairstyle, no make-up, etc.

ASPECTS OF SEX/GENDER

BIOLOGICAL SEX (anatomy and physiology):

Male -------------- Intersexed ---------------- Female

GENDER IDENTITY (psychological sense of self):

Man --------------Transgender -------------- Woman

GENDER EXPRESSION (communication of gender):

Masculine -------Androgynous ----------- Feminine

GENDER ATTRIBUTION (how person is perceived):

Male --------------Ambiguous ---------------- Female

Gender Attribution is about how others see us. This ranges from easily identifying someone at a distance as a man to easily identifying someone as a woman. But we've all had the experience of walking down the street or in the mall and wondering if the person we just passed was a man or a woman. That's an ambiguous gender attribution.

I often show this diagram to clients who come in with questions about their gender identity, and ask them to put an X where they feel they are on each dimension. It gives us a starting point for our journey together. So feel free to copy this page, mark your places, and share it with your friends and family.

You'll notice that sexual orientation is not on this second diagram. That's because it deserves a separate chart. (See Chapter 14.) Sexual orientation is independent of gender identity. That means that knowing someone's gender identity, including their transgender identity, does not tell you their sexual orientation. Sexual interests and attractions are complex and sometimes fluid for transgender individuals. A male-to-female transsexual can start out apparently heterosexual (attracted to women) before transition and become a lesbian, still attracted to women. Or she can become interested in men after surgery, and become heterosexual. "He" just wasn't interested in gay sex. One of the reasons being a butch lesbian doesn't always fit for transmen is that they're often attracted to straight women, and see themselves as basically heterosexual. Others are attracted to gay men, or other transmen. And many of the transgender clients I've worked with have not been interested in sex at all. Most, however, maintain a consistent attraction to the partners they start with, although their partners may not remain attracted to them.

You can also see that because gender identity is so complex there are many possible gender identities. Some choose a term that reflects their gender and sexual orientation, such as transdyke or boydyke. Others adopt a term from another culture, such as Two Spirit (Native American). FORGE (For Ourselves: Reworking Gender Expression) has a list of over 140 terms that gender-variant people have used to describe their gender identity). Yours will be unique to you.

References and Resources

Mildred L. Brown and Chloe Ann Rounsley, *True Selves: Understanding Transsexualism*, Jossey-Bass, 1996

Annah Moore, *Right Side Out*, iUniverse, Inc., 2006

Intersex Society of North America - www.isna.org

John Neas, *Chapter 27: Reproductive System Development, in Human Anatomy*, http://cwx.prenhall.com/bookbind/pubbooks/martini10/chapter27/custom3/deluxe-content.html

FORGE (For Ourselves: Reworking Gender Expression) - www.forge-forward.org

Chapter Three

Charting Your Course

A journey of a thousand miles begins with a single step.

Lao Tzu

Actually, I read that a better translation of that quote is "A journey of a thousand miles begins beneath one's feet." The transgender journey begins with an awareness of where you are, in all its pain and promise. It begins with taking stock of your life - where you are, where you've been, and where you want to go. Contrary to common wisdom, you don't have to know when you begin exactly where you want to end up. In expressive art work we say "Trust the Process!" Trust that with the right guidance you will be able to safely explore the territory ahead and land in a place that fits for you. It's also important to understand that your gender identity will evolve over time. As you explore different steps in the process you will find out what fits for you and what doesn't. As tempting as it is to walk into the store and pick out a new identity "off the rack", pay for it and walk out, that's not likely to be very successful.

The second step in preparing for your journey is to gather information. Although your journey is unique to you, there are many others who have explored this vast territory between the two gender polarities. There are web sites, YouTube videos, autobiographies and more available on-line. One word of caution: not all of what you read on-line is reputable! There are still authors who are not trans-positive, and there is a lot of outdated information, even on TG-friendly sites. Personal experiences are just that - one person's experience. The list of resources at the end of this section is a good place to start. Reaching out to others in the transgender community can also be helpful, but use the same caution you would use in getting to know anyone else. Transgender people have issues, like everyone else, as well as the same problems you've probably had to cope with growing up gender-variant in a transphobic culture.

Reading about other people's experiences can be both exhilarating and anxiety-provoking. It may be a great relief to find stories so similar to yours. But the process of transitioning can seem overwhelming, and you will hear many stories of heartbreak and loss. Some stories will provide you with inspiration and courage; others may serve as warnings. Every journey has its Scylla and Charybdis - two sea monsters of Greek mythology so close together that it was difficult to navigate past one without getting too close to the other. You'll have the advantage of learning from others' mistakes as well as successes.

You will also come across what's called the SOC, or Standards of Care. These are guidelines for professionals who see transgender clients/patients, published by the World Professional Association of Transgender Health (WPATH - formerly the Harry Benjamin International Gender Dysphoria Association, or HBIGDA). The Standards of Care outline a typical sequence of transition events that most male-to-female transsexuals have followed: an initial evaluation by a gender specialist or qualified therapist, then a year of hormone therapy and a year of "real-life experience" (or living in role, as I prefer to call it) and then gender reassignment surgery. This is only one possible itinerary, and doesn't cover all of the steps necessary to present as a new woman! Female-to-male transsexuals and those who identify as "genderqueer" sometimes find that sequence doesn't fit their needs. Version 7 of the Standards of Care, just published, speaks more directly to those issues and other treatment options. (For a full description and explanation of the new SOC see Appendix B.)

There is ongoing debate in the transgender community about the Standards of Care. Many resent having to go through a gatekeeper to access hormones and surgery. Where there are rules restricting what people want to do, there are always some who will try to circumvent them. "Letter-shopping", getting illegal hormones via the Internet, searching out disreputable surgeons, and lying to a therapist are all common. The risks associated with all of those are tremendous; the results can be disastrous. And when transsexuals are surveyed about the SOC, "The overwhelming majority of respondents believes that the standards of care serve a useful purpose."[14]

Once you've gathered these maps, it's time to chart your own course. First think about what you're most unhappy with about your gender. Not everyone with gender dysphoria has the same level of anatomical dysphoria. Some are quite content with their genitals. And think about what you have to work with - including your physical, social, and financial limitations. The Version 6 of the Standards of Care lists what they refer to as gender adaptations that have been helpful in relieving gender dysphoria.[15] Some people find these enough, at least for a period of time while they're exploring other options. I always recommend that clients try these first. The physical changes are unobtrusive and for the most part reversible. They give you both a taste of what it's like to live as the opposite gender and a sense of progress towards cross-gender living.

---

[14] Dallas Denny and Jan Roberts, "Results of a Questionnaire on the Standards of Care of the Harry Benjamin International Gender Dysphoria Association", in *Gender Blending*, ed. by Bonnie Bullough, Vern L. Bullough & James Elias, Prometheus Books, 1997, p. 332

[15] The World Professional Association for Transgender Health's Standards Of Care For Gender Identity Disorders, Sixth Version, 2001, at: www.wpath.org

Options for Gender Adaptation

Activities:
　　Biological Males:
　　1. Cross-dressing: unobtrusively with undergarments; unisexually; or in a feminine fashion;
　　2. Changing the body through: hair removal through electrolysis or body waxing; minor plastic (cosmetic) surgical procedures;
　　3. Increasing grooming, wardrobe, and vocal expression skills.

　　Biological Females:
　　1. Cross-dressing: unobtrusively with undergarments, unisexually, or in a masculine fashion;
　　2. Changing the body through breast binding, weight lifting;
　　3. Padding underpants or wearing a penile prosthesis.

　　Both Genders:
　　1. Learning about transgender phenomena from: support groups and gender networks, communication with peers via the Internet, studying these Standards of Care, relevant lay and professional literatures about legal rights pertaining to work, relationships, and public cross-dressing;
　　2. Involvement in recreational activities of the desired gender;
　　3. Episodic cross-gender living.

Processes:
　　1. Acceptance of personal homosexual or bisexual fantasies and behaviors (orientation) as distinct from gender identity and gender role aspirations;
　　2. Acceptance of the need to maintain a job, provide for the emotional needs of children, honor a spousal commitment, or not distress a family member as currently having a higher priority than the personal wish for constant cross-gender expression;
　　3. Integration of male and female gender awareness into daily living;
　　4. Identification of the triggers for increased cross-gender yearnings and effectively attending to them; for instance, developing better self-protective, self-assertive, and vocational skills to advance at work and resolve interpersonal struggles to strengthen key relationships.

Whatever you decide to do, you'll need a guide.

Meeting Your Mentor

Every hero needs a mentor - a wise and trustworthy guide and advisor.[16] A mentor will be your ally, your teacher, your coach and your cheerleader. A mentor will also challenge you to be better than you ever thought possible. This journey of a thousand miles can begin with a single phone call. The first person to reach out to when you decide to face your gender conflicts should be a gender specialist. A gender specialist is a therapist - a psychologist, social worker or other licensed mental health professional - who has the specialized knowledge and experience to work with transgender clients. Finding one that you are comfortable with can be a challenge, but it is essential to the process.

The first challenge is finding a qualified gender specialist in your area. There are many organizations on-line that will list transgender-friendly therapists by state. If there are only medical professionals listed near you, call them and ask them about gender specialists they work with. Resource directories for the GLBT community should also have a section for therapists. (In New Hampshire we have Rainbow Resources, for example.) If you can't find one listed on one of these sites, you can call your state psychological association and ask if they know of anyone who works with sexual minorities. Not every therapist who identifies as gay or lesbian or works with sexual minorities will be knowledgeable or experienced with transgender issues, but they will probably know someone who is. And if there are no gender specialists close enough to you, a GLBT-friendly therapist who is willing to educate him/herself further can be a good match. If you are already seeing a therapist for other reasons, it's best to ask him or her if he/she has any knowledge or experience with gender issues before opening up about your conflicts. The last thing you want is to share your innermost feelings about your gender with someone who just doesn't get it.

---

[16] Christopher Vogler, *The Writer's Journey: Mythic Structure for Writers*, *Third Edition*, Michael Wiese Productions, 2007

It's also important to get reviews and/or recommendations of gender specialists in your area. There are a few out there who are known to either set up arbitrary obstacles to getting needed services or "hand out letters like candy". What you're looking for is a *collaborative* relationship with your therapist - one where the two of you work out a plan for your transition together. Your therapist should not require months and months of weekly sessions and/or expensive psychological tests. (If he or she does recommend testing, ask what it's for; there are times when it could be useful.) But a therapist who is willing to write referral letters for hormones or surgery after one or two sessions is not looking out for your interests either. Both types of therapists are either uninformed or unethical.

You may in the end have to make cold calls to therapists to find someone willing to work with you. I know how difficult it can be to reach out and make that phone call (or email). I get calls and emails every week from people who are so nervous they don't know what to say. You can call off-hours and leave a message if you don't want to talk to the clinician (or a receptionist) directly. All you have to say is that you are looking for a gender specialist, or someone knowledgeable enough about transgender issues to help you explore your gender identity. If they don't have a clue, they probably won't call you back. If someone does call you back, ask to set up an initial consultation, to see if you think you can be comfortable enough with him or her to talk about your concerns.

Ambivalent feelings towards gender therapists and the role they play are obvious in the stories you will hear and read on-line. Because of their role in evaluating clients and writing letters of recommendations for hormone treatments and surgery, therapists are often seen as gatekeepers, or Threshold Guardians, in mythic story terms. And frankly there has been a lot of very bad treatment for gender dysphoria over the years. Your therapist should be first and foremost an Ally, someone who is supportive of you exploring and expressing who you are. In your first meeting you should be able to sense whether you can trust this person or not. If not, keep looking! I have listed the criteria for an ideal gender therapist below. If you can't find anyone with experience in this area, at least find someone who is open-minded and willing to learn.

Criteria for an Ideal Gender Therapist

1) A licensed or certified mental health professional
2) with a knowledge base in human development, human sexuality, and/or transgender mental health care,
3) experience in treating anxiety, depression, and PTSD,
4) an open mind about the diversity of gender experience,
5) comfort with "cross-dressing" & other forms of gender expression,
6) a willingness to learn more about the transition process, and seek supervision or consultation with a Senior Gender Specialist if necessary,
7) a collaborative approach to treatment planning,
8) a willingness to consult with & educate family members, schools, or employers if the need arises,
9) experience writing letters of referral, and
10) access to information about endocrinologists, surgeons, and other professionals and services as needed.

Most importantly, your mentor should be willing to listen to *your* story, and not impose his or her own narrative. I mentioned earlier that therapists are sometimes blinded by their own theoretical orientation, so it can be helpful to ask about that. Psychoanalytic, psychodynamic, and strictly behavioral therapists are best avoided. The dominant theoretical approach taught these days tends to be "cognitive-behavioral", which isn't as much a theory as a set of treatment approaches. It's popular because insurance companies like it and it's easy to learn. It tends to be value-neutral, so if a therapist says that's his or her theoretical orientation it doesn't tell you much about how he or she sees the transgender experience. Humanist, Feminist, Client-Centered, Existential, Narrative and Transpersonal therapists are all likely to be open-minded and willing to learn. Counselors who identify themselves as "Christian" are not likely to be open-minded.

Some believe in reparative therapy, which has been condemned by the American Psychological Association as ineffective and detrimental. Licensed pastoral counselors or pastoral psychotherapists, however, are legitimate mental health providers who may be very open and supportive.

Many transmen and women object to having to see a therapist for referrals for hormones and surgery. After all, they say, you don't have to see a therapist for other surgical procedures. (Actually, you do - in order to have a gastric bypass you have to have an extensive evaluation.) And "WE'RE NOT CRAZY!" they argue. I agree! There's nothing inherently crazy about not identifying as the gender you were assigned at birth. Yes, there is a diagnosis in the DSM-IV-TR called Gender Identity Disorder. But to be considered a disorder, something must cause "clinically significant distress or impairment in social, occupational or other important areas of functioning."[17] It's the distress that is the problem. I often say that I don't treat GID; I treat the stress, anxiety, and depression that are often associated with growing up transgender in a transphobic culture.

You don't have to be sick or crazy to benefit from talking to a therapist! I can think of four good reasons for seeing a gender specialist throughout your transition:

1) Guidance - a gender specialist knows what works well and what doesn't, and can help you navigate the ins and outs of the transition process,

2) Support - your therapist will be there for you through all the changes and losses, to cheer you on and share in your joys and sorrows,

3) Access to resources - a gender specialist will know endocrinologists, electrologists, and other TG-friendly practitioners, and can write those referral letters you'll need,

---

[17] *The Diagnostic and Statistical Manual of Mental Disorders, Fourth Edition, Test Revision,* published by the American Psychiatric Association, 2000, p. 581

4) Resolving any shame, guilt, trauma, internal conflicts, internalized homophobia or transphobia, and the general stress from growing up transgender.

It is also necessary to see a qualified therapist to rule out other disorders that could be driving a compulsion to cross-dress and/or confusion about gender identity. There have been cases where people have sought to transition because of multiple personality disorder, schizophrenia, Munchausen Syndrome, Asperger's Syndrome, confusion about sexuality vs. gender, a desire to control inappropriate sexual impulses, sexual dysfunctions, sexual abuse, peer pressure, and even as a way to disguise their identity. I know someone with bipolar disorder who only cross-dresses when he stops taking his medication and goes into a manic episode. I have also had one client whose cross-dressing was related to an incestuous relationship with his mother. That doesn't mean that if you've been diagnosed with Asperger's or bipolar disorder that you can't transition. A comprehensive evaluation will help sort out the different issues, including gender dysphoria, and the best way to address each one.

It's also very helpful to have a mentor (or mentors) in the transgender community - perhaps someone who is further along on his/her journey than you. Or even a cisgendered "big brother" or "big sister" who can take you out shopping, or socializing at local GLBT-friendly hangouts, and can help you get through the "which bathroom should I use" dilemma. You can find transgender mentors at local support groups, GLBT-friendly hangouts, on-line, or through TransMentors International.[18] Your therapist may also be able to help you connect with others.

The important point here is that no one can complete this journey alone. It takes a lot of work to change your gender presentation (especially male-to-female). And the surprising thing for most of the people I've worked with is that there are lots of folks out there who are happy to help. So let me introduce you to the rest of your crew next.

---

[18] TransMentors International - http://transmentors.org/

References and Resources

International Foundation for Gender Education - www.ifge.org

Laura's Playground - www.lauras-playground.com

Susan's Place - http://susans.org

Hudson's FTM Resource Guide - www.ftmguide.org

Lynn's Place - www.tglynnsplace.com

Chapter Four

Assembling Your Crew

It takes a village to raise a child.

African proverb

If you decide to transition - that is, to change your gender presentation physically in some way - you will need to enlist the help of several different professionals. This can be a daunting task, but it doesn't have to be done all at once. I'll describe briefly each one, and we'll talk more about their roles later.

Primary Care Physician (Family Doctor)

Your primary doctor can be a valuable resource. He or she can help you get your physical health in good shape, prescribe antidepressants if you need them, order hormone level tests, perhaps prescribe hormones or refer you to someone who can, and oversee the physical aspects of your transition. And a TG-friendly physician can be a sympathetic Ally. A trusting relationship with a good doctor is essential for a successful physical transition.

Not every physician is knowledgeable about transgender health care, but most physicians are open and respectful. The American Medical Association has passed a resolution supporting transgender rights and access to medical care.[19] They have endorsed the WPATH Standards of Care and affirmed the medical necessity of hormone therapy and surgery. This means that any decent doctor will take your needs seriously and be willing to discuss your transition-related health concerns. Some will need to be educated, however. There are several publications available on-line for physicians as well as numerous professional books. More recent medical school graduates or doctors who trained in urban hospitals will probably have had more exposure than older rural physicians. But you'll never know until you ask!

If you already have a primary care physician, your first approach should be to bring up the subject with him or her. You can start by asking "Have you ever worked with transgender patients before?" followed by "Are you comfortable with transgender patients?" If you're not happy with the responses you get, you can say you have a friend who's looking for a referral. If your doctor seems comfortable but not knowledgeable, you can find resources geared to physicians on-line and bring them in. Some will be eager to learn more. I was pleased to see my own primary care physician at a recent Transgender Conference; he was there to support a friend and learn more about the needs of the transgender community.

If you need to find a primary care doctor, you can ask your mentor or other transgender people in your community, or look on-line for resource listings. If you have to make cold calls, you'll probably get a receptionist who may or may not know anything about the doctor's experience. But start with those two questions above.

---

[19] AMERICAN MEDICAL ASSOCIATION HOUSE OF DELEGATES Resolution: 122 (A-08) "Removing Financial Barriers to Care for Transgender Patients", May 2008, available at: www.ama-assn.org/ama1/pub/upload/mm/471/122.doc

Even a sympathetic and knowledgeable family doctor may not be comfortable prescribing feminizing or masculinizing hormones. In that case you will need to find an:

Endocrinologist

An endocrinologist is a physician who specializes in hormones. Most of them focus on treating diabetes, thyroid conditions, and other hormonal problems. A few actually specialize in treating transgender patients and are very knowledgeable. Those you can find through on-line resource listings for your state. If you're not lucky enough to live near one listed you'll need to search for one if you want to start hormone therapy. Your gender therapist and primary care physician should be able to help you out, so ask them first. If not, then you'll need to do more cold calls. The questions to ask here are: "Does Dr. X work with transgender patients?" and "Does he/she prescribe masculinizing (or feminizing) hormones?" I've known a few endocrinologists who would prescribe estrogen and spironolactone, but were not comfortable prescribing testosterone.

Psychiatrist or Psychiatric Nurse Practitioner

A primary care doctor should be able to prescribe an antidepressant or mild anti-anxiety medication if you need it. Don't be shy about discussing your anxiety or depression with your physician or your therapist and asking for additional help. Sometimes the right medication makes it possible to do things you never thought you'd be able to do. "Jocelyn" had so much social anxiety it took her several years before she would go out dressed as herself. After a few months on an antidepressant she was not only able to go out, she volunteered to play a part in a play. She now has a budding career as a model and actress. If you have more severe depression or other mental health issues you'll need to see a psychiatrist or a psychiatric nurse practitioner (ARNP). Ask your gender therapist for a recommendation and/or referral if the need arises.

Surgeon(s)

There are several types of surgery that you may be interested in on your quest for a body that feels like your own. Each of those is a surgical specialization - doctors who do chest reconstruction surgery don't usually do hysterectomies, for example. There are a handful of clinics that offer soup to nuts, but you may have to go to more than one surgeon. Since gender reassignment surgery is the goal for most transsexuals there are many reviews of the different options available on-line. What to opt for and where to go is something to work out with your gender specialist. (See Chapter Nineteen for more information on surgeons.)

Voice Coach

Chapter Eleven will go into more detail about why a voice coach is so important for transitioning from male to female. Even a few sessions can make the difference between a genuine feminine voice and one that sounds contrived. The best voice coach is a speech therapist, but some singing coaches can help too. A speech therapist who specializes in voice feminization will not only help you change your voice tone and pitch, but also learn feminine inflection and speech patterns. Testosterone will deepen a transman's voice, but if that's not an option, or if you'd like to keep a good singing voice, a voice coach can help there as well. An acting coach can help with movement, mannerisms and speech.

Hair Stylist or Barber

One of the more anxiety-producing "firsts" along the way is going to a barber or hair stylist for the first time. Hair is important in our attribution of gender, and the right haircut makes a big difference in anyone's appearance. I don't know about barbers, but I do know that most hair stylists, especially younger ones, love to help transwomen look better. Don't be shy about asking for a cut that can be styled one way or the other - a good stylist will show you how. And transmen can look better with a good haircut, not just the old buzz clippers.

Personal Trainer

Most people start on this journey woefully out of shape. And hormones don't help - both testosterone and estrogen are well known to contribute to weight gain. Transmen will need to know how to work out so that testosterone doesn't turn them into a dough boy. Transwomen are often reluctant to work out for fear of bulking up, but there are exercises that can help them tone and firm the right places to enhance their shape. Personal trainers are available in any city, in private offices and/or at local gyms.

There are several other crew members that are specific to the needs of the male-to-female journey:

Electrologist and/or laser treatment provider

We'll discuss hair removal options in Chapter Ten. Choosing a good electrologist or laser treatment provider will be an important factor in how long complete hair removal takes, how much it costs, how comfortable treatment is, and how your skin reacts. You can find resources on-line, through a support group, or from your gender specialist. Most electrologists have worked on men, and many are trans-friendly. Just ask how experienced they are working on men, and ask if they're comfortable with transsexuals before showing up dressed as a women.

Esthetician/cosmetologist/beauty consultant

Every woman who wants to look more feminine, or younger, or more professional, can benefit from seeing someone who specializes in skin care and make-up. (I first consulted one when I was a young graduate student teaching undergrads - I asked for help looking older!) And there are plenty to be found - at hair salons, spas, department stores, specialty stores, and selling Avon or Mary Kay. They're all in the business of making women look better, and they generally love doing so. Once you find one you're comfortable with you'll enjoy it too. They are some of the best Allies and Mentors around. The same holds true for nail technicians and other spa or salon services. Saving up for a facial, manicure and pedicure at your local spa is well worth it.

Image, Wardrobe, Fashion, or Color Consultant

If you have a professional job where dressing well is important, it can be worthwhile to meet with an image consultant. She (or possibly he) can help you find the right styles, colors and fit for you and your position. This can save you a lot of money spent on poor clothing choices. There are image consultants in metropolitan areas who specialize in male-to-female makeovers, and have access to wigs, breast forms, large size shoes, etc. You'll find them listed on transgender forums and web-sites. They also often provide coaching in feminine movement, mannerisms, etc. It's a great way to catch up on all those fine points other women spend years learning.

Tailor or seamstress:

Unless you have the ideal body type for the clothes you want to wear, or know how to sew, you'll need to have some clothes altered. A good tailor or seamstress can not only hem things that are too long, he or she can take in jackets, shirts, etc. so that they fit well and look better.

References and Resources

Resources for physicians:

R Gorton, J Buth, and D, Spade, *Medical Therapy and Health Maintenance for Transgender Men: A Guide For Health Care Providers.* Lyon-Martin Women's Health Services. San Francisco, CA. 2005. www.lyon-martin.org

Anne M. Proulx, DO, Sherri L. Morgan, MD, MPH, and Gordon S Walbroehl, MD *Transgender Care Resources for Family Physicians*, Wright State University School of Medicine, Dayton, Ohio, published in *Am Fam Physician.* 2006 Sep 15;74(6):924-926.

Walter O. Bockting and Joshua Goldberg, *Guidelines for Transgender Care*, Haworth Press, 2006

Randi Ettner, A Evan Eyler, and Stan Monstrey, *Principles of Transgender Medicine and Surgery,* Haworth Press, 2007.

References for Therapists:

Walter Bockting and Joshua Goldberg, *Guidelines for Transgender Care*, Haworth Press, 2006.

G.P. Mallon, *Social Work Practice with Transgender and Gender Variant Youth*, Routledge, 2009.

Arlene Istar Lev, *Transgender Emergence: Therapeutic Guidelines for Working With Gender-Variant People and Their Families*, Haworth Press, 2004.

Randi Ettner, *Gender Loving Care: A Guide to Counseling Gender-Variant Clients*, W. W. Norton & Company, 1999

Gianna E. Israel and Donald E. Tarver II, MD, *Transgender Care: Recommended Guidelines, Practical Information & Personal Accounts,* Temple University Press, 1997

Chapter Five

Preparing for Your Journey

In my view the Holy Grail of the process is to achieve a fulfilling, happy, purposeful, socially integrated and rewarding life.

Dr. Russell Reid

A Hero's Journey is not for the faint of heart or poorly prepared. Transitioning takes patience, perseverance, stamina, support, and physical, emotional, spiritual and financial resources.

Your Physical Being

If you're like most transsexuals, you have become alienated or disconnected from your body. One of the common features of being transgender is an intense dislike and discomfort with one's body. Mildred Brown, author of *True Selves*, refers to this as "anatomical dysphoria".[20] This creates

---

[20] Mildred L. Brown and Chloe Ann Rounsley, *True Selves: Understanding Transsexualism*, Jossey-Bass, 1996, p.10

a split between one's psychological being and physical being, and at times an internal war. This can manifest as an apathy towards physical care. "Maybe if I ignore it, I can pretend it's not real." Children with intense anatomical dysphoria have been known to ignore their physical needs to the point of continually wetting and soiling themselves. Adolescents often won't shower. I've known many transsexuals who would not allow a mirror in the house.

This can result in a variety of threats to physical well-being. Eating disorders are common. Sometimes overeating serves to hide or obscure a masculine or feminine body shape. The first transsexual I saw weighed over 350 pounds. And that was down from the 500 pounds he had once weighed. Some transsexuals become anorexic, using excessive dieting in order to look more feminine. Several of my clients had difficulty developing breasts, even on maximum doses of estrogen, because they weren't eating enough. (Estrogen needs a certain proportion of body fat in order to work; that's why anorexics often stop menstruating.) At times the over- or under-eating comes from not paying attention to hunger signals, or from self-punishment. Eating disorders are also often a way of coping with intense feelings of powerlessness.

Another possible consequence of anatomical dysphoria is neglect of physical health and poor hygiene. Going to a doctor, especially a gynecologist, requires acknowledging and revealing to someone else body parts that just shouldn't be there. Having sex is bad enough, but at least you can do that in the dark, and focus on your partner. Poor hygiene and self-care can also be a way of keeping potential partners away. Avoidance of doctors is very common, and can have serious negative consequences.

Anatomical dysphoria can also manifest in physical self-punishment. Tattoos, piercings, cutting, even self-mutilation, are common. These are also ways of numbing the emotional pain of gender dysphoria. Extreme risk-taking serves a dual purpose for male-to-female transsexuals; it makes them seem like more of a man when they're trying to over-compensate for not feeling like one, and it's punishing on the body. Just ask "Joyce", a former pro wrestler, or "Heather", who has had so many brushes with death she reminds me of a cat with nine lives.

Alcohol and drug abuse are also self-destructive ways of coping with emotional pain and internal conflicts. Alcoholism rates are known to be higher among the GLBT population than among the heteronormative.[21] A new study I just received found higher rates of cigarette smoking as well.[22] Both are forms of slow suicide, all too common when living as the wrong gender seems intolerable.

If any of the above applies to you, you've got some work to do before you begin transitioning. As tough as it can be to let go of the coping mechanisms that have helped you get through until now, these health habits have got to change! Hormones carry certain health risks that are increased if you are overweight or a smoker or drinker. Alcohol and drug use cloud your judgment and get in the way of working on personal issues. Self-destructive habits can cut short your new life. Somehow you have to start caring about the body you have now so that you can transform it into a body you can feel comfortable in.

So do yourself a favor, and take the following steps as soon as you can:

1) Schedule a complete physical if you haven't had one in the past year, including a pelvic exam and Pap for biological females. Consider talking to your doctor about your concerns, and asking him or her to run baseline hormone levels.

2) If you are overweight or underweight, discuss this with your doctor and set a goal for yourself. I often set a goal with clients (under 200 pounds, for example) to shoot for before starting hormones. Find a sensible diet plan, such as WeightWatchers or the Duke Diet, not a crash diet. Start integrating exercise into your schedule. Yoga, dance and Pilates are helpful for

---

[21] IOM (Institute of Medicine). 2011. *The Health of Lesbian, Gay, Bisexual, and Transgender People: Building a Foundation for Better Understanding.* Washington, DC: The National Academies Press.

[22] "Smoking Out a Deadly Threat: Tobacco Use in the LGBT Community", American Lung Association, 2010

developing a more feminine figure and presentation. Tai Chi, weight-lifting and martial arts can help build and maintain a masculine physique.

3) Stop smoking! Many endocrinologists won't prescribe hormones to anyone who smokes cigarettes. The risks of strokes, heart attack, etc. are just too high. Put the money you save by not buying cigarettes into a jar for transition expenses.

4) Give your liver a break. Limit your alcohol intake, or quit altogether if you can't set limits and stick to them. Ditto with other addictions, such as prescription painkillers, etc. You can't make a journey of a thousand miles on crutches. Join AA if you need help.

Emotional Stability

Transitioning is an emotional roller-coaster. Facing your own fears and conflicts, coming out to family and friends and coping with their reactions, going out in public "dressed" the first time, learning the nuances of a new gender presentation - all of these are full of emotional ups and downs. And that's even before you add hormones! Estrogen and testosterone have powerful effects on mood, so adding and subtracting them in your system can throw off anyone's emotional balance.

Because your journey ahead may be stormy, it's important to have as much emotional stability going into it as possible. Imagine putting a sail on a kayak and heading out to sea. You won't get very far! A sailboat needs a particular design to withstand the vagaries of the wind. It needs to be weighted properly and balanced.

There are certain emotional issues that just about everyone has to work through as they transition, and the sooner you get started the better. Just about everyone who grows up transgender acquires some guilt and/or shame about being different. Reactions from parents and peers to gender variance can be cruel and humiliating. Boys especially are subjected to ridicule, harassment, bullying and shaming. Images of transsexuals in the media don't help. The message is loud and clear: there's something wrong with you for not conforming to gender roles. That damages self-esteem, to say the least. Internalized transphobia is often the result of this cultural conditioning. We can't help but absorb and internalize the negative judgments of our culture.

The mistreatment of homosexuals and transsexuals also instills a tremendous amount of fear. Post-traumatic stress is the consequence of physical and emotional abuse. The brain is "programmed" to respond with intense anxiety to anything that reminds us of past traumatic events. It's an adaptive mechanism that alerts us to danger. Lisa Hartley, a transgender social worker, talks about "culturally-induced stress " as an ongoing issue for transsexuals.[23]

Depression is also common among transgender clients. The combination of gender dysphoria, damaged self-esteem, years of keeping a secret and being afraid of being found out, feeling guilty and/or ashamed, and trying to be someone you're not takes a tremendous toll. An oppressed minority is a depressed minority! The depression usually lifts as you progress towards your goal, but not always entirely. And post-transition depression is common, for reasons we'll discuss later.

Considering a physical transformation is likely to bring up more fear, and some guilt. The primary fears are about losing family and friends, losing a job, and being subject to harassment, ridicule and violence. These are not unrealistic fears, and must be faced squarely. Guilt can come from religious conditioning, disappointing people, feeling selfish, and/or being told "How can you do this to your family?"

There is hope and healing, however. Talking with a therapist who understands is a tremendous relief. Every week I can see the weight being lifted off of the hunched shoulders of clients sharing their stories, some for the very first time. I forget sometimes how powerful just being compassionate

---

[23] Lisa Hartley, "Culturally Induced Stress ~ It Only Hurts Because We're Different", in Leanne McCall Tigert and Maren C. Tirabassi, eds, *Transgendering Faith : Identity, Sexuality, and Spirituality*, Pilgrim Press, 2004

and understanding can be. My unflinching acceptance of their diversity opens the door to their own self-acceptance.

With the help of a good therapist, you can confront the negative "tapes" in your head telling you you're sick or crazy or bad. Safely exploring those thoughts and feeling helps you reduce the shame, guilt, fear and conflicts that get in your way. You can rebuild your damaged self-esteem, and find true self-acceptance. A good therapist can help you find your voice, find your courage, and find your faith.

This is why psychotherapy is so important. In *The Transgender Companion* Jennifer Seeley talks about two transitions - one internal and one external. Of the internal transition she says:

> This is actually the most important part of the transition. This involves figuring out what you want (remember, this can always change, and that is ok), who you are, what you want to do, how far you want to go in your transition, how you want to live, what changes you want or are willing to make in your life, etc. Even more importantly, this internal transition involves becoming comfortable and accepting of who you are.[24]

She goes on to recommend that everyone take psychotherapy seriously, not just as a way to get referral letters. So does Mara Christine Drummond, in her book *Transitions*:

> I have a personal theory that therapists help people with their gender identity disorders in three ways. Initially they assist by helping someone with an incongruent gender identity accept who they are. Then they provide guidance and expertise to help over come the anxiety and fears caused by coming out to family, friends, coworkers, etc. Finally, therapists teach transsexuals to cope with

---

[24] Jennifer Seeley, *The Transgender Companion (Male to Female)* CreateSpace, 2007,p. 36

the sadness and disappointment that arise when others fail to fully accept them in their new gender.[25]

There are times when psychotropic medication is helpful as well. The decision to try an anti-depressant or other type of medication is up to you, your therapist, and a prescribing psychiatrist, physician or ARNP. But consider talking to them about it if:

- you have severe depression that interferes with your ability to work, or even moderate depression that interferes with your capacity to enjoy life,
- you have severe social anxiety that keeps you from meeting new people or going to a support group,
- you have extreme mood swings, or periods of time when you are either overly active and ambitious or can't seem to motivate yourself to do anything productive,
- you're having trouble controlling your eating habits or alcohol consumption,
- you have frequent thoughts of self-harm or suicide, and/or
- you have another compulsive habit, such as gambling or shopping, or a sex addiction, that controls your life.

Financial Resources

Changing your gender presentation is expensive, especially if you decide you want to surgically modify your body. I'm not going to hazard a guess at total costs, because it varies so much. I suggest you don't try to add it all up at this point, or you may want to give up before you start. But it's never too early to think about how you're going to afford transition-related expenses.

The coping mechanisms people use to try to avoid the issue can also be expensive. Alcohol and cigarettes, compulsive shopping, that bigger and

---

[25] Mara Christine Drummond, *Transitions: A Guide to Transitioning for Transsexuals and Their Families*, lulu.com, 2009, p. 13

better car or truck, the "fixer-upper", are all financial drains. Sticking to a budget, like sticking to a diet, is hard to do when you're depressed.

No matter what condition your finances are in, there's no time like the present to start getting them under control. If your financial situation is less than golden, follow these simple steps:

1) If you are unemployed, find a job. Don't be afraid that you won't be able to keep it if/when you transition. Start at the bottom if you have to, and work hard. Come in early and work late, and find positive ways to get noticed. Make yourself indispensable. If you are underemployed, look for opportunities for advancement, or consider a second job.

2) Add up your **assets** (cash, money in the bank, the value of your house, car, and anything else you own) and **liabilities** (your debts - mortgage, car loan, other loans, credit card balances, etc.) Your assets minus your liabilities is your **net worth**.

3) Check your credit score and credit record with all three major reporting agencies. Close out any credit card accounts you don't use, and clean up any mistakes or old black marks on your credit. You're entitled to one free report a year, and to write in to correct any mistakes.

4) List your bills, including the ones you pay quarterly or annually. Include your mortgage or rent, loan payments, utilities, insurance, phone(s), cable, internet, etc. These are your **fixed expenses**. Figure out how much a month you spend on these.

5) For at least three months, preferably more, track every dollar you spend. That includes gas, food, eating out, entertainment, gifts, hobbies, clothes, and every cup of coffee and lottery ticket you buy. These are your **variable expenses**. Average these out to figure out how much a month you spend.

6) Next calculate your monthly take-home pay. (If you get paid every two weeks, multiply your paycheck by 26 and then divide by 12.) Subtract your fixed *and* variable monthly expenses. If you're like most Ameri-

cans, you will probably end up with a number less than zero. That's how much you're going in the hole every month. For most people that means credit card balances that keep going up rather than down.

7) Now go back to your fixed expenses and see what you can change there. Are you really using that expensive gym membership? Do you need that many cable channels? Can you save money by bundling phone, cable and internet? Are you paying too much for car or house insurance? Shop around and see where you can save money on monthly bills.

8) The real "fat" in your budget is probably your variable expenses. Where can you trim those? Consider making your own coffee, packing a lunch, eating out less, and of course, cutting out cigarettes and alcohol. If your weakness is spending money on trying to make other people happy, you might want to talk to your therapist about that!

9) Once you've trimmed the fat, go back and do another budget. Make a line item for all your fixed expenses and list categories of variable expenses (such as travel, clothes, entertainment and eating out, pet expenses, etc.) **Add a line item for savings if you can.** Figure out what you need to pay on your credit cards in order to pay them off in a year. Then put all except one credit card away, and use that one only in emergencies, or for certain expenses (such as gas or groceries.) Set a limit and pay it off every month. Set aside a fixed amount of cash each week for spending money and retire your debit card. **Make sure this new budget balances!**

10) Check your credit score after a year and recalculate your net worth. You'll be pleased with the results. Then you can really start saving for surgery, if that's your goal, or simply have more money to spend on enjoying your transition.

Social Supports

I've been leading a support group for male-to-female transgender clients for over nine years now. People come and go as they need to, stay for a while or until they complete their surgery, and drop in periodically afterwards. Every now and then attendance is low for a couple months, and I wonder why I continue setting aside the time. Then someone will call wanting to start, or come back and visit. And I'm reminded of how very important it is for people who have been isolated in their secret, thinking there's no one else like them, to meet kindred souls. Here they can come dressed up, or not, and always be welcome. They can share their joys and sorrows and hopes and fears with others who they know really understand. They can find out where in their neck of the woods they can find an electrologist, or transgender-friendly hair salon, or size 13 women's shoes. Sometimes they go out for coffee or a drink afterwards and make new friends. They have found rides to events and medical procedures, apartments for rent, even jobs.

Everyone is nervous the first time they come to the group. Some call and say they're coming for months before they find the courage to attend. Some unfortunately never make it. They're missing a great opportunity for guaranteed social support. (With a therapist-led group there is no judging others, no "harshing", and no one is allowed to dominate or intimidate the group.)

Mara Christine Drummond talks about how she was reluctant to join a support group at first. She didn't think she needed one, but finally went just to get information about resources in her area. She writes: "What I unexpectedly found was how wonderful the people who attended the group were, and how much care, kindness, support and knowledge they were willing to offer me."[26] Jennifer Seeley has a whole chapter on Support. They both acknowledge that they could not have had a successful transition without the help of others.

There are other sources of social support available as well. Family, friends, colleagues, coworkers, church members, social clubs, and service providers are all possible allies. When I stop and think about it, the number of allies and angels out there is amazing. "William" has a set of friends who are

---

[26] Mara Christine Drummond, *Transitions: A Guide to Transitioning for Transsexuals and Their Families*, lulu.com, 2009, p.11

there for him 100%; when he broke up with his girlfriend they took him in and found him a job. "Angela" has a wife who is her best advocate, cheerleader, and wardrobe consultant."Katrina" is not out at her male-dominated job, but the women in the office know, and support her completely. "Tanya" has her electrologist and her hairdresser; the three of them go out to eat frequently. "Jason" tends bar at a gay club on the weekends and is friends with all the regulars. "Sierra" goes there often and finds friends there as well. "Judy", "Janet", "Rose", and "Aidan" all found acceptance and help in a Unitarian Universalist church community.

So how do you go about finding social support? The first step is to take a look at all the people in your life now - your family, friends, classmates or coworkers, etc. We'll talk more about coming out to them in the next chapter, but for now the important question is: Do these people care about you as a person? If the answer is Yes, put them in the Save column! Don't worry about whether you think they'll accept you as transgender or not. Cultivate the relationship by being a genuine and caring friend. If they aren't positive, caring people, consider slowly detaching or disentangling from the relationship. You will have little room in your life for people who drain your energy.

To find additional support, seek out groups in the GLBTQ community. Every major metropolitan area has transgender support groups. So do most college campuses. You can find them on-line, or through your therapist. PFLAG (Parents and Friends of Lesbians and Gays) has been reaching out to include the trans community more. A local PFLAG group will have members with a variety of connections to the GLBTQ community, and plenty of potential allies. Also consider social groups that cater to your interests, such as a book club, hiking group, dance class, or a volunteer activity. Once they know you as a person your gender identity won't be as big an issue. This will also give you a chance to practice the social skills of your new gender role.

Another wonderful place to find support is one that many of you may be reluctant to consider. I'm talking about a church community. A liberal,

Open and Affirming, or Welcoming church community. Before you reject that idea entirely, read the next section....

Your Spiritual Life

Coming to terms with being transgender is likely to provoke a spiritual as well as identity crisis, or spiritual pain and distress. A great deal has been written about the spiritual distress that people often feel when confronted with a life crisis. Spiritual distress is defined as a disruption in one's faith or belief system, with a loss of hope, meaning, and faith in a Supreme Being. A spiritual crisis is a sudden disruption that shakes the very foundation of one's faith. Spiritual pain is: "(1) loss of or separation from God and/or institutionalized religion; (2) the experience of evil or disillusionment; (3) a sense of failing God - the recognition of one's own sinfulness; (4) lack of reconciliation with God; (5) a perceived loneliness of spirit." [27] Acknowledging being transgender often presents a challenge to one's faith in a Supreme Being and certainly a challenge to traditional religious values.

Chances are, the religious community you were raised in didn't have positive things to say about homosexuality or transsexuality. Even if you have left that church and/or religion, the messages you were exposed to still influence how you feel about yourself. Much of the shaming, abuse and rejection that gender-variant children are subjected to is cloaked in religious ideology, either directly or indirectly. If you grew up believing that God and/or your faith community condemns transsexuals, and you think you might be one, then you either have to believe that you're wrong/bad/a sinner or question the beliefs of your religion.

You may have grown up, as others have, praying to God every night to make you into a "real" boy or girl. When puberty hit and you realized God was not going to answer those prayers, you may have felt angry, hurt, betrayed, and/or abandoned by God. You probably felt guilty and

---

[27] Mary Elizabeth O'Brien, "The need for spiritual integrity" In: *Human Needs and the Nursing Process.* Yura, H. and Walsh, M. (Eds.). New York: Appleton-Century-Crofts, 1982, pp. 104, 105

ashamed of your urges and desires, especially if they involved sexual feelings in any way. You may have felt that there was something wrong with you, that you were being punished for some transgression. Or you may have simply given up on God and turned your back on religion and spirituality.

That is akin to throwing the baby out with the bath water. For one thing, spirituality and religion are not one and the same. Religion is an organized set of beliefs, teachings, practices, and institutions, shared by a (usually large) group of people. Spirituality is the individual and communal experience of the meaning and mystery of life, and a connection to something greater than ourselves. Some people find spirituality in their religious communities and practices; many find comfort in them. Spirituality can be experienced with or without a religious faith.

Second, not all religious organizations condemn homosexuality and transsexuality. Some celebrate it! In some Native American cultures, transsexuals were seen as closer to Spirit because they transcended gender roles. In Hinduism, there are bigendered deities. And more and more Christian denominations are re-examining their prejudice against homosexuality and transsexuality. (There is actually very little in the Bible that speaks against either, and most of it is simply a reflection of the cultural norms of the time.)

Many transgendered people have struggled and worked hard to make peace with their God and religion. Some have found a church within their religious tradition that is open and accepting. Many have found a new faith tradition, such as Unitarian Universalism or paganism, that suits them better. Others remain "spiritual but not religious", and seek expression of their spirituality in other ways, such as art, music, or communing with nature.

If you have spiritual distress relating to being gay, lesbian, bisexual or transgendered, there are ways to reconcile and restore your faith. If you have been subjected to religious abuses, there are ways to heal. There are groups within every major organized religion working to address the concerns of GLBTQ members. And a surprising number of transsexual clergy are coming out and/or being ordained. There are many churches now that openly welcome GLBTQ people, and have groups that advocate for their rights. Joining a liberal church community can be a wonderful source of both social support and healing.

However you decide to address it, resolving your religious conflicts and reclaiming your spirituality is important. Your Hero's Journey is a spiritual journey. It is your search for meaning, for hope, for universal love, and for your place in the world. It is a journey of healing, a journey towards wholeness, authenticity and inner peace.

References and Resources

Leanne McCall Tigert and Maren C. Tirabassi, editors, *Transgendering Faith: Identity, Sexuality and Spirituality*, Pilgrim Press, 2004

Jennifer Seeley, *The Transgender Companion (Male to Female)* Create Space, 2007

Mara Christine Drummond, *Transitions: A Guide to Transitioning for Transsexuals and Their Families*, lulu.com

Trans Faith Online: www.transfaithonline.org

PART TWO

INITIATION

Chapter Six

Crossing the First Threshold

The day came when the risk to remain tight in a bud was more painful than the risk it took to blossom.   Anais Nin

Once you have come to a decision about changing your gender presentation, you are ready for the next step in your transition. By now you have met with a therapist, and talked about a plan for the changes you would like to make. Once you embark on that plan, you will need to tell significant people in your life about who you are and what you're going to do. Who, when and how you come out to people depends on your situation and what changes you're contemplating. If you decide that you are who you are, can live with the body and gender presentation you have, and don't care how other people see you, then discussing your gender identity with others is purely optional. But most transsexuals opt for changes that will show. Sooner or later most cross a threshold for which there's no turning back. It's next to impossible to change your gender without people noticing. You have to "come out of the closet", as the saying goes.

There's a wide range of opinions among transsexuals about coming out (and staying out) vs. "going stealth". I've heard the term 'going stealth' used in two ways. One is to transition in such a way that it doesn't show on the outside - by dressing androgynously and hiding the physical changes produced by hormones. (This does not work as well for transmen once they are on hormones; the voice change gives them away, but working up slowly on testosterone levels can buy some time.) The other is to transition completely and then assimilate as a man or woman so completely that no one knows their history. This latter option is preferred by many transsexuals. Some want to come out only long enough to complete their transition and then go back into the closet (or into the woodwork, as some call it). Usually this involves relocating, or at least changing jobs and distancing themselves from their former life. It may be possible for you to do this, if and when you achieve a thoroughly convincing new gender presentation. Being able to simply live as you know yourself to be and be accepted as such, without any hassle or explanation, is a worthwhile goal.

There are definite disadvantages, however, to attempting to go completely stealth. One is that you will continue living with the fear of being "read" or having someone find out about your history. Another is the disconnect from others and the discontinuity of the two lives. You have to be able to leave everyone and everything behind to start over, or make great efforts to conceal or compartmentalize those connections you maintain. But the biggest disadvantage is that once again you'd be living a partial lie. Coming out is about being true to oneself and claiming one's authenticity. It's about coming out of hiding in the shadows, lifting the shroud of shame and secrecy, and saying "This is who I am." Gays and lesbians who come out to friends and family don't always have to, but they do so to reclaim their pride and dignity. Transmen and women can live out and proud as well.

There are other reasons for coming out. Every person who comes out as transgender educates the people around them. Every transperson who makes a positive impression on others fights back the tide of transphobia. It's harder to hate someone you already like! The more people see "regular folks" (as opposed to the stereotypes portrayed by the media) who happen to be transgender the more normal it becomes. If everyone goes stealth how will anyone know how many gender-variant people there really are? And every openly transgender person is available as a role model to others who need help coming to terms with their gender identity. Some of my clients were able to begin transitioning because they recognized someone as transgender and were able to ask that person for advice.

This is not meant to pressure anyone into coming out for the sake of the community. It's an individual decision, and one that may change over time or with different circumstances. I have a friend who was out and involved with the trans community for a number of years, but when he moved to a small town he decided that his history was a personal matter that he didn't need to share with anyone new. Safety is also a concern when moving to an unknown community.

Coming out is a delicate process. It requires courage, grace and support. One of the goals of the coming out process is to preserve your relationships with significant people in your life and to garner support and acceptance from them for your journey. This is not always an easy task! If you've managed to come this far on your own, this is the time to find a therapist and/or support group. Disclosing that you're transgender is a challenging process for a number of reasons:

1) You're opening up about something that you have kept secret for a long time. You've probably worked very hard at suppressing and/or hiding your thoughts and feelings about your gender, and will encounter some internal resistance to expressing them to others. It's not easy to reverse the process of holding so much back.

2) Opening up will bring lingering doubts, fears, conflicts and any posttraumatic stress to the surface. Especially fear - fear of rejection, fear of punishment, fear of losing people you care about. You'll need to be prepared to face those fears and conflicts and overcome them.

3) Being transgender is difficult to explain! Some people will get it right away, but many won't. There may be times when just the thought of having

to explain what you've been through and what you're going through now is overwhelming.

4) It is impossible to control, or even accurately predict, how people will react. You can expect a variety of reactions, many of them the opposite of what you might have predicted. The changes you're planning will be upsetting to some people, even those who love you and want to support you.

5) Coming out can be seen as your first attempt at social communication in your new gender, and you probably still have a lot to learn, and unlearn. (For more on this see Chapter Eleven.) You'll want to make a good first impression!

For most transsexuals, coming out to others is the hardest part of transitioning. It's often what holds people back from even considering making the changes they need in order to be true to themselves. Coming out can also be the most liberating and rewarding part of the process. You will be surprised at how much support you will receive, sometimes from the least likely places. The relief afterwards is so great that many kick themselves for not doing it sooner. And simply being able to be oneself is the greatest gift of all. Hiding a secret takes a lot of emotional energy that can now be freed up to enjoy the changing relationships.

When to come out to others

There are several things to consider in the timing of disclosure. The first has to do with being clear about your direction and confident in your decision. If you are uncertain about transitioning, well-meaning advice could confuse you even more. Opening yourself up to people's varied reactions prematurely can derail your progress and send you into a tailspin. And if you seem unsure of yourself when you come out, people will be less likely to support your decision. You need to be able to articulate what you want to do and why.

Once you have begun a physical transition, you need to consider disclosing before changes are noticeable. If people close to you find out that you've begun transitioning before you tell them, they may react not only to that news but also to the fact that you've been keeping it secret from them. The people closest to you also deserve to know what you have decided to do, as it will certainly impact their lives. If you are under 18, you will need to come out to your parents in order to get their permission for hormones and/or surgery. If you are married or in a committed relationship, your significant other should be involved in your decisions about any permanent changes you undertake.

That said, only you can decide when you're ready. I nudge my clients when I think they're dragging their heels, but never insist. No one should tell you that you have to disclose your gender issues. Once the cat is out of the bag it's hard to get it back in!

Whom to tell first

Often those who are most involved in your life have the most difficult time accepting your transition. For that reason, I often suggest that you pick first the person you believe is most likely to be supportive. This could be a close family member, but it could also be an old friend, your hairdresser, or your second cousin. It is impossible to know for sure how supportive someone will be, but there are a few things I've gleaned from the experiences of my clients and others:

Gender: Women are more likely to be supportive and eager to help, especially with people transitioning from male to female. Homophobia is deeply ingrained in the American male psyche, and is the basis of most transphobia. The men in your life may be uncomfortable even contemplating the changes you're considering, much less talking about them. Male family members and friends may feel like an MtF is abandoning them and/or betraying the "brotherhood". Some men can be less gracious about inviting someone into the brotherhood.

Education and exposure: People who know someone who has transitioned, or know something about gender identity issues, are more likely to be supportive, unless they have had a negative experience with a transperson. Fortunately, with more positive media exposure more people are likely to be somewhat familiar with the idea. You'll be surprised at how many people know someone who is transgender. Do not assume, however, that everyone with a degree in psychology is knowledgeable and supportive. I have colleagues who don't have a clue, or who still relate transgender issues to cross-dressing as a sexual fetish.

Social class and ethnicity: In some sub-cultures gender roles are more strictly determined than others. That may make coming out more difficult, but once you have proven yourself by their definition of a man or a woman you'll be accepted.

Religious background: Don't assume that just because someone goes to church they're going to judge you based on their religion! It depends on how liberal or conservative their church is, and how deeply they're influenced by church doctrine. Liberal Christians who belong to Welcoming or Open and Affirming churches are more likely to make an effort to understand and accept your decision. A true Christian will not judge or reject you.

The nature of your relationship with that person: Some relationships, like that of friend, or cousin, or co-worker, or bridge partner, are less gender-specific than others. By that I mean that the relationship is not defined by gender, as it is in son/daughter, wife/husband, brother/sister, and aunt/uncle. The more "gendered" your relationship, the greater the impact of your transition. My clients have been almost universally surprised at how someone they barely know can be supportive, while a partner or family member struggles to even talk to them about it.

Two other things to consider:

1) Do not tell someone who can't keep it to him or herself until you tell others who would really rather hear it from you. Tell the town or workplace gossip only when you're ready to have your transition broadcast.

2) At some point, think about who will be most upset if they don't hear it from you personally, because once the cat is out of the bag, it will roam.

How to tell people

Coming out as transgender requires educating people about what that means, and what it means to you. Most people take their gender for granted. They were born with typical genitalia, got labeled as male or female, and were given a name that reflected that. From birth they were dressed differently and treated differently based on that assigned gender. (Actually, these days you can spot a little penis in the womb with an ultrasound pretty early on, so a lot of babies come home to a nursery already color-coded for a boy or a girl.) By the age of 3 or 4 most kids have had a glimpse of the "opposite sex" and have figured out the apparent differences between boys and girls. They looked at their own body and thought "OK, that makes me a girl (or a boy)." They learned what's expected of boys and girls and men and women in their culture, and took it to heart. Puberty was still awkward, but the changes were expected, even at times welcomed. They grew into manhood or womanhood, with some struggles because of the sometimes ridiculous and often unrealistic cultural standards, but they resolved those as best they could. They have had no trouble checking off M or F on the numerous forms we fill out growing up.

These "normal" people I call 'gender-consistent'; another common term is 'cisgendered'. Consider them blissfully ignorant. All the pieces of the puzzle match, more or less. Around 90% even fall for the 'opposite sex', as expected. To them this all seems perfectly natural. You're either a boy or a girl, a man or a woman. They have a hard time wrapping their mind around anything different. Ask them what their gender identity is and you're likely to get a very puzzled look. So when you tell them you're transgender they might have no idea what you're talking about. Even the 10% who are gay, lesbian or bisexual may not understand what your problem is.

But everyone likes a good story!

> "As people we are storytellers, and we enjoy listening to the stories of others. We live our lives immersed in stories as we watch the news, read the paper, listen to family members, read a book, or

watch a movie. A good story draws us into the reality and experience of the persons within it. Stories also creep into our soul, speaking to forgotten and lost pieces of our experience, waking them from slumber and inviting them to walk into the light of conscious awareness."[28]

Your task then is to present a story that people can relate to. Simply announcing "I'm transgender" is not likely to get more than a puzzled look. Starting at the end of the story and just telling people you're changing your gender is not likely to garner sympathy and support. You need to start at the beginning of your story and lead the person you're talking to into your experience. Then the decisions you've made will make more sense.

There are two ways to start at the beginning. One is to go back to the beginning of your awareness of being different. "There's something I've been struggling with for a long time. Ever since I was .... I've felt...." The other is to say "I've been seeing a therapist for something that's been bothering me for a long time.... I have something called Gender Identity Disorder." (The second approach works well for people who need third-party verification and/or are medically-minded.) Wherever you start, describe what you've been through and how you've come to the decision to do something about it. Tell them about your struggles to fight your feelings, the sense of isolation you've experienced, the desperate and lonely times. "You cannot just tell a factual story that does not relay the emotional journey of being transsexual. The story needs to contain a human element that discloses whatever hurt and angst you have felt throughout your life."[29]

Once you have "dropped the bomb" you need to give the people closest to you some reassurance about how the transition process will and won't affect you, and them. Mary Boenke, Chair of the Transgender Network of PLAG has a long list of pointers for young people coming out to their

---

[28] Wendy J. Miller *Jesus, Our Spiritual Director*, Upper Room Books, 2004, p.45
[29] Mara Drummond, *Transitions: A Guide to Transitioning for Transsexuals and Their Families*, 2009, p. 19

parents.[30] Some of these are applicable to most relationships. Here is a summary, with my additions:

1) You care about them and don't want to hurt them. You're not doing this out of rebellion or because of anything they have done. You want to include them in your process, and continue to have a good relationship with them. You expect that relationship to improve, now that you can be more honest.

2) You have done your research, met with a therapist, and/or met with other transmen or women. You've been thinking about this for a long time, and are carefully weighing your options. You're not going to rush into anything or make any permanent changes without consultation and reflection.

3) You know that there are risks involved in what you are undertaking, but you really feel that it's the only way you can be comfortable with yourself. You know they'll worry, because they care about you. You also know they want you to be happy.

4) You will still be basically the same person inside, no matter what changes you go through on the outside. You'll most likely still like your favorite foods, pets, music, sports teams, etc. You won't lose your sense of humor, or creativity, or ability to beat them at Scrabble. (Or whatever - think of what that person values most about you.)

5) You are not planning on abandoning your responsibilities. You will still go to work or school, still care for your family and/or friends, and still pursue your future plans/dreams/ambitions. They will still be able to count on you for most of the things that matter to them. (Although you may be preoccupied for a while.)

---

[30] PFLAG pamphlet: *Some Considerations in Coming Out Trans to Your Parents and Family*, by Mary Boenke, Chair, Transgender Network of PFLAG, at: http://community.pflag.org/page.aspx?pid=703

6) You expect to change in certain ways, and not others. (Mention some of what you plan to change and what that might look like). You might end up looking like a twin brother or sister would look. The physical changes will be gradual. You will not surprise other family members (grandparents, etc.) with these changes.

7) You understand that this may be a shock to them, and that they will have a lot of different reactions. You realize that they have an emotional process to go through, similar to the stages of grief. You will continue to talk with them about how this affects them, and help them learn more about it. You know that you're ahead of them in thinking and learning about this.

8) You know the changes will take some getting used to, and you're prepared to give them time to adjust. You know that a new name will be hard, and pronouns even harder. You'll try to be patient when they slip. (And please do your best, especially with parents. Remember, they've know you as one gender for your whole life. They were told you were a boy or girl; they changed your diapers, bought your clothes, and watched you grow up.)

You will not be able to have a stock presentation for everyone, as there is no one right way to tell people. Effective communication is individual, and considers the other person and how he or she best receives and processes information. There are a few things I can advise you *not* to do, from what I've seen:

1) Do not use a medium that the recipient is not familiar or comfortable with. Do not text your parents "HI I M TRANSGENDER. TXT ME W ? (Someone actually did this, and sent the parents into crisis mode.) Consider whether this needs to be a face-to-face conversation, a phone call, or perhaps a hand-written letter. Your cousins might be comfortable with an e-mail; your aunts and uncles might not. A letter or e-mail works well for people who need time to think about things before they respond. Close family members deserve a private face-to-face meeting, if at all possible.

2) Do not show up for an initial face-to-face dressed in your preferred gender, unless that's the way you have always dressed. You can always show pictures if the person wants to see them, but that's usually a second or third step. And don't come out to your extended family by showing up at your cousin's wedding or grandfather's funeral dressed to the nines. That's disrespectful, and won't generate goodwill and support. If you've been living full-time in your preferred gender, find an androgynous outfit that doesn't draw attention to yourself.

3) Do not overload people with information. It's more important to be prepared for their questions and to respond as honestly as you can. You may want to print out some FAQs for anyone who wants more information. (Just Google Transgender 101 to find one that suits your needs.) But don't hand someone a stack of books and expect them to read them all!

4) You do not need to tell everyone your plans all at once. In fact, with family members and intimate partners it's better not to lay out the whole process at first. Let them digest a little at a time. It's sometimes best just to say that you're exploring the options. As you make decisions and initiate changes, break the news gently each step of the way. Spouses in particular often press the panic button, assuming you will leave once your "sex change" is complete.

5) Do not argue with people's values. You're not likely to change someone's fundamental beliefs and values. You might have to find a way to explain the necessity of what you're doing in *their* terms. If someone says "God doesn't make mistakes", you can say "You're right, s/he made me transgender", whether you believe in God or not. People's reactions to your coming out will vary, of course. Being respectful, confident, and open to their questions will go a long way. But remember that each person's response depends to a large degree on his or her capacity for understanding, empathy, and tolerance for ambiguity. It takes an open mind and an open heart to support someone on this unique journey. People who are rigid and closed-minded in their thinking, or who can only think of their own needs, will probably not be able to adjust to your changes.

6) Do not take someone's initial reaction as their "final answer". Most people will be shocked, unless you've already begun changing or have dropped hints along the way. Many will resist or reject the idea at first. Others may seem supportive, saying all the right things, but show over time that they don't really understand or accept the reality of your transition. Coming out is just the beginning of your dialogue with the important people in your life. There will be many talks, some filled with tears and some with anger. Be prepared to weather their ups and downs in coming to terms with your decisions. If you cut people out of your life because they are not immediately supportive, you may lose valuable relationships.

Coming Out to Children

One of the biggest concerns most people have is the impact of transitioning on children in the family. Spouses or partners will often raise this as a reason to stop or delay progress. Coming out to children needs to be done carefully, but it is not as devastating as people imagine. Kids are resilient. You don't need to protect them from the truth. Because children understand things very differently at different stages of cognitive development I'll break down some of the considerations by age.

Under age 3: No explanation is necessary. They will grow up knowing you as who you present to them. At some point later you can show them pictures and explain your history.

Ages 3 - 6: Preschool children are very fluid in their thinking. They don't have fixed concepts yet. They can think, for example, that they're going to be older than an older sibling when they grow up. The idea that a boy can grow up to be a woman or a girl to be a man is easy for them to grasp. They're just learning about the difference between boys and girls and what each is supposed to be like. This gives you the opportunity to shape their thinking about gender and gender stereotypes. There are stories and videos available through PFLAG for this age level.

Ages 6-12: At this age children have formed fixed concepts about gender and can have very concrete ideas about it. It's important to start preparing them ahead of time by opening up their thinking. You do this by your use of language and the ways you talk about men and women. Questioning their assumptions about what's appropriate for boys and girls can lead to broader discussions about the limitations of stereotypes. Having fun dressing up for Halloween or theme parties is a great way to introduce cross-dressing.

Ages 12- 18: This is your toughest crowd. I've seen the most extreme reactions at this age - either totally cool with the idea or not accepting at all. They're often questioning everything they've been told about sex and gender, but they're also subjected to a lot of peer pressure. Teenage boys especially have a hard time coping with homophobia. Open discussions about homosexuality, harassment and bullying, and restrictions based on gender will engage their interest. Sharing some of your experiences a little at a time can help prepare the way for coming out.

Ages 18-25: Young adults tend to be self-centered, and mostly interested in what the impact is going to be on their lives. They need to know that your relationship with them isn't going to change. They've been exposed to a fair amount of diversity by now, and if you've raised them well can be very accepting and supportive. But they're also at the age when they need a stable home base to launch from, so they won't be happy with any changes in the family structure.

Over age 25: Respect that your children are now grown-up, and relate to them as adults. Sit them down and explain what you're going through the same way you would to a friend.

At any age, it's best to come out to children gradually, keeping discussions simple, brief and matter-of-fact. Allow them to ask questions in their own time. Keep the dialogue open and let them know you care about how they feel about all this. Demonstrate your understanding of how your transition can make their life difficult with peers. With school-age and adolescent children, discuss what they can call you that doesn't out you or embarrass them. Most of all, reassure them that you love them and will always be their parent (or aunt/uncle/grandparent).

It's also helpful for children to have other supports. Your spouse or partner may want to rush your child(ren) into therapy, but unless the therapist is knowledgeable that could do more harm than good. It's better to bring them to your therapist or support group, or to a COLAGE (People with a Lesbian, Gay, Bisexual, Transgender, or Queer Parent) or PFLAG meeting. Introducing them to a transgender friend before you come out is a great way to introduce the topic and assess their thinking and understanding. Your therapist may also be able to connect you with other transsexuals who have children who will talk to yours.

Coming out to a Spouse or Partner

In the best of all possible worlds, your spouse/partner loves you for who you are on the inside, and will continue to love you and be with you no matter what happens. He or she doesn't care what other people think, or how much money your transition will cost. They just want you to be happy. In this utopia your intimate partner will be attracted to you before, during and after your transition, and can't wait to make love to your new body.

That's a pretty tall order, isn't it? I actually have seen this dream come true for many of my clients. It's not an easy road for their spouses/partners; they are some of the true heroes in this story. If you think about the impact that transitioning will have, and what it will require of someone who stays in a relationship with you, you can see why coming out to your spouse or partner needs to be done with love, patience and understanding.

If you married someone hoping that marriage would cure you of your "cross-dressing" or other urges, you probably married someone thoroughly heterosexual who was attracted to and reinforced the gender presentation you were trying to sell the world (and yourself). If you've been "hiding" in a lesbian or gay relationship, your partner may be solidly invested in her or his homosexual identity. Your transition will rock the very foundation of your relationship. She or he thought they were marrying/committing to a man or a woman, and the masculinity or femininity you presented was probably a big part of what they were attracted to. In a heterosexual relationship especially, your masculinity or femininity helped define their femininity or masculinity. Coming out as transgender can also prompt your partner to question his or her own identity regarding gender and/or sexuality. Even if the person you're with identifies as bisexual, your transition will change how the rest of the world perceives him or her, and that is a big adjustment.

Most spouses or partners will assume that if you want a "sex change" a divorce is inevitable. They may think that you will want to be with someone different, or they know that they don't want to be with the gender you're transitioning to. (We'll talk about how to negotiate other options in Chapter 13.) That is why I recommend giving them a little information at a time. When a married or partnered client comes in talking about wanting to transition, I suggest that they first tell their spouse or partner simply that they've started seeing a therapist about some of their own internal conflicts that have been bothering them. Then they can open up later about their gender dysphoria, how they've tried to deal with it, etc. Wanting to make physical changes is best addressed one issue at a time. Even confessions about "cross-dressing" take time for the other person to process. As you progress, you'll need to include your spouse/partner in your decision-making. Negotiating your needs and respecting his or her needs is a delicate balancing act. You may need to consider compromising your goals, or at least slowing down your progress, if you want to give the relationship a chance. Couples therapy and support groups can help hold the relationship together.

Coming Out at Work or School

Coming out to people at work or school who are not as close to you is most likely a later step in your transition. This brings up legal and other matters that we'll discuss in Chapter Eighteen. As tempting as it may be to confide in someone at work you think is sympathetic, it's usually better to hold off and wait until you have your ducks in a row for the legal name change and the switch to living full-time in your new gender role. At school or at work your best friend one day may have a problem with you the next and out you before you're ready.

Coming Out to Friends

Assuming you have chosen your friends well, coming out to them is probably the easiest of all. But it can still be fraught with anxiety. You still have to entertain the possibility that some friends won't be able to deal with your changes. If the relationship was based on a particular gender-typed activity or interest, you'll either have to reassure them that you still love watching chick flicks or fixing cars (or whatever), or let the friendship go. In any case, be prepared to accept that even casual friendships will change as you transition. There are subtle (and sometimes not so subtle) differences in how men and women relate to "same-sex" and "opposite-sex" friends.

The changing nature of social as well as intimate relationships will be discussed more in Chapter 20. It is really an eye-opener for those who cross the gender divide. You could qualify for a degree in Gender Studies before you're done.

References and Resources

Mary Boenke, Editor, *Trans Forming Families: Real Stories about Transgendered Loved Ones Third Edition*, published by PFLAG Transgender Network, 2008

PFLAG (Parents and Friends of Lesbians and Gays) - www.pflag.org

Mildred L. Brown and Chloe Ann Rounsley, *True Selves: Understanding Transsexualism,* Jossey-Bass, 1996

Tina Fakhrid-Deen, with COLAGE, *Let's Get This Straight: The Ultimate Handbook for Youth with LGBTQ Parents*, Seal Press, 2010.

COLAGE: People with a Lesbian, Gay, Bisexual, Transgender,or Queer Parent - www.colage.

Chapter Seven

Gender Presentation

If one advances confidently in the direction of one's dreams, and endeavors to live the life which one has imagined, one will meet with a success unexpected in common hours.

Henry David Thoreau

This next section assumes that you have decided to change your physical appearance to more closely match your gender identity. There are two main reasons for doing this. One is to be able to look at yourself in the mirror and see the person you feel yourself to be. The other is to be able to be out in the world and have other people perceive you as the gender you feel yourself to be. Most transsexuals want both. Passing as a man or woman, with and without clothes on, and not being read as a transsexual, is seen by many as the ultimate goal. But it's not the only workable solution to gender dysphoria.

Some people are only concerned about how they see themselves, and don't mind being seen as male, female, or in-between. I have one client who is considering chest reconstruction surgery but not masculinizing hormones. She (for the time being) has an androgynous presentation and name. She doesn't care whether people perceive her as a man or a woman. But her breasts feel totally foreign to her, and she wants the option to present as a guy. Another client came in asking about vaginoplasty without hormones. This person is living with and caring for an aging relative, and has a public persona as a crusader for an important cause. But she wanted that inner peace of knowing she's at least partly how she feels.

There are, of course, limitations to the goal of looking in the mirror and seeing your true self. For one thing, it's probably not possible to perfectly attain the image you have of yourself. (Unless you have unlimited resources for cosmetic surgery, and even then there are limitations to what can be done.) You probably see yourself as younger, prettier and more feminine (or taller, and more handsome and masculine) than you can look. It's important to understand those limitations before you start, and to accept that you'll never have exactly the body you feel you should have been born into. It may help to know that no one has a perfect match between how they see themselves and what they see in the mirror. (Some mornings I hardly recognize the older woman in my mirror.)

The other limitation is that if you change only for you and keep those changes hidden there may still be a disconnect between how you see yourself and how others see you. Being called "ma'am" rather than "sir", or vice versa, can be a very alienating experience. That alienation can intensify the more you start to become more yourself if it is not recognized by others.

There are also transmen and women who present as their true gender without hormones or surgery. "Mary" is an older transsexual who has been living full-time as a woman for many years. She looks so good that a journalist visiting our support group wrote that her "gorgeous red wig" (which is her real hair) suited her perfectly. She has decided that she doesn't need hormones or gender reassignment surgery to feel like a woman and present as one. (She did, however, decide to have breast implants.) There are also unfortunately many transsexuals who cannot afford the surgery that would help them feel complete. Their challenge is to present as best they can on the outside, knowing who they are on the inside.

In the best of all possible worlds, passing as a man or woman wouldn't matter. Men and woman would feel free to dress how they like, without judgment, without fear of harassment, violence or discrimination. A man walking down the street in a dress would be no more objectionable than a woman in jeans. Boys would wear pink tutus when they felt like it, and lesbian couples everywhere could go to high school proms in matching tuxedos without recrimination. I'm hoping my grandchildren will see that dream come true, but I doubt that I will. Unfortunately, most people like their world ordered in a certain way, and that includes seeing people as either male or female and fitting into their view of what men and women should look like. For reasons I still can't fathom they take offense at people who challenge what they believe is the "natural order of things". Until the dawn of a more enlightened society trans-people will have to live in a world populated by people of all "mind-widths".

So this part of the book is for those who would like to learn how to present, convincingly, as the "opposite sex". I'd like to start with a bit of theory about the presentation of self.

Gender presentation is one aspect of social communication. We use other aspects of social communication when we flirt, for example, or try to get out of a speeding ticket. Gender presentation is expressed in the way we dress, style our hair, walk, talk, and interact with others. It is both conscious - things we manipulate on purpose, like clothing and hair style, and unconscious - the way we move through a room, or subtle speech patterns.

Gender presentation varies from culture to culture, along with social norms. Italian men, for example, talk with their hands more than German women. There is also variation within cultures. Yet we have no problem in our own culture identifying feminine men and masculine women based on their mannerisms. The following list applies to the cues typical of mainstream Amercian culture:

GENDER PRESENTATION

Cues people use to determine gender at a glance:

<u>Masculine</u>   <u>Feminine</u>

HAIR

Short -------------------------------- Long and/or styled

BODY SHAPE

Tall, angular ----------------------------- Shorter, curvy

CLOTHING

Plain, tailored ----------------------------- Soft, flowing

ACCESSORIES

Plain ----------------------------------- Fancy, colorful

VOICE AND SPEECH PATTERNS

Low, sparse -------------------------------- High, varied

MANNERISMS

Commanding ------------------------------- Expressive

Gender attribution is how other people perceive us. In everyday life, we automatically "gender" the people we see (and hear). It's an automatic, unconscious process that happens in a split second. We do this based on a number of cues, such as voice, body shape, hair style, clothing, etc. Some cues are weighted more than others - the presence of large breasts is read as female and significant facial hair as male, generally overriding other ambiguous cues. Recognition of male vs. female faces is a subtle process that includes facial structure, coloring and contextual cues. In the absence of obvious cues, it's the overall impression that registers. It's the "preponderance of evidence" that matters. We are cognitively predisposed to resolve conflicting information and overlook what doesn't fit the general impression. Once we make that identification as male or female, it's set, unless there's a glaring inconsistency.

There are individual differences in what people pay attention to in gender-typing others. While it's impossible to predict how each person perceives gender, I'll hazard a few generalizations. Men are more likely to focus on body shape (hour-glass figure especially) and breasts. The theory is that this is pre-wired as an evolutionary advantage - for picking women who are best suited for childbearing. American teenage girls, on the other hand, are more likely to notice the brand and style of jeans someone is wearing. That is one reason why a person in transition can walk through a mall and be seen by some people as a man and others as a woman. They're noticing different cues, and putting what they see into their own cognitive schema.

The diagram at the end of this chapter shows one way communication can be divided up to explain the other main reason for different "readings" at different times. The total of our communicable experience can be divided both into what's visible (or audible) or not to others, and what's conscious, or not, to ourselves. Our conscious presentation of self is what we purposely make noticeable to others. There are things that we keep secret, and there are also things that we are not aware of but others notice. You've probably had the experience of watching two people who are obviously attracted to each other but don't realize it yet themselves. Feelings that we're not aware of "leak" through our body language and our tone of voice.

Poker players, for example, look for their opponents 'tell' - a subtle gesture or facial expression that gives away whether they're bluffing or not.

So when clients tell me that sometimes they're seen as their preferred gender when they're not even trying, and then sometimes read when they are trying, I tell them that's par for the course! You'll never be able to totally control how people see you. This is one of the most difficult adjustments in early transition. Being relaxed and confident in who you are will go a long way, however, along with becoming more aware of what your body language is communicating.

The next sections of the book are about how to dress, walk, talk and otherwise present as the gender you feel yourself to be. They may seem artificial, or superficial, but they can make the difference between fitting in as your real gender and sticking out like a sore thumb. The suggestions I make are based on the assumption that you do not want people staring at you, or worse. If you want to be a gender outlaw (deliberately mixing gender cues to defy current stereotypes) and make me people wonder, that's fine too. Reading these sections will help you make informed choices about the impression you want to make.

These are the trials and tribulations of transitioning. It can take a lot of trial and error to learn how to present convincingly as a man or woman. This is more challenging for transwomen than transmen, who may have lived in tomboy mode for many years. There will be highs, such as the first time you get called "ma'am" or "sir" out in public. And there will be times when you wonder if you'll ever pass. One of the things to remember is that body image - how we perceive ourselves - changes more slowly than our actual image. This is because of the nature of perception. We don't see exactly what is in front of us. We see what our brain perceives is there, which is based on a perceptual schema, a cognitive framework based on experience. Our brain automatically reverts to seeing ourselves in a familiar way. This is why people with anorexia can still see themselves as fat, and I can't see why my jeans don't fit me anymore. You will see yourself as your former gender far longer than others do.

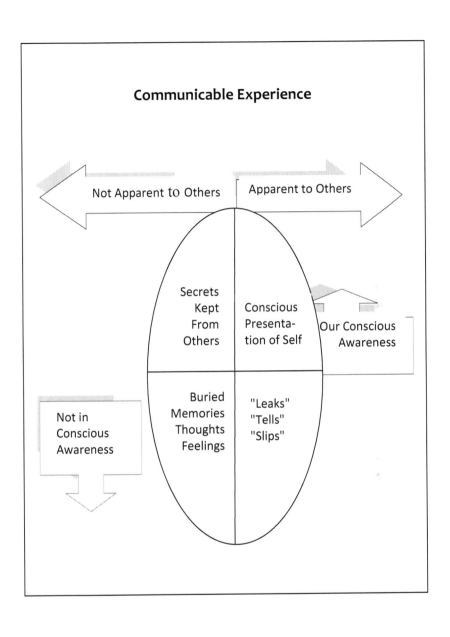

Chapter Eight

Clothes Make The Man/Woman

The body is the shell of the soul, and dress the husk of that shell; but the husk often tells what the kernel is.   - anonymous

The clothing (and accessories) we wear are a significant means of social communication. They carry not only cues about gender, they carry messages about who we are and what we're looking for from our audience. They communicate our personality and values, our social class, and even at times our profession or religion. (Think of the plain clothing style of the Amish.) Clothing communicates all this through color and style. Color is a powerful communicator, and has been shown to affect the wearer's and the viewer's emotional responses. Style includes fabric (texture, weight, and finish) and shape (cut, fit and length). Once you learn the language of color and style, you can better express the message you want to send. And it has to be learned. From what I've seen fashion sense is not encoded in the "female brain". It takes most women years to develop and refine their personal style, and we all know some who never do. Men may seem to have an easier time, with a narrower range of options, but how they dress also communicates clear messages about who they are and what they're all about.

As you start your transition, many of you have the unique opportunity and challenge of building a wardrobe from scratch. You can do this by trial and error, just grabbing off the rack what appeals to you, or you can shop with a plan. Trial and error gets expensive! You'll end up with a lot of clothes that don't fit, don't look right on you, or communicate the wrong message. One of the greatest concerns I hear about going out "dressed" is "I don't want to look like a man in drag!" The best way to avoid that is to do your homework, and learn what looks best on you. I say this for FtMs as well as MtFs, as there are particular challenges inherent in dressing a female body to look masculine. Transwomen also have the advantage of being able to talk about clothes and get advice from cisgendered women. Guys don't talk about clothes very often.

If you're a biological male who's been "cross-dressing" for a while, you may have a lot of clothes that you've picked because they're especially feminine and/or sexy. Those may have to go to the back of your closet, to be worn at home or possibly out to a club. Many transsexuals go through a phase of dressing up in a way that's not really appropriate for everyday wear. Many also dress in clothes that are "too young" for them. This probably comes from years of looking longingly at what the girls in school were wearing that they couldn't.

Clothing Choices for Transwomen

So let's start with how "real women" (as opposed to Hollywood stars and fashion models) choose what to wear every day. The reason many women often have a hard time deciding what to wear is that there are many factors to take into consideration. "Ordinary" women choose their clothing based on:

Context: This includes:

a) **Activity** - obviously going to play tennis requires a different outfit than going out for the evening. But so does going grocery-shopping and having lunch with a friend. Dress codes at work, both those written down and those that are unspoken, will vary from one workplace to the next. It is vitally important to observe what other women at work wear before you transition on the job, and to reassure your employer that you will dress appropriately.

b) **Location** - Playing tennis or having lunch with a friend at a fancy country club calls for a different outfit than going to the Y and meeting at a sandwich shop. Location also includes part of the country. Cities tend to be dressier than rural areas. If I were going out to eat in Boston I would dress up much more than I would at even the fanciest restaurant in Vermont. I've also noticed that the further south I travel, the shorter the skirts and higher the heels.

c) **Occasion** - Even dressing up for going out depends on the event or occasion. An office party requires more conservative options than a "Girl's Night Out" or a transgender event such as Fantasia Fair. Women often try to figure out what others will be wearing before choosing an outfit; they don't want to be under-dressed or over-dressed for the occasion. Being dressed far more casually than anyone there seems disrespectful, not honoring the occasion properly. Dressing "over the top" also stands out, and it's considered poor manners to outshine the hostess or birthday girl.

Season and weather: Although old rules such as "Don't wear white after Labor Day" are outdated, there are still unspoken guidelines about the colors, fabrics, and styles worn during different seasons. In some parts of the country, this is for practical reasons. Sandals don't hold up very well in the snow, for example, and wool is too warm for summer wear. Much of it is purely convention at this point, but it does influence what women wear. Defying these conventions because you're not cold will draw attention to you. You'll need to change over your wardrobe at least twice a year (in most of the country). In the fall put away shorts, short-sleeved shirts, light, thin fabrics (such as linen), light-colored outfits, sundresses and sandals.

Their body type: Most women have a basic understanding of their body shape and some idea how that influences what looks good on them. The biggest complaint women have about off-the-rack clothes is that they're designed for an ideal body type that few women over the age of 30 can attain. (Probably second is inconsistent sizing, which will certainly frustrate anyone who's been buying men's clothes for any length of time.) So they struggle with finding clothes that fit their body, often settling for clothes that cover up more than enhance their shape. With a little research you can figure out what looks best on you.

Coloring: Most women also develop a sense of what color "season" or "family" they like best. There have been several books written about how to find the colors that look best on you, based on hair and eye color and complexion. Again, with a little research you can figure this out for yourself, and save time and money knowing what colors to shop for.

Age and relationship status: We've probably all heard the comment "Why doesn't she dress her age?" or "She shouldn't dress like that at her age." This is blatant age-ism, of course, but it points out definite social norms for women. The same holds true for women who are married or in a relationship. Sexy clothes that reveal a lot of skin are seen as appropriate only for women who are young and looking for male attention. This is often heartbreaking for transwomen who have been waiting for years to be able to wear those short tight skirts and low-cut tops! The choice is yours, but be aware that if you don't look good in them you'll probably be seen as a transvestite, and even if you look fabulous you'll stand out and attract unwanted attention.

Personal style: Everyone has a personal style that shows up in the clothes they tend to buy. These have been labeled many different ways, including romantic, dramatic, artsy, sexy, classic, natural, city chic, sporty, and earthy. Most women have a hard time defining their style, but they can tell you their favorite store or catalog. Their style may be an adaptation to their career or their body type, or it could be a deliberate expression of their personality. I have a friend who shops almost exclusively at Talbot's because she knows their clothes fit her and suit her career. I have another who peruses Goodwill and consignment shops to find unique combinations of artsy clothes. Finding your personal style may take some time, but once you do you'll feel more comfortable and confident. There are numerous on-line quizzes that can help you define your style; try out several because each one has its own classification.

Clothing Choices for Transmen

Transmen also have to consider context, season and weather, their age and body type, and personal style. What men wear not only communicates gender, it says a lot about their position in life. Men are profiled by their attire, not just skin color. A client recently told me a story about how a (cisgendered) friend of his had been mistreated by emergency room staff, who called the police rather than giving him the mental health treatment he needed. The decision was based more on the person's appearance than on his behavior. "If he'd gone to the ER in a suit, I bet they would have taken him in and treated him," he complained. Transmen need to be just as aware of the image they're creating as transwomen. Being a rebel in how you dress may feel good to you, but what kind of attention does it attract?

One of the first challenges for transmen is body type, which we cover later in this chapter. Since most transmen are shorter and have wider hips than the average male, they need to dress to look taller and minimize their hips. Finding clothes that fit can be difficult, but worth the extra effort. There are plenty of on-line resources for short men; Hudson's FtM website covers these in detail.

Men also need different clothes for different occasions and activities. Context is always relevant, especially in a work setting. Advancement in the workplace is helped by dressing for the job you're in line for, not the one you're in now. If your workplace has a "casual Friday" dress code, what does that really mean? Chances are it doesn't include ratty jeans or baggy cargo shorts. Spend a little extra to get quality clothes and have them tailored if necessary. Learn to tie a tie and wear them. Save your favorite band t-shirts for weekends. Showing up at your girlfriend's parents' house in a button-down shirt (tucked in), khakis and V-neck sweater or vest will get you a lot more respect and acceptance than jeans and a t-shirt. Inappropriate attire in any context will not get you the respect you deserve.

Different seasons and weather also call for different clothing. And I don't just mean long vs. short-sleeved shirts. You'll need to change over your wardrobe twice a year, once in the fall and once in the spring. Once it's time to get sweaters out, it's also time to put away shorts, short-sleeved shirts, light-colored khakis, and sandals. And it may seem more "manly" to not wear a jacket when it's cold out, but the right jacket will balance a pear-shaped figure and add style to whatever you're wearing.

Transmen, especially younger ones, need to be especially careful about dressing their age. When you first cut your hair short and start dressing like a guy you're probably going to look much younger than your age. If you don't want to look like a teenage boy, try to avoid dressing like one! Avoid baggy pants and shorts, heavy metal t-shirts, and baseball caps. To develop your own style, start with paying attention to what other men wear, especially men you admire. You can enlist help from a female friend to find out what colors suit you best. Once you get a sense of what you like and what you look good in, follow the suggestions below for building a wardrobe.

Building a Wardrobe (For Men and Women)

Now the fun begins! As you transition, from male to female or female to male, you get to build a whole new wardrobe. Two, actually - one for each season. Even if you've been female-bodied dressing as a guy for a while, or a "cross-dresser" with a closet full of dress-up clothes, you need to start at the beginning. The first step is to assess your clothing needs based on your lifestyle. To do this, you need your calendar or planner. List all the different activities and occasions you've participated in over the past 6 months, and/or plan to participate in during the months ahead. For each one estimate how much time in a week or month you spend engaged in that activity. Include activities such as work or school, sports or hobbies, clubs or community activities, entertaining or eating out, housework and errands, travel or vacations, and downtime. This tells you the range of activities that you need different outfits for, and how many of those you need. Assuming you do your laundry once a week and wear clean clothes daily, you can then start a list of those outfits that you need. Here's a fictional example (for a man or a woman):

Work.................................... 5 days/week..........................5-10 work outfits
Working out.........................3 days/week.............................3 workout sets
Volunteer at the Y..................2 days/month.................2 nice casual outfits
Eating Out............................1 day/week ....1 dressier outfit
Housework, yard work...........2 days/week..........................jeans and tops
Running errands...................1 day/week..........................1 casual outfit
Public Speaking....................1 day/month.......................1 "classy" outfit

You can see from this that unless you have lots of occasions to go out dressed up, or work in banking, law or the fashion industry, you won't need a lot of suits or dresses. But you also can't spend all week in jeans and t-shirts. Consider your job, your neighborhood, your social group and what men and women wear in your circle. Most of you will need more "middle of the road" outfits than you realized. These are often the hardest to put together.

Once you know what you'll be dressing for you can take a look at what you have now and see where the gaps are. You can make a chart and fill in the blanks. Here's our example:

Activities/Occasions	Clothes You Own	Clothes You Need-
Work:	3 pairs of slacks, 6 shirts/tops	more slacks (or skirts) jacket or sweater to match
Working Out:	2 pairs shorts, 5 t-shirts	1 pair of gym shorts/sweats
Volunteering:	1 decent casual outfit	another casual outfit
Eating Out:	3 dressier outfits	sweater to go with them
House/yard work:	1 pair old jeans, 5 t-shirts	another pair comfy jeans
Running errands:	old jeans and t-shirts above	nice jeans, casual top
Public Speaking:	dressier outfits above	1 good suit, sensible shoes

When you start shopping for the clothes you need to add to your wardrobe, take your color chart with you. (See the section below on Finding Your Best Colors.) Choose a basic neutral color as the foundation for different outfits, such as black, brown, gray, tan or navy. If you're color blind, you'll definitely need help picking out clothes. If you shop on-line, be sure to take your bust, waist, hip, inseam, shoulders and sleeve length measurements. EBay is a wonderful source for new and used clothing, and most listings will include those measurements. Goodwill stores and consignment shops are great places to shop on a tight budget. Fashion Bug, Dress Barn and Lane Bryant have clothing for large women. Unless you have money to burn, choose more classic styles over the latest fashion. To get the most value out of your purchases, think about cost per wearing, as opposed to cost per item. The basic skirt or slacks you'll wear a lot is worth spending more on than the top you'll only wear on special occasions.

Wardrobe Essentials for Transmen

A dark well-tailored suit: Black is the usual recommendation, but charcoal (dark gray), gray and dark brown work well too. Make sure the sleeves and pants are the correct length. If you're a student or a "starving artist" or just can't imagine ever needing to wear a suit, you can skip it and put your money into the next two items.

A navy blue sport coat or blazer: This is a less formal alternative to a suit jacket that you can wear with just about any pair of pants. Wear it with gray dress pants, white shirt and striped tie for a job interview or speaking engagement, or with chinos and a blue Oxford shirt for dinner with the in-laws.

Dress pants: These are plain slacks in a neutral color; gray is versatile, but black, brown and navy are also acceptable. You'll need two pairs: wool for winter and a polyester or linen blend for summer. Plain front and trim fit work better for most FtMs than pleated or relaxed fit.

Button-down shirts: Long-sleeve and short-sleeve Oxford cotton or cotton blend shirts in white (or ivory/cream if your suit is brown) and blue are essential. With these you can mix and match with the above items and be prepared for any occasion.

Ties: You'll need three : one solid color, one conservative (think striped) and one really awesome (such as a Jerry Garcia). They should be fairly skinny, and proportioned to your height. Look at the men around you to see what they're wearing.

Chinos and/or corduroy pants: These are your more casual pants, but still nicer than jeans. Brown, khaki (light olive) and navy are good choices. Wear chinos in the summer and switch to corduroys in the fall.

V-neck vest and/or sweater: Add a light V-neck vest or sweater in the same color as your chinos or corduroys and you've got a classic outfit that will make you look longer and leaner.

Overcoat: A good all-weather coat, such as a lined raincoat, is an important investment. If you have a chance to splurge, a leather bomber jacket would be your best choice for a second coat. Double-breasted pea coats are a good choice too. Layering on more sweatshirts just adds bulk, and is best avoided by anyone over 21.

Binders: If you have more than an A cup and haven't had chest reconstruction surgery you'll probably want some way to hide your breasts. Adding on layers of t-shirts, oversized shirts and sweaters or sweatshirts may work in the winter, but it looks suspicious in the summer. Slouching to try to make them disappear leads to poor posture and back problems, and conveys a lack of confidence. Do-it-yourself methods of binding (with ace bandages, etc.) are less effective, painful, and can constrict your breathing. A binder, compression shirt, or tight flattening sport bra is the best solution. There are different kinds of binders; there are compression shirts made for men with gynecomastia, some designed for athletes, and several specifically made for transsexuals. They're all hot, constricting and uncomfortable, but some less so than others. It's worth the time and money to do some research and find one that works for you. You'll need two, so that you can hand wash and line dry them thoroughly. Whatever you use, give your chest a break when you can. Body powders can help prevent itching and rashes.

Packers/ Stuffers: Another item specific to FtMs is called a "packer" or "stuffer". This is a soft pliable form shaped like male genitals that you wear in your underwear (briefs work best) to create a realistic-looking bulge in your pants. There are a variety of brands and types; some are made for urinating while standing and some others can be adapted for that purpose. (There are also separate devices that make it possible to urinate while standing.) They also need to be washed periodically, so get two. In a pinch, rolled up socks will do. Be creative!

Essentials for Transwomen

Good bras and underwear: Every image consultant will tell you that your undergarments are essential for a good fit to your clothes. Do not guess at your bra size. Get fitted if you can. You'll need to try on several different kinds to find one that gives you the proper support and "lift". Your bra should fit snug against your body, without bunching or bulging around it. If it leaves indentations when you take it off it's too tight. You'll need at least three good bras - two in ivory, beige or nude, and one in black. If you're still developing, or under-developed, get a padded bra or one with inserts for breast forms. Choose breast forms that are proportionate to your body frame. D cup forms may be tempting, but they'll look ridiculous if you have a 36" chest. If you're developing but need to disguise the growth for now, use a figure-flattening sports bra.

The sweater or suit jacket that goes with everything: Find one in the basic color for your season. It completes an outfit and pulls separates together. If you're an inverted triangle body shape, it can be any length as long as it is fitted at the waist. This season (Fall 2011) they're calling it the "boyfriend jacket". Look for corduroy or velvet to make it special. A long belted cardigan sweater is another good option.

"Little black dress": This is a staple that stylists recommend because it can be dressed up or down with scarves and/or jewelry. But if you don't have the figure for a little black dress, try a skirt (full, not straight) or wide pants, and a plain belted tunic top. And black isn't the only color choice. Black doesn't look good on everyone. Try burgundy (dark red), royal or dark blue, or purple.

Basic "three piece suit": Men are used to thinking of a suit in a certain way, and transitioning away from that can be a challenge. For a woman, a three-piece suit is a skirt, slacks, and jacket and/or sweater in one color. Add 2-3 coordinating tops and you can make a variety of different outfits. For the inverted triangle, the skirt and slacks can be a lighter shade of the color.

Sensible shoes and classic boots: Unless you're petite, retire the 3"and higher heels. (You can use them to practice walking, which we'll discuss later.) You don't want to draw attention to your height or the size of your feet, so your shoes and boots should be understated. Simple flats or 1" pumps in dark neutral colors work best.

Nice jeans that fit well: The array of jeans styles for women can be overwhelming. (Not to mention that sizing can be totally inconsistent from one brand to the next.) Gone are the days of walking in, picking out a jeans or slacks based on your waist and inseam, and taking home a pair of that fits. You will probably need help finding women's jeans that look good on you, and even then you'll need to try on different sizes and styles. Once you find your fit and size in a particular brand that you like, buy several, in different colors.

All-weather coat: A single-breasted belted trench coat with a zip-out lining is the perfect coat for all seasons. Long thick belted sweaters work well too, in milder climates. Avoid pea coats, capes, and jackets that emphasize broad shoulders.

Essential Accessories (for men and women)

Accessories includes shoes and socks or stockings, belts, ties, hats, gloves, scarves, jewelry (including watches), eye wear, wallets, and handbags. They are the essential finishing touches to any outfit, and help define your gender and style. Whether you transition from male to female or female to male, you'll probably need to change all your accessories as well as your clothing. Here are some suggestions:

Shoes and socks or stockings: Transmen will need two pairs of casual shoes (one in brown and one in black), one or two pairs of dressier shoes (brown and/or black), a good pair of boots, and sneakers and sandals for casual wear. And lots of brown and black socks (no white, except for sports). If you have small feet, try the kids department. Transwomen will need several pairs of flats for work and casual wear (in your basic seasonal colors), two pairs of dressier shoes (one in a light color, the other black, brown or navy), a good pair of boots, dressy and casual sandals, and sneakers or walking shoes. And plain tights or stockings (no fish-net stockings please; they're for catching fish, not admiring looks).

Belts: Transmen need three good leather belts - one in dark brown, one in black, and one casual. Transwomen need several, in basic colors to start and then as need to match a particular outfit.

Hats, scarves and gloves for winter wear: You don't have to match your winter coat, but try to keep them in the same color family. Red, white, and gray go with black; green, tan, yellow and orange go with brown, and blue and purple with either.

Ties and scarves: Ties and indoor scarves serve the same function; they both dress up and "pull together" an outfit. To pull together an outfit, you pick a tie or scarf that has colors from your shirt or top, pants or skirt, and jacket or sweater. This is where you can be creative and express yourself.

Eyewear: If you wear glasses, pick out new frames the next time you go in for an eye exam. Don't be afraid to ask for help! There will be different racks for men's and women's frames, and you should be able to order either in your size.

Jewelry: Not for women only! In my experience, trans-men and women either shy away from jewelry altogether or get carried away and wear too much. Transmen can wear a masculine watch, stud earrings, chunky rings, and certain kinds of arm wear (called cuffs). Transwomen can have fun with earrings, rings, bracelets and necklaces. But keep them simple and coordinated with your outfit. A medium-length strand of colored pearls is the perfect go-with-everything necklace.

Wallets and bags: This is another area where transmen can get away with less. You can use a tri-fold wallet, but don't carry your whole life in it; it just adds bulk to your back pocket. And don't be afraid to carry a "man-bag", such as a messenger bag or laptop carrier, especially if it has a hip logo. Transwomen need at least three handbags - one for summer, one for winter, and one for evening - preferably medium-size. (Too small a hand-bag will make you look bigger.) Learn to organize what you carry in them with a matching wallet and small cosmetic bag.

Dressing Your Body Type

As mentioned earlier, everyone has a distinct body shape/type. Very few of us are built like the models we see on TV or even in magazines and catalogues. Most clothing lines are designed for tall, thin, evenly proportioned people. If you have such a figure you can pick out clothes off the rack and not worry about fit. The rest of us have to figure out how to fit into and look good in clothes not designed with us in mind. In addition to often needing to have clothes hemmed or tailored, we also need to understand which styles are more flattering, and which are best avoided. Here are two common body types and how to dress them:

The Inverted Triangle

Most male-to-female transsexuals have what is called an inverted triangle body shape. This means you have broad shoulders, a long torso, narrow hips, and long legs. Your chest measurement is larger than your hips; your size in tops and jackets, etc. is larger than your size in skirts and pants. In addition, many MtFs are taller than the average woman. Hormones will move body fat from your middle to your hips and bust, but won't alter your basic bone structure. The challenge with this body type is to balance the upper and lower halves of your body to create the illusion of an hourglass figure. You want to de-emphasize your height, the width of your shoulders, and the narrowness of your hips. You can do this by choosing certain styles of clothing.

Tops - loose flowing fabrics and styles are best. Narrow V-neck knit tops with set-in, 3/4-length sleeves, in solid colors are great. Add long scarves and long necklaces to enhance the slimming effect.

Jackets and sweaters - any length jacket as long as it is fitted at the waist. No pockets, epaulets, shoulder pads or other details on the jacket. Try a wide belt over a long sweater.

Jeans and pants - any length is good, as long as it is not tapered. Pockets and other details are great. Try flared boot-cut jeans in a light denim.

Skirts - flared, a-line, tulip, tiered, pleated, and other full skirts are best. Colors, patterns and details are all good. You want to add width and volume. Just above the knee and mid-calf are the best lengths. Short skirts show too much leg, accentuating your height, and long skirts will also make you look taller.

Dresses - full, flowing dresses, belted at the waist are best. Drop-waist and wrap styles are also good. Just be sure that there is more detail and volume on the bottom half than the top. Knee-length and mid-calf are the best lengths.

You will do best to avoid:

On top - high necklines, wide shallow necklines, big collars or lapels, skinny straps, halter tops, cap sleeves, puffy or gathered sleeves, empire waist, busy prints, bright colors, horizontal stripes, stiff or bulky fabrics, shoulder pads, pockets and other embellishments. No double-breasted jackets!

On the bottom - pencil skirts, short tight skirts, long straight skirts, tapered pants, skinny jeans, and leggings or jeggings.

The Petite Pear

Most female-to-male transsexuals have the opposite problem. They tend to be shorter than the average male, and to have wider hips than shoulders. Hormones will build up your upper body (with exercise! but may move fat from your hips to your belly. You want to create an illusion of being taller and more of a rectangular shape. To do this, you need to reverse the emphasis above. Choose:

Shirts - well-tailored shirts (trim fit if you're not too heavy) in crisp fabrics and light or bright colors with pockets are best. Tuck in your tailored shirts, especially if they're a different color from your pants. Polo shirts are better than plain t-shirts. Prints and plaids are great. Add a V-neck vest that matches your pants to create a long straight line. If you wear a tie, make it a short skinny one or you'll look like a boy in your Dad's clothes.

Jackets - long or short is fine, but make sure it has wide shoulders and lots of pockets or zippers or other embellishments. Military-style jackets are great. Bulky sweaters are OK if you're still binding and hiding your chest, but don't buy them too big. For a suit jacket try one with thin vertical stripes (called pinstripes).

Pants - straight, clean lines, with few pockets or embellishments. No plaids, patterns, or light colors. Low-rise jeans give an illusion of a longer waist and thicker torso. Pants with front creases add a long line. Make sure your pants are hemmed to the proper length and don't sag or bag around your ankle. Match your belt, socks and/or shoes to your pants if at all possible. Cowboy boots and "stacked" shoes add height.

It's best to avoid:

Tight jeans, baggy pants, long baggy shorts, cuffed trousers, horizontal stripes, over-sized shirts, double-breasted suit jackets, full-length trench coats, and anything that's too big. You don't want to be dwarfed by your clothes.

Finding Your Best Colors

Color theory and color analysis is a complex topic, beyond the scope of this book. For our purposes, I will focus on what has been called color seasons. This is an analysis of what colors look best on people, based on their natural coloring. Wearing "your colors" will make you look healthier and more attractive. It will also draw attention to your face and hair, which allows people to use those cues more in reading your gender. There are several systems for delineating as many as 12 color seasons; I'll describe the basic four season analysis.

Color seasons are based on an analysis of color as being either "warm" or "cool". Warm colors have a red, orange, or yellow base to them. (Think of a Southwest desert panorama at sunset.) Cool colors are at the other end of the spectrum and have a blue, gray, or green base. (Think of a white sandy beach, clear blue sky and blue-green ocean.) Different tones of a shade can make a color warm or cool. Teal and mint green are cool; avocado and moss green are warm. Add a light vs. dark/deep dimension to that and you end up with four seasons. If you have certain skin tones you will look better in warm colors; other skin tones will look washed out in them.

I didn't really believe in the importance of color seasons until I took advantage of a free consultation with a color stylist. I was amazed at how radiant my skin looked with the right colors and how gray with the wrong ones.

The first step to identifying your season is to look at your hair, eye and skin color. Here is a description of each, with the possible hair, eye and skin colors:

	Hair Color	Eye Color	Skin Color
Spring:	golden blonde	blue	creamy ivory
	strawberry blonde	green	peach
	copper	warm hazel	golden beige
Summer:	ash or light blonde	clear blue	porcelain
	light brown	cool hazel	ivory
	gray	green	cool beige
Autumn:	copper	brown	peach
	red	green	golden beige
	auburn	amber	"ruddy"
Winter:	black	brown	porcelain
	brown	dark green	beige
	gray	steel blue	dark

You may not be able to recognize yourself immediately in one of these seasons. Take a look at yourself in the mirror in good lighting. Is your overall impression of yourself more golden or more silver/steely? If you're not sure, ask someone to help. There are professional stylists and image consultants who can determine your best colors (and styles). Or you can do some research on your own and try draping different colors around your face and asking someone which ones make you look more radiant.

Each season has certain colors that look best with that coloring. If you have a limited color vocabulary, you may be challenged by a list of colors for each season. I recommend that you go on-line to one of the sites listed in the resources for this chapter and find the color palette for your season. Print this out and take it with you when you go shopping. You can also send away for fabric swatches in your season's colors.

References and Resources

Andy Paige, *Style on a Shoestring*, McGraw-Hill, 2009

Veronique Henderson and Pat Henshaw, ***Color Me Confident***, Octopus Publishing Group, 2010

JoAnne Richmond**, *Reinvent Yourself with Color Me Beautiful*,** Taylor Trade, 2008

Clinton Kelly and Stacy London, ***Dress Your Best: The Complete Guide to Finding the Style That's Right for Your Body***, Three Rivers Press, 2005

Style Makeover HQ - www.style-makeover-hq.com/body-shape.html

Determining Your Seasonal Color Palette: www.organicfamilycare.com /determining_your_seasonal_color_palette.htm

Carol Thompson Cosmetics - www.carolthompsonbeautysecrets.com

Hudson's FTM Resource Guide - www.ftmguide.org

Chapter Nine

Skin Care:
Not for Women Only

A man's face is his autobiography. A woman's face is her work of fiction.

Oscar Wilde

This section on skin care is for those transitioning from female to male as well as male to female. This is an important and often overlooked topic. Those raised male aren't usually taught how to take care of their skin, and those raised female often reject it as being too feminine. Add to that the effects of hormones on the skin and you have a recipe for disaster. No amount of make-up can make bad skin look good, and acne scars last forever.

Let's start with some basics on how to have a healthy complexion. You can't have healthy skin without taking care of your overall health! There are several factors dermatologists emphasize when discussing skin health:

Diet and Nutrition: Your skin requires certain nutrients in order to maintain itself. Some of these are water-soluble, but some require healthy fats, such as Omega-3, for absorption. A diet rich in fruits and vegetables, good fats, and plenty of water is essential. (The recommended 6-8 glasses of water a day may seem excessive, but that includes all non-caffeinated liquids.) A basic multivitamin/mineral supplement is helpful, because no one's diet is perfect.

Sleep: Lack of sleep really does lead to dark sagging skin under the eyes.

Sun, wind, and air pollution: These are all known to "age" the skin. (Think of an image of an old farmer or sailor, with skin like wrinkled leather.) Protecting our skin from these will not only prevent skin cancer but also help maintain youthful-looking skin. Tanning is especially harmful.

Smoking and excessive alcohol consumption: These also have been shown to have negative effects on skin quality. One more reason to quit smoking and limit your drinking!

Skin Care: This refers to what you put on your skin to cleanse, moisturize, etc., as well as professional treatments. This includes the whole body, but we'll be focusing on the face.

In order to know how to take care of your skin, you need to figure out what type of skin you have. There are five different types: normal, dry, oily, combination, and sensitive. Normal skin is well-balanced, soft and smooth, and is not easily irritated. Dry skin feels tight, and can be itchy, flaky and rough. Oily skin feels greasy and is prone to acne. Combination skin has some drier patches and some oilier sections, usually the chin, forehead and nose. Sensitive skin irritates easily, and is often red and blotchy. Skin type may vary with the weather, becoming drier in the winter in northern climates, and can change if you move to a different climate. Men tend to have larger pores and more active sebaceous glands, resulting in oilier skin.

Masculinizing and feminizing hormones change the nature of your skin. Estrogen softens and sensitizes skin, and testosterone makes it oilier. Once you start hormones your skin type will change and you'll need to change your skin care routine. The way you used to take care of your skin can damage it if you don't.

This may seem like yet another burden, especially with the array of skin care products out there (and the relentless advertising of new products). It can be helpful to consult an esthetician, especially if you have problem skin. They will have wonderful, but probably expensive, products to offer as well as advice for your problem areas. A consultant at a Clinique counter or the Body Shop can also be very helpful, for less money. Mary Kay has a good skin care line, and ProActiv® is often recommended for acne associated with starting testosterone. You can start with a travel or sample set to try out different products. Or just go to a drugstore and get the best set of products you can afford. (I could proselytize about the virtues of natural and organic skin care products, but I realize that they are more expensive and often harder to find.) You will need four to eight different products for a complete skin care routine, to address four basic processes:

Cleansing: This needs to be done twice a day, without fail. If you wear make-up, you'll need a cream cleanser (or cleansing milk) followed by a toner. Use matched products (same brand) geared to your skin type. A clear, all-in-one cleanser is best for oily skin, or if you don't wear make-up. If you wash your face in the shower, make sure you use a good quality facial soap.

Exfoliating: This is a process of gently scrubbing the skin to remove a layer of dead skin. (Our outer layer of skin is continually dying and sloughing off.) A facial scrub geared to your skin type once or twice a week is sufficient. There are also masques that can be used, no more than once a week, to deep clean and purify the skin.

Moisturizing: Any type of cleanser strips the skin of some of its natural oils. Every time you wash or cleanse your face you need to finish with a moisturizer. You don't have to spend a fortune, however; just find one (or two) designed for your skin type. You can use a thicker cream at night, and a lighter lotion in the morning.

Protecting: Dermatologists and estheticians all recommend using a sunscreen with an SPF of 15 to 30. I use a daily moisturizer in the morning with an SPF of 15 and apply a sunscreen designed for faces with an SPF of 30 when I go out in the sun for any length of time.

You can also add treatments for particular problems, such as acne, but use those sparingly. Once you've figured out what works best for you, set up a morning and evening routine and stick with it.

Common Sense about Scents

The only complaint I ever get about the work I do is that my group room sometimes smells like a cross between a men's locker room and a perfume factory. There's an old saying:"Women don't sweat. Horses sweat, men perspire, women glow." It was told to young ladies to admonish them to be circumspect in their language and to curtail excessive physical activity. But it does point to a difference in men's and women's smells as well as their propensity to perspire heavily. Women actually have more sweat glands than men, but men's are more active; they perspire more under the same conditions. Male and female hormones influence the subtle (pheromones) and not so subtle smells that accompany heavy perspiration.

Hormone treatment tends to change the quantity and quality of perspiration. Before hormones, male-to-female transsexuals need to be fastidious with their hygiene, showering daily or even twice a day if need be. (Use scented body lotion after a shower if this dries your skin out too much.) An effective antiperspirant is essential. No amount of perfume will cover up male body odor. Shoes are a common and often overlooked source of problematic odors. (The soles of the feet and palms of the hands have the highest concentration of eccrine sweat glands.) Foot powders and inserts such as OdorEaters can help, but shoes will have to be discarded if they become foul-smelling. These same suggestions apply to female-to-male transsexuals after beginning testosterone. It's especially important for transmen who use a binder; they can get really rank.

Perfumes and colognes can help convey a feminine or masculine aroma if chosen well. It's important to try out a perfume or cologne before you buy it. Any scent interacts with our own body chemistry, so one that smells great on one person might not on the next. It's also helpful to ask for other people's opinions, because smell sensitivity varies. No matter what you choose, use it sparingly! Given the number of people these days with chemical sensitivities, excessive perfume or cologne is a real turn-off.

Using Make-up

This next section is for anyone wanting to use make-up to create a more feminine look. I'm surprised at how many transwomen shy away from using make-up. It's one of the easiest ways to resolve the "Is that a man or a woman?" question. It can make you look years younger as well. The purpose of applying make-up is not to make your face prettier by "painting" it. The purpose of make-up is to highlight the aspects of the face that you want noticed and downplay the parts you don't. Just as with clothing style, where the ideal is an hourglass figure, there is an ideal female face. Make-up is used to create the illusion of that ideal face, or at least a more feminine one. For MtF transsexuals, that means camouflaging the masculine aspects of the face and accentuating feminine ones.

Experts in facial feminization surgery have researched the typical differences between male and female faces. And for $30-100,000 you can have your face surgically altered to more closely fit the female form. For some transsexuals this is as important, or even more important, than genital reconstruction. For others it's a near impossibility. Feminizing hormones will soften facial features and skin, but they can't change basic facial structure. If you can't afford FFS but still want to have a more feminine face, it's worth your while to learn how to use make-up. It's also a way to resolve ambiguity; make-up, like jewelry, is an add-on that is read as female.

So let's start with the typical differences in facial structure between men and women.

Men	Women
Wide high foreheads, receding hairline	Curved, contoured foreheads, framed with hair
High and thick brows, protuding brow bones	Arching brows, no visible brow bones
Straighter noses, or curved outward	Softer, more curved noses
Low, flat and rectangular cheek bones	Curved cheek bones, fuller-looking face
Wider, larger, more muscular jaw	Narrower jaws and softer, rounder jaw line
Wider, protuding chin	Gently pointed or curved chins
Straighter, thinner and longer lips	Plump, puckered lips, more open mouth

Most men have a square or rectangular face. Since the ideal female face is a soft oval, you can see where the challenge lies. But just as we can use color to balance the triangle-shaped body, we can use different color make-up to contour the face to look more oval. Darker colors make objects recede visually, and lighter colors make them seem closer and larger. All you need is a concealer or full-coverage foundation in a slightly darker shade than your regular foundation and a powder in a slightly lighter shade. If you use the darker color in the four "corners" of your face and the powder under your eyes and on your chin you'll create an illusion of an oval shape.

This is just one example of what you can do with the right make-up. You can hide a five o'clock shadow, make thin lips look fuller, highlight your eye color, and create a healthy youthful glow without looking like you have gobs of make-up on. This is another area where doing your homework and seeking consultation from a professional will make a big difference. Almost every day spa and many hair salons have estheticians who can give you a make-over and teach you how to do it yourself. Mary Kay representatives and department store cosmetic counters are good places to find help. There are also plenty of books, web sites, and videos available. It may seem like a big investment at first, but you'll save money by avoiding trial and error. If you know what you need you can plan your purchases, starting with the basics and adding more as you can afford them. You'll avoid a mess of cosmetics that you don't use.

Essential make-up kit: These are the basic ingredients for creating a more feminine and flattering face:

Concealer or darker foundation: A cream concealer works best, or a full coverage foundation, slightly darker than your natural skin tone. For covering a five o'clock shadow, use a slightly orange tint. Dermablend is a popular brand, especially formulated for full coverage. Concealer is also used to contour your jaw line if you have a square or rectangular face. A lighter concealer is good for dark "bags" under your eyes.

Foundation: A medium or full coverage foundation is best. Do not use the same color as your concealer! This should match your natural skin tone. Use over your forehead and everywhere you haven't applied concealer. Apply with a wedge-shaped cosmetic sponge for best results and blend in. Don't forget under your chin. Mineral powders work well too, but take more time to learn to use.

Finishing powder: This is a sheer or "translucent" powder that you apply with a brush, in a lighter shade than your foundation. It adds light to your face. Apply lightly anywhere you want to highlight, but especially on your temples and across the middle of your face.

Coordinating eye shadow duo or trio: You may want two or three sets - one in a neutral color and one or two in colors from your seasonal color palette. Apply the lighter shade over your entire eye lid. The darker color goes from the lower inside corner to the lower outside corner and gets blended up to the outer outside corner. Eyeliner is optional - use a dark color designed for your eye color or season.

Mascara: Use a high quality waterproof mascara that doesn't smudge easily. Brown works best for day wear and black, blue or purple for a more dramatic effect.

Eyebrow mousse: This is like mascara for your eyebrows. Use a color matched to your hair. You can also use an eyebrow brush and pencil. Brush your eyebrow hair gently up and then across to shape.

Blush: Use a color from your seasonal color palette, or a neutral bronzer. Brush from the middle of your cheekbone back and up to your temple. Blend in with your fingers.

Lipstick: Use a shade that matches your blush. If you're over 25, do not use lip gloss! Lip liner, in a matching or slightly darker shade, is optional - use just outside your natural lip line if you have thin lips, or inside if you have full lips.

<u>Reference and Resources</u>

The National Skin Care Institute - www.skincarenet.org

Carole Jackson, *Color Me Beautiful MakeUp Book*, Ballantine Books, 1988

Kevyn Aucoin, *Making Faces,* Little Brown and Co., 1999
        and *Face Forward,* Little Brown and Co., 2001

Gettysburg College. "Why Cosmetics Work: More Depth To Facial Differences Between Men And Women Than Presumed." *ScienceDaily,* 21 Oct. 2009. Web. 23 Aug. 2011

Chapter Ten

Hair, There and Everywhere

Hair brings one's self-image into focus; it is vanity's proving ground. Hair is terribly personal, a tangle of mysterious prejudices.

Shana Alexander

Hair style and the presence or absence of facial hair is one of the most obvious gender markers, and one of the first for children to recognize. For this reason alone, I often recommend that clients who are beginning a physical transformation start with their hair. Hair growth and beard removal take time, so starting before hormones gives you a head start. It also allows you to see something changing in those impatient months before you can start hormones or before the hormones have taken effect.

The subject of hair is one that shows the envy that often pops up between those transitioning male-to-female and those transitioning female-to-male. The MtF would do anything for a smooth face and body and a full head of hair, while the FtM covets the beard that the MtF is desperate to hide or eliminate. We will consider the challenges that each face separately.

For those transitioning from female to male:

Hair style: Ever since the late 1960s, men have had more options regarding hair length and style. I mentioned earlier the photo I still have of my college boyfriend and I with equally long (and stringy) hair. That was considered quite radical back then, and was associated with being a "hippie" (or worse). Hair styles for men have gone through a lot of changes since then. In the 1970s, shoulder-length hair was common for men, as well as long and straight. In the 1980s, rock stars and teenagers added layers and color to their long hair, usually light blonde or black for dramatic effects. The 1990s brought an even greater variety of long and short hair styles for men, but less of the "big hair" of the '80s. Shorter hair became more popular again. Since 2000 the shorter hair styles for men have prevailed, but hair color and highlights have become commonplace.

To maximize a masculine look these days it's better to go with short hair. Finding a short hair style that doesn't make you look like a teenager can sometimes be a challenge. Getting out a shaver and doing a buzz cut probably won't do it. Shaving your head will not make you look like a guy; it will make you look like you're recovering from chemotherapy. (Trust me on this; I've seen it.) Your best bet is to go to a good hair stylist and tell her or him what you'd like to achieve. Cutting your hair in stages can help you see what looks best on you, and can help others get used to the changes. Once you find a style you like, you'll need to have it trimmed regularly.

One of the possible effects of testosterone that many FtMs are not prepared for is male-pattern baldness. This could happen gradually with age, or sooner than expected based on the men in your family. If you end up losing your hair, you'll just have to work with what you've got left.

Facial Hair: The only effective way to get facial hair is with long-term testosterone treatment. Theatrical make-up is expensive and time-consuming, and substitutes like dotting mascara on your face do not yield realistic results. Shaving your face does not promote hair growth, and minoxidil (Rogaine) is not approved for facial hair. Testosterone treatment will cause you to grow facial hair, but is not guaranteed to give you a full beard. Some transmen never develop more than a moustache and/or goatee. It depends on your age, coloring, and genetic background. Some genetic males cannot grow a full beard. It takes years, not months, for facial hair to develop fully, and it doesn't always grow in evenly. So be prepared to work with what you get. I know it's exciting to see and feel as facial hair starts to come in, but it may be better to shave as it grows in rather than have odd patches. Hudson's FTM Guide (available on-line) has suggestions for beard and mustache styles. Whatever you do, keep it trimmed and neat.

For those transitioning from male to female:

Hair style: If you have a full head of hair you have the opportunity to let it grow long and wear it in a feminine hair style. The possibilities are endless! You'll need help from a good hairdresser/stylist as it grows out; different cuts will be needed at different lengths. Don't be afraid to tell a hairdresser what you want; most of them are friendly and eager to help. As your hair grows you'll have time to try out different lengths and styles. A good hair style balances the shape of your face and helps create the illusion of that ideal oval. Bangs are good for hiding the high male forehead, for example, but need to be done in a way that doesn't give you a square face. As always, doing your homework by figuring out the shape of your face and research-ing appropriate hairstyles can save some costly trial-and-error.

If you've had long hair for a while, your challenge will be to make it look more feminine. Some of the options including cutting and layering your hair, getting a "perm" for texture and curl, and/or adding color and/or highlights. I have one client who's had long hair since "he" was a rock musician in the '80s. It's been harder for friends to see the changes during her transition, because she's always had an androgynous look. Cutting, coloring and curling her hair has helped.

Once you find a hair style you like you'll need to maintain it. Even a simple hair style needs to be trimmed every 6 to 8 weeks. Hair dye grows out and fades; it needs to be repeated every 6 to 8 weeks. Highlights blend in and last longer; refresh every 8 to 12 weeks. "Permanent" texture or curl grows out and falls; perms need to be done 2 to 4 times a year to maintain curl and body.

Maintaining a hair style is not cheap! I was trying to figure out this morning how much money I've spent over the years on haircuts, perms, color, highlights and hair products. I gave up before I got to age 40. My guess is that most women spend from $150 to $750 a year on their hair, depending on how often they have it cut and whether they color or curl it. You'll have to figure this into your transition budget as well. If your funds are limited, try doing your own hair color, or even highlights, or trading off with a friend.

If you have male-pattern hair loss, you have an even bigger challenge. There are no miracle drugs or treatments that will grow a full head of hair back. I have one client (out of probably a hundred) who has had some hair recovery with hormone replacement therapy. Propecia® (finasteride) can help slow down hair loss, but is not effective once you have lost a certain amount of hair. Propecia is a synthetic compound initially used for treating prostate cancer; it works by reducing the main cause of male-pattern baldness, Dihydro-Testosterone (DHT). When DHT accumulates in your hair follicles, it shrinks them and causes them to thin and fall out. Propecia prevents DHT from forming by stopping the enzyme 5-alpha-reductase from converting testosterone to DHT. There are often sexual side-effects (low libido, inadequate erections), but those may or may not be an issue for you during your transition. Some transsexuals welcome these, and start on finasteride as soon as they are able. Minoxidil (Rogaine®) is a topical treatment that may also help.

Hair transplants work if you have minor hair loss, but they are expensive and painful. They can fill in a receding hair line and bring it forward, helping to minimize a masculine forehead. There are different kinds of hair transplant procedures; the latest is called Follicular Unit Transplantation. Basically, a hair surgeon takes a thin strip (or tiny sections) of your scalp that has hair on it, isolates 1 to 3 follicles and literally transplants them into other areas of your scalp. As you can imagine, this can be quite painful afterwards. Often more than one treatment is necessary, but done by a good surgeon the results are permanent and natural-looking. I've seen several clients who were very pleased with the results. The cost depends on how much scalp you need covered, but the estimates I've seen start at $4-5,000 and go up.

Another viable option is a wig or hair piece. You may already have one if you've been "cross-dressing" for a while. But chances are you bought it over the Internet because you liked the look, not because it suits your face. A good wig needs to balance your face and look natural; platinum blonde and copper red are fun, but not good choices for everyday wear. You can have as many fun wigs as you like, but when it's time to invest in one to wear when you want to pass, choose wisely and get the best human hair wig you can afford. A decent human hair wig costs from $100 to $500, and you'll need two. For best results, your permanent wig should be carefully chosen and fitted by a wig specialist. Wig specialists tend to be very understanding and sensitive to their clients' needs, since they often work with women who have lost their hair due to chemotherapy. We have one in our area who's wonderful with transgender clients; she'll meet them after hours to ensure their privacy. If that's not an option for you, there are plenty of places on-line. Web sites or boutiques that cater to cross-dressers are not necessarily the best places to find a permanent wig, as they are often looking for more dramatic hair styles. You might also be able to find wigs that others have worn while they're growing their hair out and don't need any more. I have several that have been donated so that new clients can try them on to try out different styles.

Wigs need care, just as natural hair does. Human hair wigs need to be shampooed every week or two if you wear them regularly, or more often in hot humid weather. You'll probably also need to take them in periodically for reshaping and restyling; that's one of the reasons for having two of them. You can style human hair wigs yourself, carefully, but they'll last longer the less often you wash and style them. Synthetic wigs will melt if you use any kind of heat on them; leave restyling them to a professional. They tend to hold their style longer and are less affected by weather conditions, but they don't hold up as well as human hair wigs.

Hair Removal

This brings us to one of the biggest challenges of transitioning from a male gender presentation to female: getting rid of unwanted body hair. We'll separate this into two sections: body hair and facial hair (beard).

Body Hair

Starting at puberty, male hormones start to change body hair from the soft fuzz of childhood to thicker, coarser, and generally darker hair. There is no way to completely reverse this process. Reducing testosterone and adding estrogen, however, will have some impact. Hair on your arms, legs, chest and back will become thinner and finer. For some, this will be enough to make the difference between a masculine and feminine appearance. Until then, or if hormones don't help enough, there are a variety of hair removal methods that can be effective. You can experiment with these (one at a time) to find which one works best for you.

Shaving: This is the quickest, easiest, and least expensive way to remove hair on your arms, legs, underarms, bikini area and chest. Most women incorporate shaving their legs and underarms into their body care routine. It does have to be repeated more frequently than other methods, however, from daily to weekly, depending on hair color and texture. Use a razor designed for women, with a moisturizing shave gel or cream, and replace the blade frequently.

Depilatories: These are creams that dissolve and remove hair at the surface of the skin. They work well on arms, legs and chest, and need to be repeated less often than shaving. They are very irritating to the skin, however, so please do test a small patch first. Use gloves or wash your hands immediately after using. Do not use any type of depilatory anywhere on your face! They are not effective on facial hair and will only irritate it.

Waxing: This is a painful process best done by a professional, but it lasts longer than shaving or depilatories. A coat of warm wax is applied to your skin then yanked off when it's cooled. It's probably your best choice for hair on your back, unless you have someone who can shave your back for you. It can be done on your legs as well but will probably leave your arms red and sore. Brazilian bikini waxing is best left to masochists and those who have a high pain tolerance. Depending on your hair color and texture you can go 2-4 months between waxings.

Tweezing/plucking: Individual hairs can be plucked out with tweezers. This is painful, time-consuming and effective only for small areas. It is important, however, to learn how to shape your eyebrows using tweezers. You can find plastic templates that define the ideal female brow and pluck around them. Or have your hair stylist or esthetician wax around your brow periodically, and pluck stray hairs as they come in.

Laser and electrolysis: These methods will be described below, because they are the best choices for beard removal. They can certainly be used on body hair as well, especially if you do not take feminizing hormones. If you do plan on starting hormones most people advise that you wait until you see what effect they have on your body hair before committing to the expense of laser and/or electrolysis. If you plan on having genital recon-struction with one of the surgeons who requires hair removal from the scrotal area you will need to do that with laser and/or electrolysis as well. (I did say transitioning was not for the weak of heart. No pain, no gain.)

Beard Removal

This is the most painstaking (literally) task of adopting a feminine gender presentation. Once you have beard growth all the hormone treatment in the world will not make it go away. Unless you can commit to shaving and applying make-up several times a day, you'll want to start working on permanent facial hair removal. The infamous "five o'clock shadow" is next to impossible to hide completely, and will get you read more often than not.

There are two primary approaches to beard removal: laser treatments and electrolysis. You will see lots of information on-line about the pros and cons of each, as well as differing accounts of how effective, expensive and painful they are. The only way you'll find out what will work best for you is to consult qualified specialists. Your skin, your pain tolerance, your hair color and texture, and your budget will determine the best solution for you. Most of my clients start with a series of laser sessions and then follow with electrolysis, lots of electrolysis. I'll describe how each of these treatments work and explain why the combination works best for most people.

Laser and Flash Lamp Hair Removal: Laser is an approved method of *permanent hair reduction.* It works by disrupting hairs in the active growth cycle. Lasers designed for hair removal emit specific wavelengths of light that are absorbed by dark hair pigment. Typically they work best when there is a high contrast between the (darker) color of the hair and the (lighter) color of the skin. There are some that work better on darker skin, such as Nd:YAG, but none that work on lighter hair. The laser beam heats up the hair shaft, which causes those hairs in the active growth cycle to die and fall out. It does not destroy the hair follicle, which is why it is not considered permanent hair removal. Because it only disables hair in the active growth cycle it needs to be repeated at regular intervals. Hair grows in three stages; only a certain amount will be in the active stage at any one time. A typical treatment package consists of 6 to 8 sessions spaced 6 to 10 weeks apart, with more as needed.

Flash lamp treatments, such as IPL (Intense Pulse Light) have become popular because they're less expensive than laser methods. It is not technically a laser treatment, but it works in a similar way. It was developed for other types of facial treatments and does not use a specific bandwidth of light. It can potentially cause more skin damage than other methods. Many of my clients, however, have had good luck with IPL. Any of these treatments will heat up your skin and leave it red for a few days. If you have sensitive skin try a small test area before committing to a series of treatments.

All laser treatments must be done by qualified practitioners; in some states it must be done by or supervised by a physician. Consult several well-qualified specialists if you can, and beware of anyone who says their method works wonders for everyone. A good practitioner will be honest about which method will work best for your hair and skin. Costs of laser and IPL treatments vary, depending on how much dark hair you have, the type of treatment you choose, and the size of the area to be treated. Normal side-effects are itching, pain, tingling, or numbness during treatment, redness, swelling and pain or numbness for a few days after treatment. Extreme redness, swelling or pain, or any bruising, discoloration or scabbing of the skin is not good; stop treatments if you experience any of those and consult a dermatologist.

Electrolysis: Electrolysis is the tried and-true and time-tested method of hair removal; it's been around since 1857. It is the only method with FDA approval for *permanent hair removal*. Electrolysis works, as its name suggests, by targeting each hair follicle with an electrical current. It does not depend on hair color or skin color, so it can be used by everyone. It is, however, very painstaking. For each individual hair, a needle is inserted to deliver the current at the root. Given that the average person has 500-1000 follicles per square inch, it takes a lot of time to clear an area of facial hair. And given that a hair follicle can only be destroyed during an active growth phase, clearing must be done repeatedly.

There are three types of electrolysis:

> **Galvanic:** This is the original method developed; it creates an electrochemical reactions that kills the hair follicle directly. It is slower but more effective than:

> **Thermolysis:** In this method the electrical current is delivered at a higher frequency, and generates a thermal (heat) reaction that impairs the hair follicle. It is faster than Galvanic, but not as reliable. A more preferred method is called:

> **Blend Electrolysis:** This is a hybrid of Galvanic and Thermolysis, and uses AC and DC currents simultaneously. It is considered to be more effective and relatively less time-consuming. It also tends to be more painful.

Pain tolerance varies from individual to individual, but most people describe electrolysis as the equivalent of bee stings - multiple bee stings.

There are a variety of topical anesthetics available that help; the most popular is called EMLA (Eutectic Mixture of Local Anesthetics). They're available by prescription from a physician, dentist or oral surgeon.

Electrolysis can only be done by a licensed practitioner. (Home methods are not effective.) It's important to find a skilled practitioner experienced with male beards. Many are TG-friendly, since transsexuals are good customers, but be sure to ask around in your community. Poorly administered electrolysis can result in scarring, hair regrowth and infections.

Even with blend electrolysis it takes from 100 to 400 hours, over 1 to 4 years, to completely eliminate facial hair. Some electrologists will give reduced rates for longer sessions or frequent customers, but obviously the costs of these sessions will add up. That's one of the primary reasons for doing laser or IPL treatments first. You can typically get decent results with 6-8 sessions of laser or IPL, then follow with electrolysis over another year or two for total clearing. If you have a light red or blonde beard you don't have much choice, but you will probably see the results faster from electrolysis than those with dark hair.

Whatever you decide, start as early as you can and stick with it. Once your facial hair decreases, foundation is easier to apply and covers more evenly, and your face will start to look more feminine. This can be a significant ego boost and help your whole transition go more smoothly.

References and Resources

Hudson's FTM Resource Guide - www.ftmguide.org

How to Care for Your Wig - www.headcovers.com/care_wigs.php

Laser Hair Removal Guidance - www.laserhairremovalguidance.com

American Electrology Association - www.electrology.com

Hair Removal Forum - www.hairremovalforum.com

Chapter Eleven

Walking the Walk
& Talking the Talk

Act the way you'd like to be and soon you'll be the way you act.

Leonard Cohen

Presenting as a man or a woman involves much more than your hair, clothes and body shape. No matter how manly or feminine you look you can give yourself away by how you move, how you sit, and certainly how you talk. Most people starting to transition are well aware that their voice needs to change in order to sound like a man or a woman. But the voice is just one aspect of the way women and men tend to communicate different-ly. There are other noticeable gender differences in communication style. These differences contribute to gender attribution - whether someone is perceived as male or female. I mentioned earlier that many of my clients are frustrated by how often they are read when fully dressed and then pass when they're not even trying. This can be partly because of the particular way the observer is reading gender cues, but I suspect it also has to do with these other areas of gender communication. For those of you who wish to present more convincingly as a man or woman, this chapter will explain how to "walk the walk" and "talk the talk".

As always, how much you want to change how you present is up to you. Some of my clients want nothing to do with femininity training; they just want to be who they are and get on with their lives. Some find it too difficult to pay attention to softening their voice and slowing down their walk in their daily lives. Some transmen don't want to give up their emotional expressiveness, or the way they laugh. Others have naturally adopted more masculine ways of being in the world.

Differences in how men and women communicate have been studied extensively over the past 30 years. There are differing views on the subject, of course. Some authors have dramatized the typical differences, making it seem like men and women are completely different. Others say the differences are minimal. In almost any study of differences between the genders it should be noted that the range of scores is always greater than the difference between the average scores. What that means is that there is greater variability within each group than between them. There will always be women who score as high or higher than the male average, and vice versa. And there are differences in communication style related to social roles and status, as well as cultural differences. So when we talk about male-female differences, we're talking in generalities. Generalities can quickly become stereotypes, and attempting to fit a stereotype can make you appear like a caricature of masculinity or femininity.

That said, there are some interesting differences in how men and women use speech, language, and non-verbal communication. There is evidence that some of these differences are biologically-based. Girls typically acquire language earlier than boys, and are more verbally fluent from an early age all the way through school. Some studies indicate that the female brain is less specialized and more internally connected than the male brain, making their cognitive style more holistic and access to different parts of the brain easier. The area of the brain responsible for interpretation of emotion based on facial cues has also been shown to be more developed in women.

Most of the differences in how men and women use verbal and non-verbal communication, however, can be attributed to socialization. Perceptions and expectations of girls and boys are different from the time they are born (or even sooner these days). These perceptions and expectations determine what is reinforced and what is punished. Your communication style has been influenced by the social expectations of the gender you were assigned. Those raised as boys know very well the limits to expressive communication that were enforced. Being too emotionally expressive was seen as weak or "gay", and severely punished. For girls, being too direct was punished; hurting someone else's feelings was seen as a major infraction of the unspoken rules of being a girl.

Learning about these differences can help you become more convincing in your gender presentation. In order to change how you present, however, you also need to become more self-aware. When we get dressed to go out we can look at ourselves in the mirror to check how we look and correct anything out of place. But we don't often get the chance to observe from the outside how we move through the world. You'll need to slow down and pay attention to how you're walking, sitting, talking, etc. This requires increasing your self-awareness, which can be enhanced through mindfulness training.[31] (Mindfulness training can be done through consistent meditation practice.) Feedback from others, and even being videotaped by someone, can really help. As always, it's up to you how far you want to take these changes. Sometimes it's simply a matter of *unlearning* the persona you were forced to adopt in order to survive in your gender role. As the old persona drops away you may find yourself moving more naturally feminine or masculine. I have seen gracious women emerge from some pretty tough exteriors! The butterfly emerging from a cocoon is an apt metaphor.

We'll start with an overview of the general differences in gender communication and then focus on voice and speech patterns. Nonverbal communication can be broken down into different categories; within each category there are one or more typical gender differences.

---

[31] What is Mindfulness, by Shinzen Young, available at:
http://www.shinzen.org/Retreat%20Reading/What%20is%20Mindfulness.pdf

Proximity and use of space: This refers to how close people are in conversation, who approaches whom, who moves away, etc.

> ➤ Men tend to claim more space as their own. They maintain greater distance from other men in conversation, and react more negatively to being crowded. On the other hand, they are more likely to intrude on a woman's personal space. In the middle seat of an airplane, men are more likely than women to claim the armrests.

> ➤ Women tend to take up less space. They stand or sit closer to each other in conversation, and lean towards a person they're listening to in order to communicate interest and empathy. They are more likely than men to move away from people who speak loudly.

Posture, position, and orientation: This refers to the position of one's body in relation to other people and to physical surroundings.

> ➤ Men tend to stand (and walk) with their legs apart and to hold their arms away from their body. They usually sit with legs open, knees pointing out, or stretched out with ankles crossed. They're more likely to stretch their arms out or up (hands behind their head) when sitting. This is another way they claim more space.

> ➤ Women tend to keep their arms close to their body, and to sit with knees together or legs crossed at the knees. They rarely raise their arms when sitting. They keep their hands in their lap or on the arms of the chair. They stand (and walk) with their legs closer together. Again, women tend to take up less space.

> ➤ Men tend to stand at an angle when talking to each other, not facing each other directly. A face-to-face position indicates confrontation. Women are more likely to face each other in conversation.

Body movements and gestures: This includes the way people move their whole body as well as hand, arm and head gestures.

> ➤ Men tend to have sharper and straighter body movements, and to walk more stiffly. They're more likely to "lumber", meaning walk with their legs apart, leaving footprints on two tracks further apart, or "strut".

> ➤ Women tend to have more fluid body movements. They walk with their legs closer together and hips swaying, leaving footprints closer to a single track. They "glide".

> ➤ Men use more hand and arm gestures in social situations, especially broad sweeping gestures. Women use fewer and smaller gestures, but tend to use more when conversing with a man. They also often tilt and tuck their head when talking to a man, a sign of deference.

Physical contact: This includes any form of touch, from a handshake to sexual groping. Who touches whom varies from culture to culture, but is often a sign of dominant role status.

> ➤ Men tend to keep their physical contact with other men to a minimum. Any touch initiated by one man to another is likely to be rough - a firm handshake, a slap on the back, or a high-five.

> ➤ Women tend to hug more, but their hugs with women are often a ritualized greeting, with a peck on the cheek that never really lands on the cheek.

> ➤ Women are more likely to use physical touch, such as a hand on the other person's hand or arm, as a comforting gesture. If men use touch to comfort, it is more likely to be a pat on the back.

> ➢ Men are more likely to interpret any touch from a woman (other than a handshake) as a sexual overture. Women are actually less likely to see a man's casual touch as a sexual invitation.

Facial Expressions: The face is a complex communicator with a myriad of small muscles around the eyes and lips. Psychologists have studied what they call micro-expressions - fleeting facial expressions that betray hidden feelings. Most of the time we are not aware of how much we reveal on our face.

> ➢ Women are more astute at reading emotions communicated through facial expressions. Men have a harder time differentiating a woman's mood based on facial expression.

> ➢ Women use more facial expressions to communicate feelings. They tend to smile more, and to smile with their whole face. Men reveal less emotion through their facial expressions, smile less, and use less of the area around their eyes.

Eye contact: Rules about eye contact vary greatly from culture to culture. To avert one's eyes is a sign of respect in many cultures; to stare someone down a sign of dominance. In our culture maintaining eye contact is generally seen as a gesture of intimacy.

> ➢ For obvious reasons, men are less comfortable with eye contact, especially with other men. (Hence the angled position when conversing.) They tend to maintain eye contact more while talking than while listening, which has been called visual dominance.

> ➢ Women are more comfortable maintaining eye contact, especially while listening. They will position themselves in ways to enhance eye contact, but may do so less directly with a man they're interested in attracting. They tend to avert their eyes during conflict.

These differences can be attributed to differing attitudes and postures in the social world. Men are taught to exhibit dominance behaviors (taking up more space, walking boldly) and to inhibit expression of feelings (smiling less, less fluid movements). There is also clear evidence of homophobia in how men relate to men. This is especially obvious in their behavior in public restrooms. Men do not smile, make eye contact or initiate conversation; they do their business quickly and get out.

Women, on the other hand, are taught to exhibit more deference than dominance (taking up less space, smiling more) and to inhibit sexually suggestive behavior (by crossing their legs, keeping their arms in close, etc.). Women are not required to prove that they're not gay, and feel freer to show "tend and befriend" behaviors (sitting or standing closer, leaning forward, gentle touch, maintaining eye contact).

These differences are also apparent in the research on differences in men's and women's speech patterns and conversational style. These differences can be broken down into 4 categories: 1) content , 2) vocabulary and sentence structure, 3) conversational behaviors, and 4) purpose or motivation.

Content:

> Men tend to choose less personal topics of conversation, and reveal less about themselves than women. They're more likely to talk about sports, current affairs, and work. They also focus more on problem-solving: providing information, directions or answers.

> Men tend to change subjects more frequently in general conversation, and go into each subject in less depth. They discuss facts more than feelings.

> Women tend to reveal more about themselves and discuss topics in more depth. They talk more about relationships and feelings than men. They talk less about themselves and more about others. They give unsolicited compliments more often than men.

Vocabulary and sentence structure:

> ➤ Men tend to use more commands than requests. They use more qualifiers (very, a little or a lot, etc.) and more numbers. Their speech is more sparse and direct. ("Pick up a six-pack tonight, hon.")

> ➤ Men use more slang and swears, and more casual language, such as running words together ("I gotta go tada store.") Women tend to use more polite speech.

> ➤ Women tend to use more descriptive language. A typical sentence will have several adjectives, for example, and more detail. ("I've got to go to the new Safeway and pick up some Miller Lite for Bill before the kids get home.) Women use more words per phrase or sentence; on average, women use ten thousand more words per day than men.

Conversational Behaviors:

> ➤ Men are more likely to disagree, challenge and debate others in conversation. They are also more likely to interrupt or talk over the other person. They tend to talk more and listen less.

> ➤ Men give fewer non-verbal "encouragers", such as head nods and "uh-huh". They ask fewer questions and elicit more detailed information less often. They want to get right to the point.

> ➤ 3) Men are more likely to interrupt or divert a conversation by making jokes or telling their own story. They're also more likely to monologue rather than dialogue.

> ➤ Women listen more attentively, give more non-verbal and verbal encouragement to the speaker, ask clarifying questions, and generally do more to keep a conversation going. They tend to let others finish before speaking, and focus on agreement more than disa-

greement. Women also show more warmth in conversation and use a more pleasant tone.

Purpose or motivation:

➤ Men seem to use verbal communication more to compete and to assert dominance or control. They tend to approach conversations as debates to be won or lost.

➤ When not competing, men tend to be more geared towards fact-finding and problem-solving. They also use fact-finding and problem-solving to demonstrate knowledge and competence.

➤ Women tend to use conversations as a way of enhancing and maintaining connection in relationships. The content is not as important as the process; the end product not as important as getting there together.

➤ Women seek to understand and to be understood. They give and want to receive more acknowledgment and agreement.

These are all generalizations, of course, but these typical differences are worth noting. You can see why men and women don't always understand each other! You may already have a communication style more like your desired gender, but you can always learn more. It's most enlightening to go to a mall or other public place and watch how men and women walk, talk, and relate to each other. Or just pay attention at work to those around you. Pick out someone you think of as presenting their gender well and observe their movements. What is it about them that makes them seem so feminine or masculine?

Then find some way to observe your own communication style. Set up mirrors in your kitchen, or wherever you're most likely to talk on the phone. Ask someone for feedback, or to videotape you in common situations. Once you have a clearer sense of the differences between your behavior and the "ideal" feminine or masculine, pick some things to practice. Walking in heels is a great way to learn how to walk like a woman; it automatically makes your hips sway. You may need to exaggerate new behaviors at first, but try not to overdo it in public. Your goal is not to walk like John Wayne and talk like Clint Eastwood, but to learn how to project your true masculine (or feminine) style.

Finding Your Voice

To understand how and why men's and women's voices differ we need to review how the voice works and what happens to the voice at puberty. To produce speech we use our brain, our diaphragm, lungs and trachea, and our larynx, throat and mouth. Air goes through our trachea (windpipe) and larynx (voice box)as we breathe. Vocal folds (cords) stretch from the front to the back of the larynx. When we breathe, the vocal folds pull apart at the back, allowing air to pass through. When we speak, sing or scream the vocal folds close and vibrate. This vibration creates sound.

The amplification and modification of this sound takes place in the throat, mouth and nose. At the back of the throat the voice is simply raw sound. As it moves through your mouth it is turned into words by a series of precise, high-speed maneuvers; it is stopped and started, dampened and amplified, and squeezed into intelligible speech. This involves muscles on the walls of the throat and mouth and the tongue, lips, jaw and soft palette. Our unique voice is determined by the structure and functioning of all these parts of our body and how they work together. It's an amazing process that we learn to do as children without even thinking about it.

The size and shape of the vocal tract is greatly influenced by the increase in testosterone at puberty (in males and females, but obviously more so in biological males). During puberty:

- the growth of facial bones creates bigger spaces in the mouth, nose, and throat, which increases the *resonance* of the voice,
- the vocal folds grow longer and thicker, making them vibrate more slowly, which lowers the *pitch*,

- the thyroid cartilage tilts to a different angle in the neck, creating an "Adam's apple" and changing the position of the vocal cords, and

- the cartilages in the larynx grow larger and thicker, increasing the height and depth of the larynx.

These testosterone-driven changes are the basis of the differences in pitch and resonance between men and women. There is individual variability, however; there are plenty of women with "husky" voices, and plenty of men with higher voices than average. And although there are some physical limits to how high or low we can go, we are all capable of producing a wide range of sounds. Anyone who has had experience with singing knows that with practice and training we can reach much higher or lower notes than we usually use when speaking.

Once puberty is complete and full adult size has been reached, the basic physical structure of the mouth, throat and larynx will not change. When transmen take testosterone, the vocal folds will thicken, but they will not grow longer. Thus the pitch of the voice will lower, but not necessarily the resonance. For transwomen, lowering testosterone and adding estrogen does not affect the voice at all.

Pitch and resonance are only two of the ways that men's and women's voices and speech differ. Here are some of the other qualities that differentiate men's and women's voices:

Pitch: Pitch (how high or low the voice sounds) is the most obvious difference between men's and women's voices. Pitch is created by the frequency of vibration of the vocal folds; at a pitch of 100 Hertz the vocal folds are vibrating 100 times a second. A pitch of 200 Hz is vibrating twice as fast, and will sound twice as high. Speaking pitch ranges from 80 - 275 Hertz. A typical range for male voices is approximately 100 to 150 Hz, and for women 175 to 250 Hz. The range considered to be within the female register, however, is 145 to 275 Hz, with 80 to 165 Hz heard as within a male range. That means there is a 20 HZ overlap that can be heard as either male or female. In the "gender neutral" range, other aspects of speech and voice quality determine whether someone sounds like a man or a woman.

Resonance: Resonance, or timbre, is another important aspect of voice quality. Resonance is determined by the size of the voice "chamber", that is the throat space. The bigger the size, the deeper (or lower) the formant frequencies, called *deep resonant overtones*. The genetic female has a smaller mouth and throat and therefore does not have that deep rumble that you hear in most genetic male voices. These chambers place a very important role in the perception of the timbre of the voice—whether it's perceived as a rich, nasal or thin voice. Think of how different the same note would sound from a tuba and a flute. The pitch would be the same, but the resonance would be totally different.

Loudness: Resonance and the size of the voice chamber also relate to the decibel level of male and female voices. Women tend to have a softer, quieter voice than men. Men tend to speak more loudly, and to speak in an assertive, decisive tone. One of the difficulties many transwomen have in changing their voice is trying to project a female voice loudly when necessary; it's hard to have a "booming" female voice. Transmen need to learn how to project their voice more firmly.

Articulation: Women tend to speak more clearly than men. Their consonant sounds are a bit more crisp and precise. Men tend to mumble more, and to run words together more often.

Pacing and Phrasing: Pacing refers to the speed (number of words per 10-second interval), while phrasing refers to the number of words per breath. Men tend to speak in shorter bursts, and often "clip" (end abruptly) their words or sentences. If you're from northern New England, you know what clipped speech is - it's the way your typical Yankee talks. Women tend to speak in longer, flowing sentences, more like a Southern drawl.

Intonation: This is another very important aspect of speech differences. As we noted above, typically men have a 50 Hz range in their voiced, and women a 75 Hz range. What that means is that women tend to vary their pitch more within a sentence, resulting in a more melodic voice. Typical male speech is less varied in pitch, more level or monotone. Women also use more upward shifts in tone, and men use more downward shifts, particularly at the end of a sentence.

Voice Feminization

You can see from this list that there's much more to changing your voice than making it higher or lower. That is why good voice training is so important, especially but not exclusively for transwomen. Voice feminization is the process of changing from a masculine voice and speech patterns to a more feminine presentation. This is one of the hardest challenges of transitioning from male to female. It takes lots and lots of practice. There are several CDs and programs available on-line, but there's no substitute for professional help. Trying to change your pitch on your own can do damage to your voice; you need to learn proper warm-up routines, voice hygiene, etc. Specialists have the equipment necessary to test your pitch, and can tailor exercises to your needs.

Voice training should ideally be done with a Speech and Language Pathologist who specializes in voice feminization. Rebecca Shafir, MA, a specialist in the Boston area, lists five things to look for when choosing a voice coach:

1) Experience working with the transgendered population. A speech therapist who works primarily with children or the elderly will not have the specialized expertise you need. If you find a speech therapist willing to work with you who does not have a lot of experience, be sure he or she is getting training or supervision in this area.

2) A background in theater or singing is also helpful. You want someone with a holistic approach, who can help you with all aspects of speech and gender communication.

3) References from others. Find out what experiences other clients have

had. More importantly, what were the results? Do they have natural-sounding feminine voices?

4) Accessibility in person or by phone for appointments. You'll be very lucky if you find someone nearby. Chances are you'll have to drive a considerable distance, and want to be able to do some of the work by phone.

5) Good value for the fee. Some relevant questions to ask: What do you get in an hour session? Do materials come with the cost? Will they charge you for a check-up phone call? Can you leave a voice sample for a progress update?[32]

The new WPATH Standards of Care include a section on voice and communication therapy. They list competency requirements for voice and communication specialists, and offer guidelines for them. Make sure your voice coach is familiar with these before you start.

A voice feminization coach will set up an initial assessment, recording your pitch range, etc. This typically takes 2 - 4 hours, and costs $3-500. You'll get a complete analysis of your voice and speech, concrete goals, homework exercises, personalized practice tapes, and follow-up sessions by phone or in person. It will take six months to a year to achieve consistent results, with sessions becoming less frequent over time. Sessions will typically cost from $50 to $100 an hour, but they're well worth it. An artificial sounding higher-pitch voice is just as much a give-away as a deep low voice.

There are several new voice feminization programs being started at universities in different parts of the country. At this time there are programs at the University of North Carolina in Greensboro, University of Washington in Seattle, and University of Arizona, among others. Check to see if there's a Speech and Language Pathology Department in colleges and universities in your area, and ask them if they offer voice feminization.

---

[32] Rebecca Shafir, http://www.mindfulcommunication.com/index.htm

There are several advantages to a university program, including lower cost, group sessions, and access to the latest research and technology.

Another important thing to note here: You have to quit smoking if you want voice training to be effective! Smoking cigarettes (or anything else, for that matter) changes your voice quality, making it rougher and raspier. You're also more likely to damage your voice if you try to modify it before you quit smoking.

Voice Feminization Surgery

I will not review the types of surgery that are possible for altering your voice, because I have seen nothing to recommend them. The surgeries available are risky, with inconsistent results. At best, surgery can change the pitch of your voice, but not the resonance or any of the other aspects of voice quality mentioned above. At worst, you could lose your voice altogether or end up sounding like Minnie Mouse. Anne Lawrence has a comprehensive review on her web site.[33]

Voice Changes for Transmen

Transitioning the voice from female to male is often seen as a non-issue - all you have to do is take testosterone, right? Unfortunately it's not that easy. As we discussed above, the larynx, or voice box, is a hormone-dependent organ. In teenage boys, increased testosterone production causes the vocal folds (vocal cords) to thicken, lengthen and mature. The cartilage of the larynx grows, further influencing the tone of voice. This is a process that happens over time as the teen matures.

Transmen, however, usually start on testosterone treatment in a way that speeds up that process. The vocal folds will thicken, lowering the pitch of the voice. But voice quality is restricted by the size of the larynx, which is

---

[33] Anne A. Lawrence, M.D., Ph.D., "Voice Feminization Surgery: A Critical Overview", available at http://www.annelawrence.com/voicesurgery.html

not likely to change in an adult FtM. And some transmen don't experience a significant voice change with hormone therapy. Those who do often experience a period of their voice "cracking", much like a teenage boy. Many end up with a weak or chronically hoarse voice. Starting at a lower dose of testosterone and increasing more slowly may ease the voice transition. Learning to care for your voice can help as well.

Transmen can also benefit from voice training, particularly if you enjoy singing and want to be able to continue. Any singing skill you had will not necessarily transfer to your new voice if/when you start on testosterone. It's been a disappointment to some to lose their singing voice, but it's possible to regain it with voice lessons. Learning proper techniques for breathing, and opening the diaphragm and larynx, can substantially improve singing abilities.

References and Resources

Shelagh Davies and Joshua Mira Goldberg, **"Trans Care Gender Transition: Changing Speech",** Vancouver Coastal Health Project, Transcend Transgender Support and Education Society and Canadian Rainbow Health Coalition, Vancouver Canada, 2006

Tonya Reiman **"Gender Differences in Communication"**, at: http://www.bodylanguageuniversity.com/public/213.cfm

Kathy Perez, *Voice Feminization for Transgender Women.* Denver, CO: Exceptional Voice, Inc. 2004

J. Koufman**, *"Call for a moratorium on voice feminization surgery for the M-to-F transsexual in the United States."* Winston-Salem, NC: Center for Voice and Swallowing Disorders. 2005

J. Challoner, The voice of the transsexual. In M. Freeman & M. Fawcus (Eds.), *Voice disorders and their management.* Philadelphia: Whurr Publishing, 2000

Rebecca Shafir, **"Transgender Voice Training"**, at: http://www.mindfulcommunication.com/transgender.htm

PART THREE

SEPARATION

Chapter Twelve

Crossing the Second Threshold: Hormone Therapy

A ship in port is safe, but that's not what ships are built for.

Grace Murray Hopper

So far, we have been talking about changes that you can start on your own, most of them without medical treatment. I urge clients to start with those, for several reasons. The first has to do with motivation and morale. Once someone has decided that they want to change their gender presentation they usually want it all to happen yesterday! They sometimes resent having to go through a period of assessment or counseling, which they may feel isn't necessary at all. Getting started on something relieves the impatience, and keeps them from getting discouraged. The second is that starting external changes in gender presentation provides further assessment for those who are unsure of their direction. I encourage them to start with "dressing" more, changing their hair style, etc., to see how it feels. If it feels right, normal, natural, comfortable, and they want to do more, that's a good indication that this is the direction they want to take. If the thrill wears off or they don't experience any increase in comfort, then perhaps some further exploration is needed.

Usually clients relax after a few sessions and settle into working on their gender exploration and expression, and come to recognize the third reason - all these changes take time, money and effort. Once they start coming out to family and friends, dealing with their reactions and negotiating those changing relationships often becomes the first priority. The reality of the impact of changing genders hits home. Sometimes they need to slow down or scale back their plans for a while. I work hard with clients to pace their transition appropriately so that they don't get themselves into a position of having to go backwards, or "detransition" at some point. ("Detransitioning" is fairly common, for reasons we'll discuss more in the next section.) Which brings us to the fourth reason for working on the non-medical aspects first; they can be either reversed or concealed. Clothes can go back in the closet, hair can be cut short (or grown long) again, and beard removal can be explained away.

Once you start hormone treatments, you're starting changes that cannot easily be reversed, even if you stop the hormones. There comes a point of no return that is the second major threshold to cross. Your transition plan needs to consider when that point is likely to be, and how to manage the impact on your life. For the male-to-female transition it's usually the development of breasts. Up here in northern New England you can hide them with sweaters or vests for half the year, but once the warm weather returns that becomes more difficult. For the female-to-male transition, it's the voice changes that cannot be hidden. Facial hair can be shaved, but the deepening voice can only be explained as a cold for so long. Sooner or later, permanent changes will be apparent to everyone, and the final stages of coming out - the legal process and coming out at work or school - become necessary.

As eager as you may be to get that letter for hormones, work with your therapist on those issues. There are good reasons for therapy. It's not just an evaluation process - some sort of test to see if you're "really trans" or not. It's a period of preparation for the start of irreversible changes in your appearance. That said, if your therapist spends the whole time trying to figure out if you're "really" a transsexual, and/or where those feelings came from, you're probably seeing the wrong therapist.

From a gender therapist's perspective, there are three things he or she needs to be sure of before writing a letter of referral for hormone treatment: informed consent, eligibility, and readiness. Gender specialists are ethically bound to follow the guidelines outlined by the World Professional Association for Transgender Health. Any guidelines endorsed by the premier organization in a field of medicine are considered to be the "best practices" as well as "standards of care". (Other examples of these are things like the childhood immunization schedules put out by the American Academy of Family Physicians, or the requirement for psychological evaluation before bariatric surgery.) Deviations from these standards must be justified and documented. If a professional does not follow the appropriate standards of care and something goes wrong, he or she can be sued or brought before a professional review board.

The new Standards of Care (Version 7) have relaxed the eligibility requirements for beginning hormone therapy. One letter from a qualified mental health professional to the prescribing physician is still required. This letter must document that the following criteria have been met:

> persistent, well-documented gender dysphoria

> capacity for fully-informed consent

> age of majority or parental consent

> adequate control of any physical or mental health conditions.

These are minimum criteria, not a guarantee of a recommendation. Many gender therapists will still use the guidelines in Version 6 of the SOC to help them assess your readiness to begin irreversible changes.

Informed Consent

If you've ever had surgery of any kind (other than extreme emergencies) you know that you have to sign an informed consent form before they'll take you in. This is a prerequisite for any complicated medical procedure or treatment. There are two parts to it - informed and consent. Both of these require what is called the capacity for informed consent. This is a hot topic in medical and research ethics! Basically what it means is that the person has the cognitive ability to understand the procedure, and its risks and benefits, and to freely consent. Those considered not capable of informed consent would be minors (defined as under age 18, for the most part), and those with a developmental disability or major mental illness that impairs their judgment and/or decision-making ability.

The second piece of this is "informed". This usually boils down to being aware of all side-effects, limitations and possible negative outcomes. I make sure that clients have done enough reading (not just You-Tube viewing) to know not only what to expect from hormone therapy, but also what *not* to expect, and how to recognize possible complications.. Only then can I be assured that the person is making a truly informed decision. Informed consent also includes a realistic understanding of the impact that the physical changes brought about by hormones will have on your life. Your therapist will need to know you're reasonably prepared for the consequences of permanently changing your gender presentation.

Readiness

Readiness criteria for hormone therapy were more explicit in Version 6. Version 7 simply says that other medical and mental health issues must be adequately controlled. V.6 included "consolidation of gender identity, mental stability and a reasonable assurance that the client will take hormones responsibly." Complete consolidation of gender identity is an ongoing process that takes longer than a few months, but a degree of clarity and consistency is essential. What this means to me is that the client has explored the gender continuum mentioned in Part One, found his/her place, considered the different pathways ahead, and started in a direction that makes sense.

Mental stability is always relative; everyone has ups and downs and days when life is overwhelming. But because transitioning is already a roller-coaster ride, and hormones can affect mood, it's important to have a base of emotional stability before you start. If you have significant post-traumatic stress and are highly reactive, for example, this should be treated first. Extreme mood swings or severe depression may require medication, and those with moderate anxiety and depression might benefit as well. I try to make sure a client has a reasonable amount of support and decent coping skills before adding hormones to the mix. I also don't recommend starting hormones in the middle of a difficult divorce, for example, or any major life upheaval.

Your therapist will also have to rule out the rare conditions that could possibly be causing a false self-diagnosis as transsexual or temporary urges to change gender. He or she will and should ask you questions about your history, including physical and sexual abuse, mental illness in your family, sexual obsessions or compulsions, sexual orientation and experiences, and other things that may not make sense to you at the time. Please be open and honest. There are no right or wrong answers! Having masturbated as a teen when "cross-dressed", having been molested as a child, or having an uncle who had a 'nervous breakdown' should not keep you from getting hormones.

The therapist will also want to make an assessment about your likelihood of taking hormones in a responsible manner. That means taking them consistently (not skipping or starting and stopping), and not taking more than the prescribed dosage. It also means not taking them in any way that could be obviously harmful. The dilemma is that self-medicating with black-market hormones is not a responsible use of medication. I understand that there are a lot of reasons why transmen and women seek out hormones on the Internet or from other illegal sources. If someone comes to see me and says they've been self-medicating I don't insist that they stop, because I know that stopping abruptly is not medically sound. But I do talk about the risks and try to arrange medical management by a qualified physician as soon as possible.

The Standards of Care do not require any assessment beyond this. Your therapist's evaluation should not be based on whether you're a "true" (or "primary") transsexual, whether you know you want surgery or not, how well you pass, whether your family approves (unless you're a minor and/or completely dependent on them financially), or how well you fit stereotypes of masculinity or femininity. Your sexual orientation should not be a determinant of your eligibility for hormones. If you identify as gender-queer, or want masculinizing hormones without the possibility of chest surgery, be prepared to discuss how that's going to play out in the "real world" (not just college), but that should not exclude the consideration of hormone treatment.

From time to time I hear horror stories of therapists who spend months and months doing their assessment, and require costly and time-consuming psychological testing. Unless there are questions about capacity for informed consent psychological testing should not be necessary for an adult. It shouldn't matter what other psychological diagnoses you might have as long as your judgment and decision-making abilities are sound. At the other extreme are therapists who will give you a blanket letter of approval for hormones after one or two sessions - for a substantial fee, of course. If you run across one of either kind, run the other way!

Once your therapist has been assured that you're capable of informed consent, know what you're doing, and will use hormones responsibly, he or she should help you find an endocrinologist or other physician who can prescribe them for you. You should have already broached the topic with your primary physician and had a complete physical. If your physician is knowledgeable and comfortable prescribing masculinizing or feminizing hormones, a letter from your therapist to him or her is all you need. There are also clinics in major cities where outside psychotherapy is not a re-quirement; the evaluation of informed consent, eligibility and readiness are done by their counselors or members of the medical team. (I can think of four off the top of my head - Fenway Health Center in Boston, Callen Lorde in New York City, Whitman-Walker in Washington DC, and the Mazzoni Center in Philadelphia.) Most endocrinologists rely on a therapist's assessment of the client's eligibility and readiness. It is ultimately their decision to prescribe or not, based on medical as well as psychological criteria. They have clinical practice guidelines to follow as well.[34]

If you don't have access to one of the major centers, and your therapist and physician do not have a specific referral in mind, you'll need to do some research on-line or make some cold calls. Look up Endocrinologists in your geographic area, and call and ask "Does Dr. X prescribe feminizing (or masculinizing) hormones for transgender patients?" All endocrinologists prescribe hormones, and all *can* prescribe the kind you want, but not all of them are knowledgeable or comfortable in this area, so you have to be specific. It may take a while to find a knowledgeable endocrinologist, or to get an appointment with one, so don't wait until the last minute to start looking.

Introduction to Hormones

Before we talk about the specifics of masculinizing/feminizing hormones, it would be helpful to review some basic physiology. Hormones are the chemical messengers of the body; they orchestrate a variety of physiological changes throughout the body. There are a number of other essential hormones that you've probably heard of but take for granted unless something goes awry; they regulate physical growth, metabolism, mood stability and a host of other functions of the endocrine system. The ones that affect the reproductive system and secondary sex characteristics are androgens (testosterone), estrogens and progesterone. Estrogen and testosterone are present in males and females throughout our lives. As we outlined in Chapter Two, the genetic markers of XX or XY trigger the development of the ovaries or testes which begin producing the requisite amount of masculinizing or feminizing hormones in utero. This furthers the differentiation into a male or female fetus, resulting in (usually) a boy

---

[34] Wylie C. Hembree, Peggy Cohen-Kettenis, Henriette A. Delemarre-van de Waal, Louis J. Gooren, Walter J. Meyer III, Norman P. Spack, Vin Tangpricha, and Victor M. Montori, "Endocrine Treatment of Transsexual Persons: An Endocrine Society Clinical Practice Guideline", in *J Clin Endocrin Metabolism*. September 2009, 94(9)

or girl baby. This sequence does not always proceed according to plan, sometimes producing intersex conditions of one sort or another.

The ovaries and testes continue to develop as the child matures, producing moderate amounts of both estrogen and testosterone. There is evidence of a surge in testosterone in boys around the age of 3-5, but other than that hormone levels are stable until puberty. At puberty the increase in hormone production in girls results in breast development, full development of the uterus and ovaries, widening hips, an increase in both height and body fat, the growth of pubic and underarm hair, and the onset of menstruation. In boys the increase in hormones brings about an increase in the size of their genitals, a marked growth spurt, the development of coarser thicker pubic and body hair, a broadening of the chest, muscle development, facial hair, increase in libido and aggressiveness, and deepening of the voice. These changes take place over a period of about five years. Girls start to show signs of developing at age 9-13, boys around 11 years old, and both are still developing until 16-18. Female breast development takes an average of four years.

It is important to note that the endocrine system is a complex system of interrelated hormones. The onset of puberty is controlled by the luteinizing hormone (LH), which is secreted by the pituitary gland, at the direction of the hypothalamus. Puberty cannot be reversed or recreated with hormone therapy after it has happened! Sorry to say, but once you are through puberty, the damage has been done. That is why transgender children are treated with hormone blockers at what is called Tanner Stage II (the beginning of noticeable changes) to delay further development.[35]

Once full maturity is reached, hormone levels in males are usually stable until about age 30, when they start a very gradual decline. There is considerable variability in testosterone levels, with a range from 250 ng/dl to 850 ng/dl. Average T levels in men run around 5-600, but can drop to 350-400 with advancing age.

---

[35] Norman Spack, MD, "Transgenderism", Fall 2005, available at http://www.imatyfa.org/permanent_files/spack-article.pdf

Women's hormone levels are more complex. Natal women have estrogen, progesterone and testosterone in their system, as well as other hormones that regulate their production. Testosterone is produced by the ovaries and adrenal glands, and regulates libido, among other things. Total testosterone ranges from 6 to 86 ng/ml in women, with less than 25 or over 100 considered abnormal. Estrogen and progesterone fluctuate over the menstrual cycle, and during and after a pregnancy. Hormone levels drop significantly after menopause. Estrogen levels can fluctuate from 50 to 400 pg/ml, depending on the day, and end up around 50 pg/ml or less after menopause. Progesterone levels typically range from .5 to 20 pg/ml, again depending on the point in the menstrual cycle, and drop to nearly zero after menopause.

With all this in mind, let's take a look at hormone treatments.

Feminizing Hormone Therapy

There is no magic formula that is going to transform you into the woman you have always wanted to be. You cannot turn back the clock and reverse the effects of puberty. It is possible, however, to change the proportions of estrogen and testosterone in your body, which will bring about changes that will enhance your feminine appearance. There are two components to this:

Antiandrogens/testosterone blockers: Lowering testosterone levels is essential in order for estrogen treatment to be effective. The most commonly used antiandrogens are spironolactone (Aldactone®) and finasteride (Propecia® or Proscar®). Spironolactone is the most commonly prescribed. Antiandrogens alone will have some feminizing effects, such as slowing male-pattern baldness, and reducing sexual functioning. Using antiandrogens also means that you'll need less estrogen than if it had to "fight" the testosterone in your system.

Estrogens: Estrogen is the cornerstone of feminization treatment. It works directly on your body's development, and also contributes to lowering testosterone levels. Estrogen can be taken as a pill (oral application), patch or gel (transdermal) or injection (intramuscular). Estrogen patches are associated with fewer side effects, but are less convenient than pills. Injections have some benefits where access to health care is limited, but they do not provide a steady hormone level. There are different chemical formulations of estrogen supplements; some have been shown to have fewer side effects than others. There is a growing interest in bio-identical formulas that can be compounded in some pharmacies. These are metabolized more effectively, so less is needed for the same effect.

There are also two types of supplements that are sometimes used by transsexuals:

Progestagens: Progesterone is not necessary for women to feel feminine; as noted earlier it drops to practically zero after menopause. It's inclusion in HRT for post-menopausal women was discontinued after a comprehensive health study demonstrated significant health risks (including depression and weight gain). Most transgender health programs do not include progestins (such as Provera®) in their treatment protocols, because of the increased risks of side-effects. There is a difference, however, between progestins (which are synthetic) and micronized progesterone, which is considered bio-identical. Some anecdotal evidence suggests that progesterone helps with breast development, but this has not been substantiated by research. If you do not have sufficient breast development with estrogen alone, discuss the pros and cons of adding micronized progesterone with your physician.

Phytoestrogens: These are herbal supplements, such as soy isoflavones, that may mimic the effects of estrogen. Some people swear by them, but there is no evidence that they are actually effective. They are easily obtained, and sold widely over the Internet, but do not live up to their hype. It's just not possible to verify the strength or potency of any particular supplement, and negative side-effects are possible at high doses of even all-natural herbal supplements.

The specific hormone regimen that your doctor will prescribe will depend on a number of things. First and foremost, it will depend on your pre-existing hormone levels. If you are older or have lower testosterone for any reason, you will need less testosterone-blocker, and perhaps less estrogen, to achieve the desired effect. Second, it will depend on your age, general health, and any other risk factors you have that could contribute to adverse effects of hormones. And last but not least it depends on the particular prescribing practices of your physician. The prevailing approach is to reduce testosterone levels and raise estrogen levels to the ranges considered normal for a biological adult female. Most physicians take a conservative approach to hormone therapy - first, do no harm - and start on low doses and increase as needed. THIS IS IN YOUR BEST INTEREST. You do not want to take any more of any kind of medication or supplement than you need.

With that in mind, here are the hormones commonly recommended by endocrinologists:

Estrogen:

Oral (pill):	estradiol	2.0 - 6.0 mg a day
	OR	
Transdermal (patch):	estradiol patch	0.1 - 0.4 mg twice a week
	OR	
Parenteral (injection):	estradiol valerate	5-20 mg IM every 2 weeks
	or cypionte	2-10 mg IM every week

Antiandrogen:	spironolactone	100 - 200 mg a day
	and/or finasteride	up to 5 mg a day

Antiandrogens are eliminated after an orchiectomy or gender reassignment surgery, and estrogen levels adjusted. Some physicians drop estrogen levels to match postmenopausal women; this may not be adequate for feminizing effects. Discuss this with your prescriber.

Feminizing Effects of Hormone Therapy:

You can expect to see some changes soon after starting hormone therapy; others take much longer. One to three months after starting FHT you should begin to notice:

Sexual changes: These include a decrease in sex drive, fewer spontaneous and/or morning erections, decreased ability to produce sperm and ejaculatory fluid, and difficulty achieving and/or maintaining an erection when stimulated. Some transwomen experience an abrupt and complete drop in sexual functioning, while others retain the ability to function to some extent when aroused. Some say that their male sexual functioning disappears, but not their experience of themselves as sexual beings. They report more "whole-body" sensual/sexual arousal, often to the point of orgasm (without ejaculation).

Skin changes: One of the first effects that many notice is a change in skin texture and sensation. Estrogen promotes a softening of the skin, increase in skin sensitivity, and a decrease in oil production from the sebaceous glands. The increase in skin sensitivity is mostly pleasurable, except when it comes time for electrolysis! As skin becomes less oily it becomes less susceptible to acne; however, a change in skin care is necessary to avoid overly-dry skin. (See Chapter Nine.)

Changes in body shape: FHT results in a decrease in muscle mass, an increase in body fat, and a redistribution of body fat to hips and buttocks. The advantage in upper arm strength that men have over women is fueled by the differences in hormones; once you decrease testosterone and increase estrogen you will lose that advantage. You will not be able to lift as much weight as you are used to, and need to adjust your expectations of yourself. This can be difficult for those who depend on their upper-body strength for their job. Several of my clients had to give up physically demanding work; pushing themselves to do more ended up causing back problems. The increase in body fat may also be disturbing to some transwomen. If you have been losing weight in order to look more feminine you'll need to adjust your expectations here too. It's vitally important to maintain a good diet, even if you gain weight. Cutting your calories too much will inhibit the positive effects you want from estrogen. The increased body fat will, with time, settle in your bust and hips and/or buttocks. Don't despair if the first women's jeans you bought no longer fit! That's a good sign - it means your figure is filling out and becoming more feminine.

Changes in mood: Hormones have a powerful effect on mood and emotional well-being. Testosterone tends to be a mood enhancer; it's no coincidence that depression in men increases with age. Dropping testosterone levels, especially without or before estrogen replacement, can have a dampening or "flattening" effect on mood. But reducing testosterone can also have a calming effect, since high levels are associated with increased aggression and irritability. Estrogen, on the other hand, is associated with increased emotionality. Some transwomen experience significant depression on hormones, especially those who add progestin or take more than the recommended dose. Another way to describe the emotional changes is that testosterone is an invisible emotional shield; take it away and people feel more vulnerable. Most transwomen (and their partners) aren't prepared for the spontaneous tears and emotional outbursts that can erupt when they start hormones. Many partners report, however, that they like the emotional changes. They say that their partner is not only happier but kinder and gentler.

You can expect to see the following *gradual* changes (over 1 - 2 years):

Changes in body hair: Your hair texture will change along with your skin texture. The hair on your arms and legs will become thinner and finer, and may appear lighter. Hair on your torso (chest, back and abdomen) will begin to fade, and possibly disappear altogether. This can be hastened with waxing, as remaining hair will grow back more slowly. However, hormones cannot eliminate facial hair.

Slowed or stalled hair loss: Male-pattern baldness is dependent on testosterone, so lowering it will stop or at least slow down the loss of hair on your head. Hormone therapy will not grow hair back, unfortunately. (See Chapter Ten for more about how to cope with hair loss.)

Nipple and breast growth: Ever so slowly you will start to see, and feel, changes in your breasts. The areola and nipple will become larger, and more sensitive. The breast area may become sore, or at least very sensitive to touch, as it grows. You can expect to see some swelling by six months, and full development in two years. There is no way to predict how large your breasts will become. Some use the "one cup size smaller than the women in your family" formula, but that's just an estimate. Increasing your hormones above the recommended levels will not get your breasts to grow faster or larger.

Decrease in testicular size and volume: Over time, your genitals will seem to shrink. Your testicles will stop producing sperm and ejaculatory fluid, and your penis will not be able to become as full and erect as it once did. This will be an advantage when it comes to tucking them out of the way. You must realize, however, that this means you will most likely become completely impotent and sterile. If you are married or in a long-term relationship with a woman, you must disclose this to your spouse or partner. Some MtFs have frozen their sperm, just in case they decide they would like to impregnate someone. Contact a sperm bank or talk to your physician about this if you have any concerns. Your sperm count may drop as soon as you start taking hormones, so it's best done sooner rather than later.

Limitations of Feminizing Hormone Therapy:

After 2 to 4 years on hormones, you will reach the limit of the changes you can expect to see. Your breasts will not get any bigger without surgery or a significant weight gain. Hormone therapy can only do so much after puberty is complete. Your bone structure will not change, so your hips will not widen and your shoulders will still be as broad. Your facial features may soften on hormones, but your facial structure will not change. Your facial hair will not go away, and any hair lost on your head will not grow back. You will not have a natal woman's breasts, with functioning mammary glands. Hormones will not alter your voice in any way; you will have to work hard to learn how to speak in a feminine voice. And FHT won't change your basic personality. In some ways it will help you feel more like a woman, but it can't make a purse out a sow's ear, as the saying goes.

Risks and Negative Side-effects of Feminizing Hormones:

Whenever you alter the body's chemistry in any way, there are risks as well as benefits. Some of these can be deadly; some are merely annoying. It's important to understand what the risks are and how to minimize them. Here are some of the more common negative side-effects:

Estrogen increases the risk of blood clots (venous thrombosis), which can cause heart attacks, strokes, lung damage, chronic leg pain, and sudden death. Smoking while taking estrogen increases those risks; so does obesity. For this reason, if you have a history of blood clots you will probably not be able to take oral estrogen. If you have several other risk factors, such as smoking and obesity, you will also not be able to start FHT until those are resolved. You will have to quit smoking and lose weight. It's that simple.

Estrogen changes the way your body metabolizes and stores fat. This increases your risk of Type 2 diabetes, heart disease and gallstones. Estrogen may also increase your blood pressure, which may need to be treated if you are not taking spironolactone. Exercise and dietary changes will minimize the risks of diabetes and heart disease. Dietary changes will be necessary to maintain a reasonable weight; you cannot continue to eat a typical American man's diet and not suffer the consequences.

Estrogen stimulates the production of the hormone prolactin. This can result in a milky discharge from the nipples, which is not a problem by itself. It can be an indication that prolactin levels are too high, which can increase the risk of tumors of the pituitary gland. For that reason, your physician should check your prolactin levels frequently in the first year on hormones, and then yearly after that. Your dosage of estrogen may need to be reduced until prolactin levels are back in the normal range.

Estrogen may increase your risk of breast cancer. Risks are greater if you have a family history of breast cancer, are over 50 and/or overweight, smoke cigarettes, and if you have been taking progestagens. For this reason your physician will recommend a mammogram as soon as you have sufficient breast development. Learn how to do a manual self-exam and get mammograms every year or two.

Estrogen may increase the risk of depression. This can result in a Catch-22 for some transsexuals. Being in the wrong body can be depressing, and not being able to get the physical changes that result from FHT can be even more depressing. Adding hormone-driven depression, however, doesn't help either. Fortunately, depression is treatable. If you have any signs that your mood is worsening on hormones, it's imperative that you tell your doctor.

Other possible side-effects of estrogen include nausea and vomiting and an increase in frequency and severity of migraines. Nausea and vomiting can be reduced by using estrogen patches or injections. If you are prone to migraines, or have epilepsy, let your doctor know. These can be treated with medication.

Spironolactone lowers blood pressure. In fact, it was originally developed as a treatment for high blood pressure, until the demasculinizing side-effects were discovered. Because it is a diuretic it changes the sodium/potassium levels in your body. This can result in orthostatic hypotension - dizziness when you stand up quickly. It can also lead to problematic changes in your heart rhythm. Be sure to stay well-hydrated, and consider Gatorade or other sports drink with strenuous exercise or on hot days. Spironolactone can also result in a skin rash.

Decreasing hormone levels increases the risk of osteoporosis. Our body needs hormones in order to maintain adequate bone density. If you take an antiandrogen, such as spironolactone, without adding sufficient estrogen you run the risk of compromising bone density. This can lead to back problems, hip fractures, etc. For this reason, anyone on long-term FHT needs to get their bone density checked as they get older.

Any oral medication puts a strain on liver functioning. This increases your risk of liver disease. (So does excessive alcohol consumption.) For this reason you will need to have your liver enzymes checked annually, and consider estrogen patches or injections if you have a pre-existing liver condition.

You can see from this list that medical supervision of hormone therapy really is necessary. At your first visit your endocrinologist will review your complete medical history and will order baseline hormone levels, if you haven't had them done yet. He or she will discuss the best hormone regimen for you, considering your goals and any pre-existing conditions you have. You will probably not get a prescription for hormones on your first visit! The physician will want to check the lab test results first before deciding where to start. He or she will start you at a low dose, and retest your levels after three months. Your medications will be increased until the test results are in the normal range for a woman.

DO NOT TAKE MORE THAN THE RECOMMENDED DOSAGE. This will not help you develop faster, but it will increase the risks associated with hormone treatment. You also need to continue seeing your physician regularly once you have started hormone therapy. Not only will you want to have your hormone levels tested regularly to see how well the FHT is working, you'll also need to have your liver enzymes, cholesterol levels, and serum prolactin checked every 3-6 months to start, and annually after everything is stable.

Masculinizing Hormone Therapy

Masculinizing hormone treatment for those transitioning from female to male is in some ways simpler than feminizing hormone treatment; all you have to do is add testosterone. But it too has its risks, benefits and limitations. Testosterone is one of three androgens that occur naturally in our body; the other two are dehydroepiandrosterone (DHEA) and dihydrotestosterone (DHT). Testosterone is the sex hormone responsible for the development of masculine secondary sex characteristics that occurs at puberty. This includes an increase in the size of boys' genitals, a marked growth spurt, the development of coarser thicker pubic and body hair, a broadening of the chest, muscle development, facial hair, increase in libido and aggressiveness, and deepening of the voice.

In adults, testosterone affects mood, metabolism, muscle mass, and libido. It supports sexual performance and functioning in men. Testosterone treatment is used in small amounts for males with testosterone deficiency and/or declining T levels that occur with age, and in women with low libidos due to declining hormone levels after menopause or an oophorectomy. It is used in higher doses for full masculinizing effects. Androgen therapy works in two ways: 1) by directly increasing testosterone levels, and 2) indirectly, by suppressing the hypothalamic-pituitary-gonadal feedback loop that stimulates the release of estrogen from the ovaries. Thus there is no need for an additional "estrogen-blocker".

Testosterone can be delivered in several ways:

Intramuscular (injection): A weekly or biweekly shot is the most common method of administration. It is the least expensive and most direct. You get more "bang for your buck" with injections, and they bring about the desired results more quickly than the gel or patch. It does not, however, deliver a steady amount of testosterone; T levels will rise and fall over the week or two week period. Side-effects and mood changes are most noticeable 2-5 days after an injection. There are risks associated with frequent or improper injections. You can learn to give yourself injections, but it is advisable to have someone trained to give them to you. Either way there are procedures that must never be skipped, and needles must be disposed of properly.

Transdermal (gel or patch): Testosterone can be applied directly to the skin via a patch or gel. The gel must be smeared on daily, after showering and/or swimming, and allowed to dry. The patch may cause skin irritation, and can come off with exercise or sweating. Both can rub off on another person with intimate contact; this is especially hazardous for a pregnant partner or children. The advantage is that the gel and patch provide a steady supply of testosterone, with less mood fluctuations. The cost, however, is as much as ten times the cost of injections. There is also a new mode of delivery called Buccal testosterone that is applied to the upper gum twice a day.

Oral (pills): Testosterone treatment at the levels needed for full masculinizing effects is not generally prescribed in pill form. Oral medications have to pass through the liver, and can cause damage in large doses. Because oral testosterone is rapidly degraded in the liver, you'd have to start with an even higher dose in order to end up with enough free testosterone to have any effect. It is also not as effective at stopping menstrual periods as the other forms of testosterone.

Other androgen supplements: There are a number of dietary supplements available that purport to act like testosterone. It might seem to make sense to look at DHEA and DHT supplements, since those are also androgens, but they are not the androgens responsible for masculinizing effects. Don't be fooled by any claims made by places selling such supplements! There is no evidence that they are effective. In fact, there is evidence that they end up raising estrogen levels, and lowering HDL levels (the good cholesterol). And with all such supplements there is no government regulation, so you can never be sure of what you're actually getting. One in particular - Androstenedione - is listed by Consumer Reports as one of the top 12 supplements to avoid.[36]

There are other avenues being developed for the delivery of testosterone, such as sublingual drops and subcutaneous implants, but their use has not become routine among endocrinologists. It is generally safer to stick with what has been proven to be helpful rather than looking for the "latest and greatest" method. It is also safer to stick with hormones prescribed by a knowledgeable physician. It's risky enough playing around with one's body chemistry with prescribed hormones. To self-medicate in any way is asking for trouble you don't need. "Cheryl" abused sex steroids as a semi-pro wrestler; this contributed to the development of the obesity and diabetes that she struggles with daily.

So do yourself a favor and find an endocrinologist or knowledgeable primary care physician and make an appointment. At your first visit your physician will review your complete medical history and will order baseline hormone levels if you haven't had them done yet. He or she will recommend the best hormone regimen for you, considering your goals and any pre-existing conditions you have. You will not be able to take testosterone if you are pregnant or breastfeeding, or have an androgen sensitive breast

---

[36] "Dangerous Supplements: Still at Large." Consumer Reports, May 2004

cancer, severe liver disease, uncontrolled coronary artery disease or endo-metrial cancer. You probably won't get a prescription for hormones on your first visit! The physician will want to check the lab test results first before deciding where to start. He or she will start you at a low dose, and retest your levels after 3 months. Your testosterone will be increased until the test results are in the normal range for a man.

The specific hormone regimen that your doctor will prescribe will depend on a number of things. First and foremost, it will depend on your pre-existing hormone levels. Second, it will depend on your age, general health, and any other risk factors you have that could contribute to adverse effects of hormones. And last but not least it depends on the particular prescribing practices of your physician. The prevailing approach is to raise testosterone levels to the range considered normal for a biological adult male. Most physicians take a conservative approach to hormone therapy - first, do no harm - and start on low doses and increase as needed. THIS IS IN YOUR BEST INTEREST. You do not want to take any more of any kind of medication or supplement than you need.

It is important to remember that testosterone is a DEA controlled sub-stance in the United States. This is due to the history of testosterone abuse by athletes and bodybuilders. You will have to get a new prescription every six months. DO NOT TAKE MORE THAN THE RECOMMENDED DOSAGE. This will not help you develop faster, but it will increase the risks associated with hormone treatment. Taking a higher dose can actually slow down the masculinizing effects; extra testosterone in your system can be converted to estrogen.

With that in mind, here are some typical dosage recommendations:

Intramuscular injection:
Testosterone cypionate (Depo-Testosterone)   100-200 mg every 2 week
        OR Testosterone enanthate (Delatestryl)   OR 50-100 mg weekly

Transdermal:
Dissolved testosterone crystals   2.5 - 10 g per day
        (Androgel® or Androderm®) :

Your physician will need to check your testosterone levels periodically and adjust your dosage as needed. If you have your ovaries removed your dose will probably be cut in half; once your body is not producing as much estrogen you won't need as much testosterone to maintain the masculinizing effects. Without ovaries you will need to stay on testosterone (or other hormone replacement therapy) or risk significant loss of bone density.

Masculinizing Effects of Testosterone

You can expect to see some changes soon after starting hormone therapy; others take much longer. Within a few months after starting MHT you should begin to notice:

Mood and libido changes: You will probably notice these changes first. Increased energy and enhanced mood are common. You may become more irritable or more aggressive. You may also find that your range of emotions is narrower. Your interest in sexual activity will definitely increase. Your close friends and intimate partner(s) need to be made aware of this potential! Although you may welcome it at first, some transmen report that this can become a burden. If you have had anger or mood management problems, be sure to work on these with your therapist. I have seen too many transmen drop out of therapy as soon as they get their prescription, and then return in crisis after relationships have crashed and burned.

Skin changes: Testosterone will increase the size and activity of sebaceous glands, resulting in oily skin and acne. This can usually be managed with good skin care (see Chapter Nine), but occasionally prescription medication is needed. Acne may develop on your back and chest as well as your face, and can result in permanent scarring if not treated properly. You may also notice an increase in perspiration and body odor. Your skin texture will change, becoming rougher or coarser. There is one spot, however, that will become drier, and that is your vagina. If you have intercourse or other vaginal penetration you will probably need to use lubrication. Your clitoris will increase in size, by about 1 - 3 centimeters (about an inch) to start and up to 5 cm (2 inches) after a year or two.

Body hair: The hair on your arms and legs will become thicker and coarser, looking darker. You will also develop hair on your chest, back, abdomen, buttocks and even in your ears. How much and how thick and dark will depend on your genetic make-up. Take a look at the men in your family as a guide to what you can expect.

By six months you should observe the following changes:

Cessation of ovulation and menstruation: If you are on the right dosage of testosterone your periods will eventually stop. You will probably become infertile, which may or may not be reversible if you stop taking hormones. The possibility of becoming sterile (permanently infertile) is something you need to consider carefully and discuss with an intimate partner. Think about and discuss all possible scenarios; it's one thing to say when you're 20 that you don't ever want to bear a child, but you may feel differently when you hit 30. There are plenty of cisgendered women who put off a decision about childbearing until their thirties and then discover that they cannot conceive; you increase the odds considerably by taking testosterone for a number of years. There is also no guarantee that you'll stop ovulating, however, so be sure to use birth control if you have vaginal intercourse with a man! Getting pregnant while on T is not healthy for you or a baby.

Body shape: You can expect a weight gain on testosterone, as much as ten percent of your body weight. Most of this will be in the form of increased muscle mass. Your body fat may shift from your hips to your waist, giving you a more rectangular body shape. Over time, your breasts may "deflate" to some extent. Your appetite may increase, and your metabolism may change; if you eat more without exercising you risk becoming overweight or obese. (This is one of the reasons for taking off any excess weight *before* you begin hormones.) With proper exercise your upper body strength will increase. If you are young (under 21) you may also experience a late growth spurt. You may become taller, or your feet and hands may become larger. I have one client whose feet grew a whole shoe size.

Voice deepening: As discussed in Chapter Eleven, men's and women's voices differ in a number of ways, including pitch, resonance, loudness and intonation. During puberty testosterone affects the growth of facial bones, the development of the Adams's apple, and the length and thickness of the vocal chords and cartilage in the larynx. The result is a larger voice box in teenage boys than girls. These testosterone-driven changes are the basis of the differences in pitch and resonance in men and women. Once puberty is complete and full adult size has been reached, the basic physical structure of the mouth, throat and larynx will not change. When you add testosterone as an adult the vocal folds will thicken, but they will not grow longer. Thus the pitch of the voice will lower, but not necessarily the resonance. Three to six months after starting MHT you'll notice your voice beginning to "crack" and become lower. It may sound like you have a perpetual cold for a while. It can take up to a year for your voice to reach its final register. To keep from getting hoarse and to protect your voice as it changes, drink plenty of liquids. Speech therapy or voice training can help develop a more masculine voice, and/or retrain your singing voice.

It will probably take a year or more to see the final changes in your appearance:

Facial hair: A beard is that one marker that is always read as unmistakably male. It takes a while (up to four years) to develop, however, and may appear in patches. Nothing is more obviously "trans" than a long wispy goatee that really does look like a goat's beard. You might consider shaving until you have a sufficient amount of facial hair for a reasonably full beard or a decent mustache and/or goatee. For more style suggestions, see Chapter Ten or Hudson's FtM website.

Male-pattern baldness: If you are genetically predisposed, you may begin to see the beginning of male-pattern baldness. This may be welcome, or not. Topical treatments such as Minoxidol can be used to reduce hair loss.

Risks and Negative Side-Effects of MHT

Polycythemia: Polycythemia is a condition that results in an increased level of circulating red blood cells in the bloodstream. Basically, this means a thickening of the blood. People with polycythemia have an increase in hematocrit, hemoglobin or red blood cell count, above the normal limits.

This is a serious condition that increases the risk of blood clots, stroke, pulmonary embolism, and heart attacks. It also puts a strain on the kidneys. It is imperative to have a CBC (complete blood count) every year.

Increased insulin resistance: One of the metabolic changes that occurs with increased testosterone is increased insulin resistance. This increases your risk of developing Type 2 diabetes, especially if you are overweight. Given the increased appetite, you will really have to watch what you eat, and exercise regularly.

High blood pressure and high cholesterol: As your physiology becomes more masculine you'll become more prone to the conditions that commonly afflict men. Testosterone lowers HDL levels (the "good cholesterol") and can raise LDL levels and triglycerides. These increase the risk of heart disease and stroke. Obesity also increases your risk. The first transgender client I saw was unable to get his weight below 300 pounds, and died of a heart attack at the age of 38.

Elevated liver enzymes: Testosterone puts a strain on liver functioning, which shows up as elevated liver enzymes. This is a risk factor for liver disease. Obviously alcohol abuse and other risk factors such as Hepatitis-C and HIV would make the risk of liver disease even higher. Your liver enzymes should be tested before you begin MHT and periodically after.

Cancer risks: Just as there are estrogen-sensitive cancers, there are androgen-sensitive ones too. Testosterone use may be linked to an increased risk of liver, breast and uterine cancer. There is a possibility that MHT increases the risk of ovarian cancer, which is the deadliest form of female reproductive cancer. It has been shown that long-term androgen exposure results in polycystic ovaries. There haven't been enough studies of the long-term use of MHT to be sure of the overall cancer risks. It's vitally important to continue (or start!) getting mammograms and Pap tests along with a complete annual physical.

Neurological disorders: Testosterone has been shown to worsen several neurological conditions: migraine headaches, seizure disorders (such as epilepsy), and sleep apnea. If you have or suspect you have any of these it's important to get it checked out and treated. They shouldn't preclude getting or staying on hormones, so be honest with your physician about these.

Limitations of Masculinizing Hormone Therapy

Testosterone is not a miracle cure for gender dysphoria. It will not automatically make you passable or more comfortable with yourself. It will not magically cure depression or social anxiety. Nor will it transform you into the man you've always wanted to be. As mentioned earlier, once puberty is complete and secondary sex characteristics are developed they can't be undone. Your breasts will not disappear, and your clitoris will not grow into a penis (or anything capable of penetration). You will probably go through a period (perhaps a year or two) where you look like a teenage boy. MHT will also not change your basic body structure. You won't get taller, and you will still have wide hips, so you may have to hunt for guy clothes that fit.

I hope you can also see from this list that MHT affects your whole body and needs to be monitored by a physician. Before you begin testosterone you should have a complete physical, with pelvic exam and Pap test (and pregnancy test if you are sexually active with men), and have your hormone levels, weight, blood pressure, lipid profile (cholesterol levels), liver enzymes, complete blood count, and glucose levels tested. These should all be checked again three months after you start testosterone, then every six months for another year or two, and then every year for as long as you're on it. Mammograms should continue until chest reconstruction surgery. If you have Polycystic Ovary Syndrome (see below), as do many transmen, you'll need to monitor the effects of testosterone even more carefully.

References and Resources

Olivia Ashbee and Joshua Mira Goldberg, **Hormones: A Guide for FTMs** Vancouver Coastal Health,Transcend Transgender Support & Education Society and Canadian Rainbow Health Coalition, February 2006

Olivia Ashbee and Joshua Mira Goldberg , **Hormones: A Guide for MTFs,** Vancouver Coastal Health,Transcend Transgender Support & Education Society and Canadian Rainbow Health Coalition, February 2006

Louis J. Gooren, Erik J. Giltay and Mathijs C. Bunck, "Long-Term Treatment of Transsexuals with Cross-Sex Hormones: Extensive Personal Experience", *J Clin Endocrinol Metab*, January 2008

Eva Moore, Amy Wisniewski and Adrian Dobs, "Endocrine Treatment of Transsexual People: A Review of Treatment Regimens, Outcomes, and Adverse Effects", *The Journal of Clinical Endocrinology & Metabolism*, Vol. 88, No.8, 2003

Tsuyoshi Baba, Toshiaki Endo, Hiroyuki Honnma, Yoshimitsu Kitajima, Takuhiro Hayashi, Hiroshi Ikeda, Naoya Masumori, Hirofumi Kamiya, Osamu Moriwaka and Tsuyoshi Saito, "Association between polycystic ovary syndrome and female-to-male transsexuality" in *Human Reproduction* Vol.22, No.4 pp. 1011–1016, 2007

Slabbekoorn D., Van Goozen S., Gooren L., Cohen-Kettenis P. "Effects of Cross-Sex Hormone Treatment on Emotionality in Transsexuals." IJT 5,3 2001, www.symposion.com/ijt/ijtvo05no03_02.htm

Polycystic Ovary Syndrome (PCOS)

Polycystic Ovary Syndrome is a health condition that is very common among female-to-male transsexuals. PCOS is a hormone imbalance where the ovaries produce higher levels of androgens than normal. This results in:

➢ hirsutism (excessive hair growth)
➢ acne, oily skin, dandruff and sometimes rough dark patches of skin
➢ weight gain and obesity, especially around the waist
➢ insulin resistance and diabetes
➢ infrequent, absent or irregular menstrual periods
➢ anovulatory cycles and infertility
➢ thinning hair
➢ many small cysts on the ovaries, often painful
➢ anxiety or depression
➢ sleep apnea
➢ higher risk of miscarriage and other pregnancy complications

If you suspect that you have PCOS, please discuss this with your doctor. The associated symptoms can be treated in a variety of ways. Because androgen levels may already be high, masculinizing hormone treatment must be started slowly and carefully. MHT could increase the risk of obesity and Type 2 diabetes.

Chapter Thirteen

Allies and Challengers

To be nobody but yourself in a world which is doing its best day and night to make you everybody else, means to fight the hardest battle which any human being can fight, and never stop fighting.

e.e. cummings

Once you have crossed the second threshold, the changes and challenges in your life will accelerate. When your appearance noticeably changes, you will find out who your real friends and allies are. You will find many supporters, some where you least expect it. Allies are the people in your life who truly support your growth and change. Not everyone who says they support you, however, is a true ally. There are degrees of acceptance and support. The Unitarian Universalist Association Welcoming Congregation Handbook presents these as stages of understanding:

1. **Repugnancy:** People at this stage have no tolerance for anything outside their norms of gender and sexuality. They are ignorant, homophobic, transphobic, and self-righteous. They will do everything they can to keep you away from their children.

2. **Toleration:** At this stage, people can tolerate people who are different, as long as they keep their distance. They are basically judgmental, but will keep their opinions to themselves, most of the time. They may say they're OK with your changes, but they still don't want you near their children.

3. **Acceptance:** With some education and understanding, people can move to accepting that some people are different and shouldn't be discriminated against. They are OK with transgender people in their church or workplace, but wouldn't hire one as a babysitter.

4. **Affirmation:** Some people seek to truly understand the experience of gender-variant people and get to know them at a deeper level. They have transgender friends and celebrate their unique contributions. They have no problem with their kids getting to know them.[37]

It's important to recognize these different stages or levels of understanding. There may be some people in your life who said they were fine with your transition, but when it starts to show they may react differently. Their reactions can be confusing, disappointing, and hurtful. There are two types of reactions I call Sirens and Saboteurs.

Sirens: In Greek mythology, Sirens were mythical beings who lived on an island in the Mediterranean. Their singing was said to be so enchanting that sailors were lured to their deaths, crashing their ships into the rocks near the shore in their attempts to get closer to the sound. Odysseus, so the legend goes, stuffed his crew's ears with wax and had himself tied to his mast in order to avoid the temptation. On our journey through life, Sirens

---

[37] Scott W. Alexander, Meg Riley, and Keith Kron, editors. *The Welcoming Congregation Handbook: Resources for Affirming Bisexual, Gay, Lesbian and/or Transgender People,* Unitarian Universalist Association, 1999

are those who lure us away from our chosen path with promises of one sort or another. The relationship that pulls us away from our own values and priorities with promises of a wonderful life together, or the job that offers fame and/or fortune, but no fulfillment, are examples of Sirens.

I have one client who drops in every year or two to consider transition options. Then he's off again in another direction, lured away by a big construction contract, or an old flame who has reappeared in his life. I've seen clients who finally got out of one controlling relationship, only to end up in another. There are several who have decided to have yet another child, pushing back their transition plans. There's another who spent all her time and money for five years building her dream house, ending up nearly bankrupt when her company down-sized.

Fame and fortune can also be powerful sirens that draw people away from transitioning. I have seen many clients delay transitioning because they believe that they can't transition at their present job, and it pays too well to consider leaving. We'll discuss how to deal with this more in Chapter Eighteen, but I suspect that it's more than the money that holds them back. The male ego is made, not born. Those who were raised male often see career and financial success as a measure of their worth. They can be attached to the status their money and position provides.

Security is the most seductive Siren of all. It's hard to transition without taking some risks. Clinging to the safety of a familiar but unsupportive relationship, or the financially-rewarding but stifling career, provides security but not growth. You have to leave the shore to explore new lands.

Saboteurs: Saboteurs are those people in your life who manage to undermine your progress. Some are clearly opposed to your transition. Some are wolves in sheeps' clothing; they appear to be fine with your transition, but they're really not. Consciously or unconsciously they put up roadblocks that can derail you if you're not careful.

Saboteurs are usually subtly critical of your transition. They don't like the way you dress or wear your hair. They think your new name doesn't suit you. They're also the ones who are quick to say they can't see any changes in your appearance, and have trouble switching names and pronouns. They're also worriers, always pointing out the negative possibilities. They ask those "Are you sure...?" questions that convey a lack of confidence in your decisions. They seem to have your best interests at heart, but they do not. They're unable to cope with your changes, but can't come right out and say that to you.

Significant others who are unable to stop someone from transitioning directly may resort to subtle (or not so subtle) sabotage. They may say they support your transition, but every time you plan to dress up and go out or attend a support group meeting there's some sort of crisis. Suddenly they're not feeling well, or they pick a fight over something, or don't come back in time with the car you need. They may run up the credit cards so that you can't afford your clothes or transition-related expenses. They ask for frequent delays, stalling for time "to adjust". It's never a good time, in their view, for you to tell the children, or start hormones, or take the next step. They want you to be happy, but....(fill in the blank with excuses).

Some of these reactions may be temporary, as people adjust. Deciding whether to stay in a relationship with someone who is having a hard time with your transition is a major challenge. The two questions I hear most often are: "How can I transition without destroying my marriage and/or family?" and "How can I get my wife/girlfriend/boyfriend/parents/kids to accept me?" Where it was once thought that transsexuals had to leave their marriage and family in order to transition, it is now considered more beneficial to preserve as many close significant relationships as possible. If an existing support system can stay intact, all the better! That's not an easy task. We are all, unless orphaned and/or estranged, embedded in family systems, as well as communities. One thing we know for sure about family systems (or any other kind of system) is that when one person changes it affects everyone. And not everyone likes change, especially of this magnitude. I'll address these two questions in this chapter, but first, let's set the stage....

What happens when an irresistible force meets an immovable object? That's an old riddle that came to mind as I started this chapter. The irresistible force is your need to be yourself. The immovable object is often your spouse or significant other. Many of the clients I have worked with were married when they started transitioning. Some still are. I have seen a wide range of responses from spouses. On one end of the spectrum is the wife who said to me that she would rather have her husband commit suicide than become a woman. (Sadly, the last I heard from the client he was in the state hospital.) At the other end are partners who embrace the changes and become champions of transgender rights. They are often bisexual (whether they knew it before the transition or not). They are usually progressive in their thinking, or at least open-minded. In between are those who struggle with coming to terms with the changes their spouse or partner proposes. Some come to accept and even appreciate the changes, some make an uneasy peace with it, and others just can't make the transition that's required of them.

So let's look at the changes that are required of someone when their spouse decides to transition.

Cognitive changes: In Chapter Six we talked about "cisgendered" people and how they take their gender identity for granted. They have grown up in a binary world where gender was predetermined (by biology) and immutable. They have a hard time wrapping their mind around anything different. It takes a higher level of thought, a different cognitive perspective, to be able to not only understand the different aspects of sex and gender but also see them as a continuum and not a dichotomy. Some people don't have the cognitive flexibility to "get it". Changing their way of thinking about sex and gender is too threatening to their sense of order. For some it shakes the foundation of their own masculine or feminine identity.

Physical changes: As much as we like to think that we fall in love with a person's personality, our initial attraction is usually to a person's physical appearance. Sexual attraction is a big part of the glue that brings and holds relationships together. Even if an intimate relationship starts out as friends, at some point there is that spark of attraction to their physical being that turns it into something more. With time we get to know our partner's body intimately, and that body is what we respond to sexually. We take comfort in the familiar feel and smell of our partner's body. It's a big adjustment when that body starts to change, when breasts or facial hair grow, skin feels different, and even the smells become unfamiliar. When a spouse's gender changes, there's no guarantee that there will still be any sexual attraction left. Some spouses find they are still just as attracted physically, or even more so; most are not.

Sexual orientation: Most people identify as either heterosexual or homosexual. In our social world an intimate relationship is seen as either heterosexual (between a man and a woman) or homosexual (between two men or two women). If one person in the relationship changes gender, it changes the relationship from hetero- to homosexual or homo- to heterosexual. It changes the nature of the relationship for *both* partners. One of the biggest objections I hear from spouses is "But I'm not....(gay or lesbian, or heterosexual)!" It takes a major redefining of their sexual orientation to stay with a transitioned partner. Some may end up saying "Well, I guess I'm bisexual (or pansexual)." Others hang on to their sexual orientation, and say that they are who they are and just happen to be in a different kind of relationship now. Some simply can't handle the idea of now being in a homosexual (or heterosexual) relationship. Some women depend on their husband being masculine in order to feel like a woman; when "he" transitions it threatens their feminine identity. And many lesbians are deeply committed to their lesbian identity and community and/or don't want to be seen as heterosexual.

Social changes: No matter how a couple ends up redefining their relationship, it will be perceived by others as different. To now be perceived as gay, or straight, by the rest of the world is another big adjustment. It takes a man who is very secure in his masculinity, for example, to handle being seen as gay once his wife transitions. If a couple has been living in a heteronormative world they will now be open to all the discrimination and harassment that comes with being seen as homosexual. And unless they've been traveling in open-minded social circles they will probably see friends drop away. One of my clients is very religious and his wife is very involved in the local church. Not only will "he" be ostracized once "he" transitions, but she will be as well.

Role changes: Every couple works out certain roles and responsibilities that each partner takes on. This is less true in homosexual relationships, but in most heterosexual relationships these are often typed by gender. Wives often depend on their husbands to do the "heavy lifting", and those interactions in the world where a man has an advantage. They garner some safety and security from having a man around. They lose that when their husband transitions. Their "new" spouse may be just as tall, and still know how to do all those manly things, but the physical strength is just not the same. And again, the perceptions by others are not the same.

Financial sacrifices: A transitioning spouse is asking his or her partner to sign on to an undertaking that can cost thousands of dollars. It's a lot to ask of someone, especially when it wasn't part of the initial agreement. A spouse or partner who stays may have to give up or put off his or her plans for school, or retirement, or a car that runs consistently. That is difficult to accept, especially when the partner is also increasingly self-involved, as is typical when transitioning. This is where the most resentment shows up, and the accusation "You're being selfish!" often comes from.

Pressure from others: Before you come out to family and friends your partner will feel the burden of keeping the secret as much as you do. Once the word is out, your spouse or partner may feel pressured by family and/or friends to leave. Certainly other people will have things to say about the situation. Partners often have difficulty finding unbiased support and advice on how to stay in the relationship. (Although I've also seen partners who want to leave have trouble getting others to villainize their spouses as much as they do.) Unless there is a support group for spouses nearby, your spouse will probably be the only one she (or he) knows who is going through this.

If you add all this to the realization that the person you've been in a relationship with for X number of years is not exactly who he or she appears to be, and that he or she has been keeping a secret all that time, it's no wonder that partners often react badly to the initial disclosure. Their world has just been turned upside down. The list of emotional reactions to the news includes shock, disbelief, anger, anxiety, confusion, depression, despair, self-blame and self-doubt, and feelings of betrayal, rejection, and abandonment. But you can also often add to that (with time): relief at finding out what's really going on, curiosity, empathy, and concern and understanding.

That list sounds a lot like the stages of grief, doesn't it? Family members almost invariably go through the "stages" of grief in reaction to the news that their loved one is changing gender. They have to let go of their old image of that person, and mourn the loss of the son/daughter/parent/husband/wife they thought they had. Despite everything we hear about the only thing constant being change, we all somehow expect that at least someone's gender will be a constant.

Arlene Istar Lev, in her book *Transgender Emergence*, writes about the process of family emergence.[38] She outlines four stages:

1) **Discovery and Disclosure:** This is the initial discovery of the family member's gender variance. It could come from intentional disclosure by the family member, or by accidentally walking in on him or her, or discovering computer files or emails or some other telling trace of information. Sometimes the partner or family member has been aware of the gender variance, but then discovers that the person is planning on a full transition. The initial reactions are usually shock, disbelief, anger, confusion, anxiety and feelings of betrayal. These may alternate with periods of denial, resistance, and avoidance of the person or of the subject. A partner may shut down emotionally, hoping that if he or she ignores the problem it will go away.

2) **Turmoil:** This initial stage is often followed by a period of chaos and conflict in the relationship. Trust has been shattered; everything will be called into question. There will be lots of questions, and plenty of tears and angry words. This is perfectly natural! It is important to allow the person his or her feelings, even if they're painful to listen to. Some families break apart at this stage. One transwoman was forced to leave the house

---

[38] Arlene Istar Lev, *Transgender Emergence*, Haworth Press, 2004

she had built very shortly after disclosure. The wife went from zero to furious in a matter of hours, and got stuck there. Unfortunately she also turned the kids against "him". But usually once the heat of emotion has died down, the family member can move on to:

3) Negotiation (Bargaining): At this stage, they have at least accepted that the gender issues are not going away. Most family members will attempt to negotiate compromises. This is the point where parents try to get their gender-variant adolescents or young adults into counseling. Spouses may go along with "cross-dressing", go to support group meetings, even go shopping for their partner. They are often feeling out what they can live with, and where their limits are. There is still, however, some degree of denial or hope that their family member will reconsider and not go through with a full transition. This is a trying time for those who do want to transition. Their family members will try to put limits on their gender expression, but often inconsistently. I've heard many clients complain about mixed messages from their spouses. "She bought me new clothes last week, and then freaked out when I wore them!" It's like the children's game of "Mother, may I?" - two steps forward, one step back, lover may I? Some couples get stuck in this dance for a long time.

4) Finding Balance: At some point many couples and/or families find a workable solution to the conflicts that erupt after disclosure. It may be a precarious balance, with an uneasy compromise, but they find some way to continue as a family with a transgender family member. This may or may not involve that person fully transitioning. Some people decide that being able to be who they are in their own home is good enough, and choose to spare their family some of the impact of a full transition. Some couples decide to continue living together, but as best friends rather than intimate partners. This is more common in longer-term relationships, with children involved. They go about the business of being a family, in a different family form.

Here are some examples of couples who have managed to stay together and find that balance. (Names and identifying details have been changed, and some similar stories merged.)

Mitch is married to a much older man who used to be "her" tennis coach. They have been through a lot together, including some serious health challenges. Still, he hesitated to bring up the subject of transitioning, not knowing how the husband, and his friends, would deal with the changes. How would he feel about being in a relationship now perceived as homosexual? Would that alienate their friends? To his surprise and relief, both his husband and their friends have been very supportive. There have been some difficult adjustments; Mitch's husband is not comfortable holding hands or showing affection in public.

Caroline has been married for 10 years, with no children. Her wife has been supportive of her "cross-dressing", helping her with her make-up and attending TG events with her. Her wife understands, and wants her to be happy, but also has needs of her own. There are times when she says "I want my husband tonight." Caroline is certain that she wants to go further, but they both want to preserve their marriage. They are in the midst of dealing with extended family issues, so Caroline has put off plans to transition for now. She works at home and can dress as she pleases during the day.

Maddie and Janice were proud of being a same-sex married couple even before that became legal in New Hampshire. Maddie has had her struggles with transitioning because of some health issues, but Janice has been supportive every step of the way. They have been very involved in the transgender community, and Janice started a support group for spouses of transsexuals. Their kids were taught early on that this is just the way some people are born, and have also been supportive and involved.

Alex identified for many years as a butch lesbian, and was in a long-term lesbian relationship. His partner identified as a lesbian, but is comfortable seeing herself as bisexual. Their transition has been very smooth, except for financial challenges. Their friends, gay and straight, have accepted Alex as a transman. They have maintained their ties to the gay and lesbian community; Alex now works weekends at a GLBTQ-friendly bar.

So how can this happen? There is no sure-fire way to get your family to accept you as you are and go along with your transition plan. There is no way to protect them completely from the social impact of your transition. Leaving your family and moving to another town to spare them the direct impact is not the answer; that just deprives them of their spouse/parent /child. There are, however, ways to maximize the likelihood of your spouse and/or family being willing to come along with you on your journey.

Let them know as soon as possible what's going on. The sooner you can tell them the less likely it is that they will feel betrayed by your keeping a secret. As mentioned in Chapter Six, don't tell them everything at once. Be honest with your partner first about your struggles, past and present. Tell him or her you've been getting help and trying to resolve these feelings. Present it as a problem to be solved together, even if you already have a solution in mind.

Affirm your commitment to the relationship. Tell them how much they mean to you, and how much you'd like their support. Reassure them that you want to stay in the relationship and will do everything you can to make it work. This should be part of every coming out conversation. You may assume they should know that, but it's essential to say it, often.

Acknowledge their feelings. Be willing to listen to their anger, grief, fears, and despair. Let them know you understand, and that they are certainly entitled to their feelings. Never try to talk someone out of their feelings! Assure them that their reactions are normal, and that you want to help them deal with all this.

Give them time to process the disclosure. You can't resolve all the potential conflicts in one sitting. Some partners may press for details, including exactly how far you plan to go. Do not give in to that pressure! Others will need a lot of time to think about what you've said, and won't be able to give you answers to your questions right away. Don't pressure them!

Remember that you've been thinking about all this for a long time; they have probably never given it a thought.

Allay their fears. Discuss their reactions when you can both be rational about them. Many spouses will think it's their fault; reassure them that it has nothing to do with them. Some will assume you're going to leave when you transition, or want to be with someone different. Assure them that you are not going to transition overnight, or do anything to threaten their safety and security.

Point out the positives. The reward for your family is a happier healthier spouse/parent/child. If you can show them the better person you are becoming, and reassure them that there will be a benefit for all of you, it gives them hope. Point out the things that they like about you that you feel are part of your true self.

Include them in your decision-making. One of the gestures that can be very meaningful for parents is to ask them what they would have named you if you were born a boy/girl. (If you can't stand the name, you can use it as a middle name, or use the middle name they would have chosen.) Include your spouse in decisions about the timing of different aspects of your transition. That means:

Be patient! You'll have to go at a pace your family can tolerate if you want them to come with you. Be willing to do the "one step forward, two steps back; lover, may I?" dance. This can be excruciating, especially if you've come to a decision about what you want after years of struggling. But it's worth the effort if you want to preserve the relationship.

Be persistent. Because there is a common tendency towards denial and avoidance, it is also important to continue to broach the subject. You may need to "push the envelope" from time to time, and keep asking for another step forward. At the very least, don't let your partner restrict you from doing things that don't directly impact him or her, such as attending support group meetings.

Be creative in the bedroom. The sexual adjustments necessary when one person transitions take some work, and some play. There are a lot of ways to spice up your sex life and please your partner. There are plenty of toys available to play with; experiment! If there are no adult stores near you, there are some good resources on-line.

Seek support. Acceptance comes much easier for family members who can talk to others who are going through the same experience. It can be difficult to find support groups for partners, but there are on-line forums. (Google SOFFA - Significant Other, Friend, Family, and Ally.) And if your therapist sees enough transgender clients, he or she may be able to connect you with others who are in supportive relationships.

Consider couples or family counseling. I often invite clients' family members into counseling for a session or two. It helps me get a sense of what their family is capable of, and it reassures the family member that I am not somehow converting the client. For extended couples or family therapy, however, I always recommend a separate therapist. The client needs to feel that I am on his or her side, and the couple needs a therapist who doesn't take sides. There's an advantage to letting the partner pick the marriage counselor, as long as it's a TG-friendly therapist.

Children and Parents

Children will invariably be affected by your transition, to the extent that you are a part of their lives. As we discussed in Chapter Six, how they process it depends on their developmental age. Younger children are more flexible in their thinking, and adapt more easily. They will, however, need to be taught the difference between keeping a *secret*, which is not healthy, and keeping something *private*, which is often necessary. Keeping them informed, including them, listening to their concerns, reassuring them that you will still be their parent, letting them pick a name to call you, and respecting their feelings will all help preserve the relationship. Some conflicts are inevitable; be prepared to make concessions! You can't expect to pick up your teenage son from school looking in any way that stands out, for example; that will just embarrass him in front of his peers. In general, the older the child the longer it will take for her or him to feel comfortable with your changes. Teenagers might hate you for being different, and/or for disrupting their lives, and will freely tell you so. Some will need years to come around. One of my clients was very visible in her transition, and completely alienated her son and daughter for a period of time. They are now both back in relationship with her.

Parents also go through a grieving process, perhaps even more than a partner because they have known you longer. A parent-child relationship is just as intimate, and just as tied to gender. They raised (in their mind) a girl or a boy, and watched you grow into a young man or woman. They have aspirations for your life, which probably include marriage and grandchildren. If you are married with children, they probably have attachments to and concerns about them as well. Your parents were raised in a different generation, where gender roles were fixed and gender itself innate and immutable. With all the parental hopes and fears they had for you, changing gender was probably not even on the radar. They will be shocked, perhaps outraged, and certainly bewildered. They will probably wonder what they did wrong.

As parents, they will worry about the consequences of your transition, about violence and job discrimination, about your kids (if you have any), about surgery, about what other people will think, about....well, about just about everything. They will most likely try to talk you out of transitioning. They may threaten to withdraw their emotional and/or financial support. This is not because they don't care - quite the opposite. Parents want to protect their children from harm, and will often go to extreme measures to do so. They may feel powerless in the face of something they cannot protect you from, and try to keep you safe in any way they can. Their deepest fear is that they will lose you.

Provide as much information as you can to your parents. They may not be as computer-savvy as you, so don't expect them to search out YouTube videos. Send them a book or print out articles and send them. Let them know you're doing your homework and considering the risks as well as the rewards. Tell them about PFLAG or other organizations in their area. Even parents who have accepted you as gay or lesbian, or single and/or childless, or just plain different, will struggle with accepting you as the "opposite sex". You know you're the same person, but in their mind they're losing a son or daughter. They need time to absorb the shock, to understand what this is all about, to grieve their loss, and to learn how to relate to you in a different way.

Keep the lines of communication open if you can! Very few parents are willing to carry out their threats and cut you out of their lives completely. Many are surprisingly supportive, and will be there for you no matter what. What parents want most of all is to see you happy and successful. If you can show them that in your new life they will be relieved and reassured, and even proud of you for having the courage to pursue your dream. Keeping them informed and helping them adjust to changes in your appearance can be harder if you're not living with or near them. They may hang on to denial and avoidance longer than those closer to you. They will probably have trouble calling you by a different name and using the correct pronouns. Be patient with them. Remember that they picked out your original name, probably after considerable thought.

References and Resources

Mary Boenke, Editor, *Trans Forming Families: Real Stories about Transgendered Loved Ones Third Edition,* published by PFLAG Transgender Network, 2008

Tina Fakhrid-Deen, with COLAGE, *Let's Get This Straight: The Ultimate Handbook for Youth with LGBTQ Parents*, Seal Press, 2010.

COLAGE: People with a Lesbian, Gay, Bisexual, Transgender, or Queer Parent - www.colage.org

PFLAG (Parents and Friends of Lesbians and Gays) - www.pflag.org

Chapter Fourteen

Traveling Solo

Throw your dreams into space like a kite, and you do not know what it will bring back, a new life, a new friend, a new love, a new country.

Anais Nin

There may come a time when it's clear to you that your partner or family is not going to be able to accept your transition plan. At that point you'll have a difficult decision to make. You'll have to decide if it's possible for you to leave those relationships, or if it's possible to give up or scale back your plans. Neither is a good choice (unless those relationships were abusive or destructive, in which case leaving is a good thing anyway). I have seen many clients falter and slide back because of opposition from a spouse or partner. It's easy for me to say that being yourself is worth the sacrifice, or that anyone who really loves you will support you, but I'm not in your shoes, or theirs. It's a decision that only you can make.

"Detransitioning"

To detransition is to stop the train and reverse direction, to go back to your old persona after having started the physical transition. Very few transsexuals who complete a full transition try to go back to their birth sex permanently. Some who start the process go back for a period of time, due to external pressures. The most common reason is to try to make a marriage work. Annah Moore talks about this in her book *Right Side Out.*[39] Five months into her physical transition, having come out to her family, friends and co-workers, and facing a holiday alone, she flushed her hormones down the toilet and went back to being Adam. She tried to be the man her wife wanted, but in the end she became so depressed that her wife suggested she go back on the path of being her true self. She doesn't regret the year she spent trying to make it work; it helped her know for sure that she was doing the right thing by moving forward.

I have only seen a few clients try to go back to their old selves. One did so because of falling into a new relationship that was not supportive of transitioning after leaving an abusive marriage. Another went back to try to get custody of "his" son. I suspect that stopping and restarting is more common when people try to fast-forward the process. Detransitioning can be traumatic, especially if done suddenly, out of desperation. (For one thing, going off of any medication abruptly wreaks havoc on your body). It's discouraging to see the progress that you've made slip away from you. It's also humiliating to have to explain to people that you're changing back. They may see it as you admitting that you were wrong about transitioning in the first place. Once you have come out to people it compromises your credibility if you change your mind. Their perception of you is changed forever. You can't really go completely back into the closet once you're out.

If you do decide that you need to take a step (or more) backwards don't beat yourself up over it! You have the right to change your mind at any point. Don't let anyone, including your therapist, tell you otherwise. Your therapist will be concerned, of course, if he or she believes that transition-

---

[39] Annah Moore, *Right Side Out*, iUniverse, 2006

ing is right for you. We're human, and we like to see our clients make progress. It's your journey, however, and we have no right to tell you how you should do it. Others in the transgender community may try to judge you; your decision may threaten their resolve. It's really none of their business. To go forward just because you don't want to let someone else down, or because you don't want to be called a coward, is ultimately self-destructive.

At some point, if your significant other(s) can't support your transition and you can't go backwards, you'll reach a crossroads. If they don't end the relationship you may have to be the one to say "I can't stay in this relationship anymore. I can't remain the person you want me to be." It will seem selfish, and in some ways it is. You've decided that you have to put your growth, your sanity, your health and well-being, your own needs before the other person's needs and wants. To stay when you need to move forward with your life, however, doesn't do anyone any favors. You're no good to anyone else if you're miserable and full of resentment. And if you can't be yourself in a relationship, then it's not a genuine relationship. You've been relating to that person with parts of yourself, not your whole self.

You have to untie your boat and let go of the shore in order to set sail. You have to say goodbye to those who are unwilling to come aboard.

Coping with Loss

At that point it is you who will be going through the process of grief.

Transitioning will most likely involve many losses. You will probably lose at least one relationship - someone who can't understand or can't handle your changes. One out of four transsexuals reports losing a job[40]. A few lose everything in a divorce, including the house, the kids, and the spouse.

---

[40] Grant, Jaime M., Lisa A. Mottet, Justin Tanis, Jack Harrison, Jody L. Herman, and Mara Keisling. *Injustice at Every Turn: A Report of the National Transgender Discrimination Survey*. Washington: National Center for Transgender Equality and National Gay and Lesbian Task Force, 2011.

Each loss is a blow that must be accommodated somehow. Grief is the process of coming to terms with those losses so you can move on.

We grieve many things over the course of a lifetime - people die or move away, relationships break up, school ends. Even the changes we make ourselves - leaving home, changing jobs, outgrowing a relationship - involve a loss of some sort. We grieve the loss of people, pets, places and even things. Some are gradual and easier to handle; others are harsh and abrupt. The stages of grief are not discrete sequential stages as much as different aspects of grief that we cycle through when we experience a significant loss. These are the common reactions:

Denial: This can take many forms. One of the common ones is disbelief. One client kept saying "I can't believe she would do this to me!" every time his wife would do something particularly nasty during their divorce. Another form of denial is continuing to try to reconnect with someone who is clearly not capable of accepting the new you. Avoidance of certain people or difficult topics is another form of denial, especially effective if the other person is also in denial.

Bargaining: This is similar to the process of negotiation and compromise mentioned in Chapter 13, except that at some point compromise and negotiation may be a lost cause. "Maybe if I dress down I can go to (insert family event)." There comes a time when it's not possible to appease a family member's unrealistic demands. Bargaining can also take the form of "If only...(she/he could understand, would listen to me, would give me another chance....)".You have to face the music at some point and accept that the conflict is too deep to be resolved.

Anger: At some point you will need to acknowledge your anger at the person you've had to let go. No matter how much we love someone, we feel angry when they disappoint us. This can sneak up on you and/or come out indirectly if not acknowledged. It can also be turned on yourself, through excessive guilt and self-blame. It's important to remember that you're not responsible for someone else's limitations. Beating up on yourself won't help you and it won't get the relationship back.

Depression: Grief hurts. It takes a toll physically, emotionally and spiritually. Even if intellectually we can say, "Those who matter won't mind and those who mind don't matter"[41], it's devastating to lose a significant relationship. It is not, however, a sign that you shouldn't have made the choices that led to the loss. I have seen several clients cave in and go back because they couldn't cope with the sadness. It's important to allow yourself time to grieve and to heal, and to take care of yourself physically and emotionally. Delaying this can contribute to the post-transition depression that we hear about so often.

Acceptance: With time you'll think about the person (or people, or place) less often, and the periods of denial, anger and hurt will be shorter and less intense. There will come a time when you will feel OK about the loss. Not great, but OK. Some losses you don't get over; you just get used to them. Others you will realize, in hindsight. that it really was for the best. You will move on. You will be able to love and trust again, hopefully with greater wisdom.

Finding Your Tribe

In Chapter Five I mentioned the importance of finding support for your journey. This will become even more apparent if the social world you started out in begins to unravel. If your social connections have been primarily through your spouse or partner and that relationship dissolves, you may find those friends distancing themselves from you. Your extended family support system may shrink. Friends who were involved in gender-typed activities may feel less comfortable including you in those activities, or you may lose interest in them. You may have to find a new "tribe". Cultivating new interests, joining a liberal faith community, and going back to school or taking classes are all ways of finding people with similar interests and values. Many young people find communities on-line, but there's really no substitute for friends you can hang out with in real time and space. If you live in a populated area, look for transgender support

---

[41] "Be Who You Are and Say What You Feel Because Those Who Mind Don't Matter and Those Who Matter Don't Mind.", attributed to Dr. Seuss (Theodor Seuss Geisel).

groups. If you can find one, go! There's nothing quite like being with other people who understand. If you can't find a transgender support group, look for PFLAG meetings, GLBT groups, and gay clubs. You need to be aware, however, that acceptance in those groups is not guaranteed. There has been a long history of tensions within the GLBTQ community that still linger in some areas.

The T in the GLBT Community

Transsexuals have long felt like the stepchild in the GLBT family. Despite the fact that the first person to fight back at the Stonewall riot of 1969 was a transsexual named Silvia Rivera, the Gay Rights movement focused on gay and lesbian rights and issues first and foremost. Gay activists didn't want their cause hurt by the stereotypes of drag queens and transvestites. Lesbian feminists sought separatism, and often excluded anyone who wasn't a "woman-born-woman". It wasn't until the mid-1990s that the "T" was added to most gay and lesbian events and organizations. This is starting to change, but here are some of the issues that have divided the community:

The confusion of gender and sexuality. Historically, transsexuals were assumed to be homosexual, because all gay men were thought to be effeminate and lesbians assumed to be masculine. Many of the first transsexuals came from the gay community. Some gays assumed that these early transwomen were transitioning because of intense self-loathing; they'd rather become a woman to have sex with men than come to terms with being homosexual. The medical establishment didn't help with that; early gender clinics assumed that all MtF transsexuals wanted to be with men, and excluded any who said they wanted to be with women. Transsexuals seeking hormones and surgery had to deny any homosexual interests. Transsexuals were seen as leaving the gay community because they would be able to gain acceptance as heterosexual.

Limited resources of the Gay Rights movement. Gay activism arose at a time when AIDS was threatening its population and homophobia was intensifying. This was seen as a much more important issue than being inclusive of transgender rights. And because of the association with transvestite prostitutes, at least in the public's mind, MtF transsexuals were seen as an embarrassment, and a hindrance to political power. They wanted the most "normal-looking" gays and lesbians to show up at rallies and hearings. Even as recently as 2009, some gay rights activists were willing to have a non-discrimination bill passed that excluded transgender rights.

Insecurity of an oppressed population. There is an unfortunate tendency of oppressed groups to look desperately for someone they can consider beneath them. As different ethnic groups came to the United States they faced discrimination and persecution by those before them, and often went on to look down on the ones that came after them. Even among the transgender population, there have been instances where transsexuals further along in their transition have looked down on others, often those who were 'pre-op' or 'non-op' (not choosing gender reassignment surgery). People struggling to be accepted for their choices often feel threatened by those who make other choices. Women who worked outside the home were once fighting societal norms for acceptance; then women who stayed home with their children felt obliged to defend themselves. Transitioning completely, becoming ultra femme or ultra masculine, was once the be-all and end-all; now those who consider themselves genderqueer accuse those who seek that of being trapped in the binary gender paradigm. These are all the growing pains of an ever-expanding movement.

Transwomen and the lesbian community: Rejected by the gay community, and/or not wanting to be considered a gay *man*, transwomen often sought acceptance among lesbian and feminist groups. Surely they would accept their new sisters! Not always. Some radical feminist/lesbian groups were so anti-male that anyone with testosterone and/or a penis was automatically suspect. (The Michigan Womyn's Music Festival - a large gathering that draws lesbians and feminists from all over - is open only to "women born as women and living as women", thus banning all transgender people.) But more and more transwomen have come out as lesbians, still wanting to be with women. Acceptance of them in the lesbian community is growing, but many still feel excluded.

Transmen and the lesbian community: In the last 5 to 10 years there has been a dramatic increase in the number of lesbians coming out as transgender and seeking reassignment as men. The reactions in the lesbian community to this have been mixed, at best. Some lesbians feel betrayed and abandoned, seeing transmen as going over to "the other side". The lesbian community has long fought the idea that lesbians just want to be men, which is certainly not the case for most. Now that more butch lesbians are transitioning, it unfortunately reinforces that notion in the public's eye. There can be a fine line between "butch" and "trans", at least on the outside; both are rejected by radical feminist lesbians as "male-identified". Others resent transmen benefiting from male privilege, and fear the loss of allies in the fight against sexism. Some are just uncomfortable with all the testosterone-based changes.[42]

Transmen in the Gay Community: This is a relatively new phenomenon. Because so many transmen came from the lesbian community, and because of the hetero-biases of the medical establishment, it was once assumed that all transmen wanted to be with women. Not so! There are plenty of transmen who identify as gay and are attracted to gay men. The gay community has been slow to open up to them. Most gay men have a "type", and a role they prefer to play in bed. Many can't imagine how a transman would fit into their scene. But with new prostheses being developed, gay transmen can participate in all aspects of gay sexual life.

Because of these tensions, there may be gay or lesbian groups or individuals who are not as inviting as one would hope. There is, however, a generational shift happening in the wider community. The younger generation of transgender people and their allies and partners are less likely to define their gender identity and sexuality in either-or terms. They may identify as "genderqueer" or just "queer". They may resist labeling altogether. They tend to be more fluid in their sexual orientation, and open to experimentation. They socialize together, especially on college campuses, in all-inclusive groups.

---

[42] Loree Cook-Daniels, "Femmes, Butches and Lesbian-Feminists Discussing FTMs", available at: www.forge-forward.org/handouts/feminismFTM.php

Every GLBTQ community is different as well. In big cities there are more clearly differentiated gay, lesbian, and trans communities; because there are more people there can be more sub-groups. Each one will have its history, and its unique composition and predispositions. In smaller cities and towns there may be fewer barriers between groups because there aren't enough people for sub-groups to form. In the largest city near me there are only a few gay bars. Gay, lesbian, bisexual and trans-identified are all welcome there. There's a GLBTQ bowling group, which is open to all.

Social isolation is a serious side effect of growing up gender-variant. Many people who identify as trans have never felt like they belonged in a group. It's hard for them to now join a group and feel connected. It doesn't happen overnight. I've seen many clients attend a group once (including my own), and then say they don't fit in. I encourage everyone to try a group three times before making a judgment (unless it's clearly a hostile environment). It's like trying a new food - it usually takes a few bites before you can tell whether you like it or not.

Some people are more comfortable with one-on-one relationships than groups. For them, the challenge is finding new friends for support and companionship. Many, however, look for that in intimate relationships before they're ready, because that's all they know how to do.

Dating

Dating during your transition, and even post-transition, is not easy. I recommend to my clients that they focus on friendships only until they're through most of their transition. If you've been married or in a long-term relationship for a number of years the prospect of getting out there and meeting potential partners is daunting enough. Add to that the complications of presenting differently now than you will in a year or two and it can get very messy. You're emotionally vulnerable, and could get hurt in any number of ways. So let me start with the cautions first, and then discuss ways to explore dating when you're ready.

Caution #1: Dating out of desperation. If you're desperate to find some-one you may fall for the first person who shows an interest in you. If you are still presenting as your assigned gender that person will be attracted to that gender. Or even if they're attracted to transsexuals, they may attracted to a particular type (pre-op TS girls, for example). They will most likely resist or undermine your efforts to continue your transition, even if they seem supportive. You don't need someone else's agenda influencing you as you try to find your way. Trying to please them can slow down your transition, or derail it completely. Find a way to face your loneliness and get support from friends until you feel strong enough to make good choices.

Caution #2: The "Experimenter". There are plenty of people who are interested in transgender partners for the novelty of it all. They are often just interested in a sexual encounter, not a serious relationship. They may have seen some she-male porn and have unrealistic fantasies. Or they may think it's cool to be with someone trans until it comes time to introduce you to their friends and family. That's fine if all you want is a casual hook-up, but if you're someone who attaches easily you'll probably end up getting hurt. The problem here is that few people are up front about being experimenters. They seem genuinely interested at first, but can do an abrupt about-face once they get in too deep.

Caution #3: Reactions to the "bait and switch". If you are presenting as your desired gender but haven't had gender reassignment surgery, potential partners can end up feeling deceived when they find that out. The greatest risk of violence occurs when a man is attracted to a transwoman, not knowing she's transgender, and then finds out at an inopportune moment. (We'll discuss safety issues more in Chapter Fifteen.) Women who feel deceived or betrayed can also be nasty, and may out you in anger.

Caution #4: Codependence. I know, this word has been used so much lately that it's lost its meaning. The original term was coined to describe a person who is dependent on someone addicted to drugs or alcohol. The codependent person is as caught in the addiction as the user. I use the word to describe someone who is so dependent on someone else that they make excuses, cover for his or her problems, and try desperately to fix her or him in order to get their needs met. If you get hooked into someone with an addiction or other major issues, their problems can easily take over the relationship and end up consuming all your time, energy and money.

Having considered all of the above, if you want to start dating you need to establish a goal for yourself. Are you just out for a good time? Do you want someone with whom to share certain activities or interests? Are you looking for a long-term relationship? Generally speaking, the goal of dating is to find someone you want to spend time with who also wants to spend time with you in equal measure. Out of all the people in the world there's a pool of potential partners in your age range, with your interests and affinities, who might be compatible. That pool is constricted by the number of variables that are in play. (Available male partners for educated women over the age of 45, for example, form a fairly small pool.) The challenge is to first find your pool, and then go fishing!

One way to find potential partners is by socializing among your peers. If you're young and in school, there are GLBTQQIA groups. If you're over 21 there are GLBT-friendly bars and clubs in most cities. If the bar scene is not your style there are support groups and other organizations. Liberal faith communities that are welcoming or open and affirming, such as your local UU or UCC (Congregational) church, are a great place to meet people. Any club or group that caters to your particular interests, whether that's a book group or a rod and gun club, is a place to meet like-minded people.

One of the best but also riskiest ways to find potential partners is on-line. There are GLBT forums, on-line discussion groups, and singles sites for just about every group imaginable. The advantage to on-line dating sites is that you can get the important questions answered before you bother meeting someone. The risk is that not everyone there is honest or has the best of intentions. The best strategy is to write an honest profile outlining exactly what you're seeking. Then take your time getting to know someone before you get together in real life. Always meet in a safe public place for the first time, and never give out your full name, phone number or home address until you do. Even then, who you meet may be very different from what you expected. On-line relationships, especially long-distance ones, can be based more on fantasy than reality.

If you meet someone in a club or elsewhere who shows an interest in you and has no idea that you're transgender, proceed with caution! Suggest a coffee or lunch date first (with no alcohol, so you can keep your wits about you). If you hit it off and want to see him or her again find a way, before the second date, to let them know what you're going through. It's not fair to either of you to start a relationship with a false impression. Anyone can fall in love hard and fast. If you don't get that second date, at least you won't have wasted your time and/or gotten your hopes up.

Sexuality

Understanding your sexual orientation is important once you start dating. It's a confusing issue for many transsexuals. Some transsexuals start out identifying as gay or lesbian because they're attracted to the same sex as their assigned gender. But for many, even though the attraction is there, it doesn't feel right. "I was attracted to men, but not as a man; I didn't want to have gay sex" is a common comment from those transitioning male to female. The stone butch lesbian wants to make love to a woman, but doesn't want to be pleasured, or sometimes even touched, herself. It reminds "her" (if "she" is really a transman) that the body parts are all wrong. These are common sentiments of primarily heterosexual transwomen and transmen. Once their gender is straightened out they tend to identify as straight. It was once thought that all transsexuals were like this.

That doesn't explain, however, the increasing number of transsexuals who have been in a heterosexual relationship and are staying with their spouses, or who continue to be attracted to once opposite-sex, now same-sex partners. The majority of my clients who transitioned from male to female were married at some point, partly as a cover story or to prove that they were "normal". A few tried to be "studs" and date numerous women. Most of those are still attracted to women and are now affirmed lesbians. The majority of my clients who are now transmen identify as straight, but there are several who consider themselves bisexual, and a few who have always been attracted to gay men.

The truth is that transgender individuals can be gay, straight, bi- or pan-sexual, or even asexual, just like everyone else. The National Transgender Discrimination Study[43] found that 93% of their respondents fell into four equal groups: heterosexual (23%), homosexual (23%), bisexual (24%), and queer/pansexual (23%). The rest identified as asexual or "other". Some of my transgender clients have avoided sexual relationships altogether or been involved in only a few. They're not sure of their sexual orientation. Some say "How could I possibly enjoy sex when I hate my body?" Others admit that they learned to disconnect from their body in order to perform sexually.

One client shared with me this morning a dream she had that surprised her. In the dream she was telling a man how attracted she was to him. This surprised her because she was married to a woman, and assumed she was still attracted to women. In thinking about the dream, and her limited experiences with dating, she realized she had no idea what her sexual orientation really was. She asked, quite honestly, "How do you tell?" She wasn't sure if she dated and got married (when she lived as a man) because she was attracted to her wife or because it was just something she was supposed to do. She admitted that when she was with a woman she became aroused by imagining she *was* that woman. I don't believe for a minute that this experience, common among transsexuals, is a sexual fetish. I believe that for many this is simply the only way they can feel like a sexual being, because they can't relate to their given genitalia.

I explained to her that most people know their sexual orientation because they know by looking at men and women who they'd rather have as a sexual partner. But most people are cisgendered, so they're imaging having sex with someone in a body that feels normal and right to them. They want to make love to someone as themselves. The transsexual doesn't have that clarity because they aren't themselves yet. So my client's confusion about

---

[43] Jaime M. Grant, PhD, Lisa A. Motet, JD, and Justin Tanis, with Judy L. Herman, PhD, Jack Harrison and Mara Keisling. "National Transgender Discrimination Survey Report on Health and Health Care". published by the National Center for Transgender Equality and the National Gay and Lesbian Task Force, October 2010

her sexual orientation is perfectly normal. I suggested that she simply allow herself to remember whatever bits and pieces of past experiences she could in order to uncover some of her original sexual attractions. If nothing solid emerges then she can just start from here and explore who she's attracted to now.

Many transsexuals find that their perceived sexual orientation changes when they transition. Some attribute it to changing hormones. I suspect it has more to do with new possibilities opening up. They can now acknowledge feelings for men or women that didn't feel right before. I've heard several say "I want to date a man *as a woman,* to have someone treat me like a lady. " Some are more open to being bisexual or pansexual. Once you've gone beyond the gender binary it seems natural to go beyond the "gay or straight" dichotomy as well. One of my clients identified as a gay man before transitioning; after her transition she fell in love with a woman. She's now perceived as a lesbian, but identifies as bisexual.

It's fine to take your time while you're transitioning to figure out your sexual orientation, and to let it evolve. When dating or considering relationships keep in mind that your whole life is in transition, including your sexuality. Let your partner(s) know that.

One of my clients has three words of advice for transsexuals: Marry someone bisexual! She is very happily married to a bisexual woman who loves both her male and female personae. I would add "or pansexual/omnisexual". A distinction can be made between *bisexual* and *pansexual* (also sometimes called *omnisexual).* Bisexual people are considered to be attracted to both men and women. Pansexuals are attracted to men, women and others. Some are specifically attracted to their type, such as tall and slender with long hair (regardless of gender); many say that it is not the gender they're attracted to, but the person. And there are people who are specifically attracted to transsexuals.

Bisexual people have also had their difficulties with acceptance by the gay and lesbian communities. They have been seen as confused, or not willing to come all the way out of the closet. They have been accused of wanting the best of both worlds without committing to one. They have been resented for being able to live in both worlds and fall back on heteronormative privilege. Bisexual women have been shunned by the lesbian feminist community for consorting with men. Bisexual men have been accused of spreading AIDS. It is assumed that they go back and forth at whim and are never faithful.

The truth is that sexual orientation, like gender, is a complex continuum. There are different aspects to sexual orientation, including sexual attraction, sexual behavior, emotional affiliation, and political affiliation. Keppel and Hamilton write, "Sexual identity (how people think of themselves) sometimes has little to do with their sexual behavior. Three different people may have the same distribution of sexual behavior in the past and/or present, but have three different sexual identities: homosexual, bisexual, or heterosexual."[44]

Figure 3 (at the end of this chapter) shows a model of sexual orientation developed by Bobbi Keppel and Alan Hamilton, based on the work of Fritz Klein. It breaks sexual orientation into eight dimensions that represent different aspects of interpersonal orientation/identification. Each aspect can be rated on a 7-point scale, from exclusively heterosexual to exclusively homosexual. The ratings can be done for past, present, and your ideal. This gives a much more complex picture than "gay or straight". Breaking out the different dimensions is particularly important for people who are already "out of the box" of gender. Here are the questions to ask yourself to rate each of these dimensions:

1) **Sexual attraction:** To whom are you sexually attracted? Who do you look at lustfully? Who do your eyes follow down the street? What images arouse you?

2) **Sexual behavior:** With whom have you actually had sexual relations? With whom are you currently sexually active? With whom would you like to be sexually active?

---

[44] Keppel, Bobbi, and Alan Hamilton, "Using the Klein Scale to Teach about Sexual Orientation." Brochure published by the Bisexual Resource Center, Cambridge, MA

3) **Sexual fantasies:** Who do you fantasize about? Who is in your romantic/sexual daydreams? If you fantasize when you masturbate, who is in those fantasies?

4) **Emotional preference:** Who do you love? With whom do you fall in love? With whom do you enjoy talking intimately? Who do you trust?

5) **Social preference:** With whom do you socialize? Who do you like being around, hanging out with? With whom do you spend most of your time?

6) **Lifestyle preference:** What is the sexual identity/orientation of the people you consider your "tribe"? (This includes an option of "All".)

7) **Sexual identity:** How do you think of yourself? How do you define your sexual orientation? (This includes an option of "Other" or "No label".)

8) **Political identity:** What sexual identity most describes your political affiliation? What group are you most aligned with politically? (This can be different than your own personal sexual identity.)

Take some time to think about your past and present feelings, and your hopes for future relationships. What is most important to you? Answering these questions will help you define for yourself your sexual orientation. Revisit this page at different times in your transition, to see if any of your answers have changed significantly.

References and Resources

Jillian Weiss, "The Lesbian Community and FTM Transsexuals: Détente in the Butch/FTM Borderlands", The Journal of Lesbian Studies 11, 219-227 (2007)

Sheila Jeffreys, *Unpacking Queer Politics: A Lesbian Feminist Perspective*. Cambridge: Polity, 2003.

Judith Halberstam, "Transgender Butch: Butch/FTM Border Wars and the Masculine Continuum." *GLQ: A Journal of Lesbian and Gay Studies* 4 (1998): 287-310.

Joanne Meyerowitz, *How Sex Changed: A History of Transsexuality in the United States*. Boston: Harvard University Press, 2002.

Joan Nestle, Clare Howell and Riki Wilchins, Eds. *GENDERqUEER: Voices from Beyond the Sexual Binary*. Los Angeles: Alyson Publications, 2002: 228-237.

Figure 3: Aspects of Sexual Orientation
(adapted from Fritz Klein by Bobbi Keppel and Alan Hamilton)

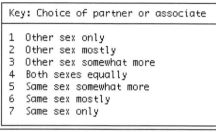

Key: Choice of partner or associate

1 Other sex only
2 Other sex mostly
3 Other sex somewhat more
4 Both sexes equally
5 Same sex somewhat more
6 Same sex mostly
7 Same sex only

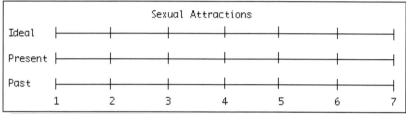

Sexual Attractions

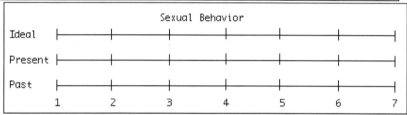

Sexual Behavior

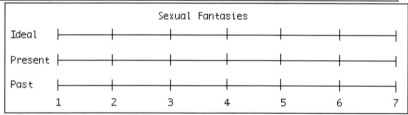

Sexual Fantasies

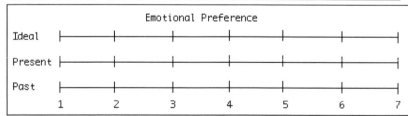

Emotional Preference

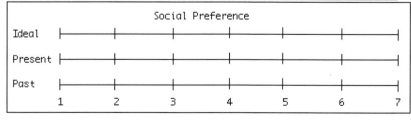

Social Preference

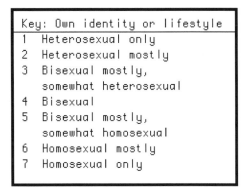

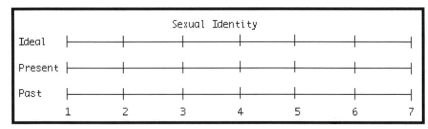

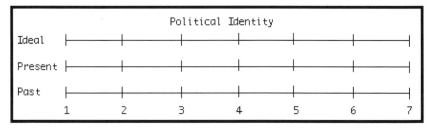

From **Sexual and Affectional Orientation and Identity Scales** by Bobbi Keppel & Alan Hamilton, published by the Bisexual Resource Center. Reprinted with permission.

Chapter Fifteen

Trials and Tribulations

It is important to expect nothing, to take every experience, including the
negative ones, as merely steps on the path, and to proceed.

Ram Dass

This is the most difficult chapter to write. I'm filled with tremendous
sadness and anger every time I read about yet another example of the
challenges that transgender individuals face in our society. In mythic
terms, every journey has its obstacles to avoid or overcome, battles to fight
and dangerous stretches of turbulent waters. The treatment of transgender
people in our culture, however, goes far beyond the usual difficulties of
changing life course or pursuing a dream. It's hard to believe that people
are capable of such ignorance and hatred.

Transgender people experience discrimination, harassment and violence in
many different areas. This maltreatment arises from both homophobia and
transphobia. Homophobia is an intense fear or dislike of someone based
on their (assumed) sexual orientation. Transphobia is the reaction of fear
or loathing to anyone who appears gender non-conforming - that is, their
gender presentation doesn't match their perceived biological sex. Homo-

phobia and transphobia are inextricably linked because sexual orientation is often inferred from gender-atypical appearance and/or behavior (the butch woman and the effeminate man). Likewise, sexual orientation is often inferred from transgender status. To the ignorant person it's all the same, and it's all abnormal.

It's hard for me to grasp the basis of homophobia and transphobia. I've lived most of my life in liberal communities in the Northeast and associated with people with values similar to mine. No one I know feels their marriage or family is threatened by granting full equal rights and privileges to gay and lesbian couples. I do, however, recognize xenophobia - the fear of someone from a different culture than our own. When I lived in Austin Texas for two years I had my first experiences with both groups of young black men and Texans who chewed tobacco and carried firearms. Both made me a little uneasy! The less we understand about a culture or sub-culture the more uncomfortable we are. Our social thinking is such that we tend to generalize from known examples of a certain class of people to all people in that class. (Hence the mistreatment of males wearing turbans, many of whom were Sikhs, after the terrorist attacks on September 11, 2001.) The smaller the number of examples, and the less we know them personally, the more likely we are to stereotype. If our only exposure to a group is through the media, our characterization of them will be even more distorted.

Transphobia is starting to break down to the extent that both media portrayals and personal experiences are changing. Familiarity with the transgender experience helps allay fears. My clients are often surprised by the number of people who say "Oh, I understand - my cousin/coworker/friend transitioned a couple years ago". Xenophobia, however, is only one source of transphobia. Transphobia is also based on "genderism" - the belief that there are two discrete genders, present and recognizable at birth, based on a distinct biological difference. Genderism also posits that one's "real" gender is based on genitalia, and that gender presentation should match. Gender is a fundamental attribution and assumption that we make whenever we see someone, and the basis for codes of conduct in relation to that person. To not be sure of someone's gender is to not know how to relate to that person. If you've ever seen the embarrassment when someone mistakes someone's gender and uses the wrong label - saying "ma'am" instead of "sir", for example - you know what I mean. The person is suddenly off-balance, having been caught in a faux pas. The degree to which someone treats people differently based on their gender may determine some of their response to being surprised. Men are particularly prone to sexualizing and "genderizing" all their interpersonal interactions. (Many men, for example, don't believe that a man and a woman can be close friends, with no sexual undertones. That says a lot about how they see women.) Their surprise at realizing a woman they've been talking to is (in their minds) "really a man" is doubly threatening. From their point of view they have been deceived, subject to a bait and switch. It activates not only their transphobia, but also their homophobia.

Research studies have verified what many of us have suspected for a long time - that homophobia is in part a reaction to suppressed homosexual feelings. In one study of "exclusively heterosexual" males, only the homophobic men showed an increase in arousal to male homosexual erotic images.[45] Homophobic men (and perhaps women) are projecting their own intolerable feelings onto those they perceive as homosexual; they are hating a part of themselves. Psychologists have a term for this: "shame rage". When some people (especially men) feel humiliated it is so intense and intolerable they fly into a rage. They feel so awful they want to die, so they strike out at the source of their humiliation. To be "deceived", and to find themselves aroused by another "man" is the ultimate humiliation.

In these times of changing social norms and role expectations for men and women, some people are able to adapt and embrace the new freedom to access both their femininity and their masculinity. Those who are more rigid and authoritarian, who need rules and order, are easily threatened by anything "out of the box." A review of research into sexual prejudice (attitudes and beliefs condemning gays, lesbians and bisexuals) found that there are higher levels of prejudice among those who are older, less edu-

---

[45] Henry E. Adams, Lester W. Wright, Jr., and Bethany A. Lohr. *Is Homophobia Associated with Homosexual Arousal?* Journal of Abnormal Psychology, 1996, Vol. 105, No. 3, 440-445

cated, more authoritarian, more fundamentalist (in their religious orientation), and more politically conservative.[46] There are areas of the country
where sexual prejudice is more or less common as well; people in the
Northeast tend to be more open and accepting than those in the South
and Midwest.

Discrimination

Prejudice and discrimination against transgender people shows up in many
forms. It is systemic and institutionalized at a societal level. It can be
personal, either intentional or unintentional. And it is pervasive. The
National Center for Transgender Equality and the National Gay and
Lesbian Task Force combined efforts to launch a comprehensive study of
the discrimination against transgender and gender non-conforming people.
Their report, *Injustice at Every Turn: A Report of the National Transgender
Discrimination Survey*, is 228 pages long.[47] It documents the experiences of
the 6450 people who responded to their lengthy survey. (It is worth noting
that this was a voluntary sample, not a random sample, and thus inflates
the prevalence of acts of discrimination. People who had had negative
experiences were more likely to respond than those who had not.) To
most of you reading this, these findings will probably not be a surprise.
Here are some of the results:

Education: Transgender and gender non-conforming students in grades K-
12 reported harassment (78%), physical assaults (35%) and sexual assaults
(12%). Six percent of these students were expelled, and 15 percent left
school because of mistreatment. Teachers and school officials were often as
bad as peers. Harassment and bullying have strong negative effects on
students' self-esteem, school attendance, and grades. The suicide rate for
harassed teens is staggering, with half of GLBT teens reporting suicide

---

[46] Gregory M. Herek, "The Psychology of Sexual Prejudice, Current Directions" in
Psychological Science, Volume 9, Number 1, February 2000, 19-22
[47] Jaime M Grant, Lisa A. Mottet, Justin Tanis, Jack Harrison, Jody L. Herman, and
Mara Keisling. *Injustice at Every Turn: A Report of the National Transgender Discrimination
Survey*. Washington: National Center for Transgender Equality and National Gay and
Lesbian Task Force, 2011.

attempts. Those harassed and/or abused by teachers were more likely to quit school and end up with lower income. [48]

Every transgender student I've worked with has encountered some resistance or harassment in school. One young student was treated well by her teachers and other students, but the parents fought with the principal for months over the child's right to wear her preferred attire to school. Another was treated well enough by the school administration, but not supported in his struggles with harassment by peers. Several transgender youth I know have had to change schools as they transitioned. Others are just plain scared all the time, and work very hard to conceal their transgender status. Charter and private schools may be more welcoming than public schools, but that creates an additional burden for families with a gender-variant child.

Employment: The majority of the NCTE and NGLTF survey respondents reported negative consequences at work. A quarter of them reported losing a job because of their transgender status, another quarter not being hired or being passed over for promotions, and 50 percent reported being harassed at work. The unemployment rate for the survey respondents was twice the national average. Many of the unemployed were homeless, and sought work on the streets, ending up with HIV or in jail. Sixteen percent of their respondents resorted to illegal work. The end result of discrimination in education and employment is a high rate of poverty. Fifteen percent lived on less than $10,000 a year, again twice the rate of the general population. Racial prejudice compounded these problems, with multiracial, black and Latino transgender men and women faring far worse.

On a more positive note, however, the vast majority reported feeling more comfortable and more productive at work after transitioning. Most of my clients have been fortunate in their on-the-job transitions. I have seen many clients transition successfully at their workplace, some of them in

---

[48] Suicide Prevention Resource Center. (2008). *Suicide risk and prevention for lesbian, gay, bisexual, and transgender youth.* Newton, MA: Education Development Center, Inc.

traditionally-male occupations. Most have been surprised by how supportive their coworkers and managers were and how well it went. I've only known three who lost their job after coming out to their employer. I have seen, however, clients endure some subtle and not-so-subtle harassment for non-conforming behavior.

Housing: Survey respondents reported various forms of housing discrimination, with 19 percent having been refused a home or apartment. One-fifth reported being homeless at some point, and the rate of current homelessness among respondents was twice the national average (2% versus 1%). The worst reported discrimination was in homeless shelters, where 55 percent reported being harassed, 29 percent turned away, and 22 percent assaulted by residents or staff. This was highly correlated with both unemployment and family rejection. The rate of homelessness among GLBTQ youth is particularly distressing; they have been rejected by family and have little hope of making enough money to live independently. Many turn to sex work and drug trafficking just to stay alive. The homeless are also more vulnerable to violence and harassment in public settings.

Public Sector: Survey respondents reported discrimination and/or harassment in a wide variety of public venues: retail stores, hotels and restaurants, transportation, government offices, hospitals and clinics, even social service agencies. Particularly distressing is the number who reported mistreatment by police and emergency services. There have been reports of EMTs refusing to help someone they discovered was transgender. Transgender police officers hear first-hand, before they come out at work, the jokes and demeaning comments about not only transmen and women but also gays, lesbians, and women in general. There is still little diversity education and sensitivity training in law enforcement.

Health Care: High unemployment rates also mean lower access to employment-based health insurance. Difficulty accessing and affording health care is one of the biggest obstacles to transitioning. Almost half (48%) of the study participants postponed medical care at some point due to inability to afford it. Many sought care at low-income clinics and emergency rooms rather than doctor's offices. Affordability is not the only obstacle. Nearly a fifth (19%) of the respondents had been refused medical treatment because of their transgender status. Others reported having to educate their health care practitioner (50%), and being subject to harassment or mistreatment in a health care setting (28%).[49]

In spite of this, the vast majority in this study had sought and received some form of transition-related health care. Seventy-five percent received counseling related to their transition, 62 percent had accessed medically supervised hormone therapy, and 20 percent had had some form of gender reassignment surgery. This speaks to the tremendous drive and determination of transgender men and women to do whatever is necessary to achieve congruity between their gender identity and their physical being.

Violence

Violence against transgender people is finally receiving the media attention it deserves. As I write this there is a protest forming in Baltimore over the very public beating of a transwoman in a McDonald's, recorded by an employee who did nothing to intervene. Hundreds of people (including her family) are coming out to show their support for the victim. The perpetrators have been arrested and the employee fired. For every incident that makes the news, however, there are many more that are either not reported to the authorities or not considered newsworthy. There are three types of violence against transmen and women that need to be addressed:

Hate crimes: A hate crime is a crime against a person because of who he or she represents. They are usually perpetrated by a member of a cultural majority against a minority. The legal definition is an act that involves threats, harassment, or physical harm and is motivated by prejudice against someone's perceived race, color, religion, national origin, ethnicity, sexual orientation or physical or mental disability. You'll notice that "gender

---

[49] Jaime M. Grant, PhD, Lisa Mottet, JD, Justin Tantis, DMin, with Jody L. Herman, PhD, Jack Harrison and Mara Keisling, *National Transgender Discrimination Survey Report on Health Care.* National Center for Transgender Equality and the National Gay and Lesbian Task Force, October 2010

expression" is not included in the legal definition. That's because hate crime legislation has been slow to include crimes against transgender or gender non-conforming individuals. The FBI keeps statistics on hate crimes against sexual minorities, but not specifically transsexuals.

Statistics on hate crimes against transgender people are hard to find, for several reasons. One is that many transgender victims don't report them. They either feel they're to blame, or they don't consider it bad enough, having grown up with so much mistreatment. They may be just as afraid of the police as their attackers, and don't want to out themselves. Another is that the police response minimizes the problem, often blaming the victim and sympathizing with the perpetrator. As the protest is mounting in Baltimore, the prosecutors are still deciding whether to charge the attackers with a hate crime. The third is that there has been no concerted effort to keep track of transgender hate crimes separate from those against sexual minorities. And in truth it may be hard to differentiate, not knowing whether the perpetrator was reacting to a perceived sexual orientation or gender non-conformity.

In survey studies of the experiences of transgender individuals violent crimes may be over-represented because of a different kind of reporting bias - those who have been victimized are more likely to fill out the questionnaire. The largest surveys completed so far have been conducted in major metropolitan areas, which already have higher rates of violence. Even taking that into consideration, however, the statistics are alarming. Those studies showed that between 25 and 50 percent of their respondents had experienced a hate crime. The highest rates were for those under age 18, who were most likely to be mistreated by family members, often repeatedly. Living on the streets or in homeless shelters was highly correlated with being a victim of a violent crime, as was low socio-economic status.[50,51]

---

[50] Lombardi EL, Wilchins RA, Priesing D, Malouf D. "Gender violence: transgender experiences with violence and discrimination." *Journal of Homosexuality.* 2001; 42(1): 89-101

Intimate partner violence and domestic abuse: It was a great surprise to me when a lesbian couple came in for counseling and talked about the physical abuse of one partner by the other. (It was my first year as a therapist and I was very naive.) I somehow expected that women, long the recipients of domestic violence, would not subject each other to it. The truth is that gay, lesbian, bisexual and transgender people have the same problems with partner violence as cisgendered and heterosexual people do. Estimates about prevalence range from 10 to 50 percent, depending on the study, but a reasonable estimate is 30-40 percent, the same as for the general population.[52]

Intimate partner violence (IPV) and domestic abuse are about power and control of one person over another. It's a systematic attempt of one person to assert their will and superiority over the other through manipulation, coercion, threats, and physical and sexual abuse. Domestic abuse includes: verbal abuse (name calling, put-downs), emotional manipulation, deliberate social isolation, withholding financial, physical and emotional support, forced sexual contact, harming or threatening to harm the partner's family, friends, children, and/or pets, threatening suicide if demands aren't met, physical abuse and threats of abuse, and stalking and harassing a partner. Transgender-specific abuse also includes preventing access to transition-related services, threatening to out someone, threatening to take children away, and insults based on transgender status.

Transgender men and women, and especially transgender youth, are vulnerable to partner abuse for a number of reasons. Having grown up with bullying, harassment and other abuse by family members and peers, it

---

[51] Jeremy D. Kidd, A.B. and Tarynn M. Witten, Ph.D "Transgender and Transsexual Identities: The Next Strange Fruit—Hate Crimes, Violence and Genocide Against the Global Trans-Communities" *Journal of Hate Studies* [Vol.6:31. June 2008] 31-63.

[52] Janice Ristock, Ph.D. and Norma Timbang, "Relationship Violence in Lesbian/ Gay/ Bisexual/ Transgender/Queer [LGBTQ] Communities: Moving Beyond a Gender-Based Framework". Violence Against Women Online Resources, July 2005

may seem normal. Low self-esteem, shame, and internalized transphobia leave them more vulnerable to believing that they deserve it, or that it's all their fault. These same reasons make it more difficult for them to seek help. Family members may be of no help, or may even use the problem against the person. Lack of economic resources often makes it difficult for victims of domestic abuse to leave. Transgender-specific resources for victims of IPV are not available, and DV shelters may either discriminate or simply not know how to handle transgender clients.

Microaggressions: Every transgender client I know has had to endure some harassment, or what researchers are now calling microaggression. Micro-aggression is a term originally used to describe racist treatment of people of color, then heterosexist treatment of gays, lesbians and bisexuals.[53] Micro-aggression is the verbal, behavioral and institutional communication of hostile, derogatory, heterosexist and transphobic slights, insults and indignities. It can range from outright verbal harassment to more subtle looks and attitudes. Outing someone without their permission is a com-mon microaggresion. As most of you know, there are many forms of microaggresion, and they occur frequently in everyday life.

Microassaults are explicit derogatory comments, such as calling someone a "tranny", "she-male" or "it". Offensive jokes and comments associating transgender people with pedophiles, prostitutes and AIDS are also micro-assaults. *Microinvalidation* is anything that denies, negates or excludes the legitimacy of a person's experience. Excluding gays, lesbians and trans-gender people from the full legal privilege of marriage is an institutiona-lized invalidation, for example. Other examples include referring to your assigned gender as your "real" gender, or any references to not being a "real" man or woman. Not having a category for 'Other' on forms that ask for gender is an invalidation of those who identify as neither male or

---

[53] Kevin L. Nadal, Yinglee Wong, Marie-Anne Issa, Vanessa Meterko, Jayleen Leon and Michelle Wideman, Sexual Orientation Microaggressions: Processes and Coping Mechanisms for Lesbian, Gay, and Bisexual Individuals. *Journal of LGBT Issues in Counseling* Volume 5, Issue 1, 2011, Pages 21 - 46

female. *Microinsults* are rude and insensitive remarks, sometimes unintentional, that show a heterosexist bias. Derogatory comments about changes in appearance, or about presumed sexual orientation can be microinsults. Other examples are inappropriate questions about breast development, surgery, etc. (It's none of their business what genitals you have or don't have.)

The most subtle form of microaggression is non-verbal snubs, gestures and looks. Lesbian friends of mine mentioned a time when they were coming out of a concert holding hands and saw a mother pull her kids closer to her when she saw them. That's microaggression. Double-takes are common enough, when someone notices an anomaly and looks at you to try to figure out your gender. A double-take followed by a smile, or slight shrug of the shoulders is not bad. When it's followed by a hostile stare, look of disgust, snickering, or pointing or other rude gesture, that's a microaggression.

To call these microaggressions implies that they are small, but it doesn't mean that they don't hurt. They can undermine your determination and resolve, not to mention your self-esteem. A steady diet of everyday microaggression can be as devastating to GLBTQ youth as outright violence. It takes a thick skin to withstand these zings and arrows. Those transitioning from female to male have some protection from the increased testosterone, but male-to-female transitioners often feel more vulnerable on estrogen.

Coping with Mistreatment

Some amount of microaggression is unfortunately inevitable. I have seen several ways of coping with it. I have seen some people so terrified of negative reactions that they didn't dare go out as themselves until they felt they passed perfectly. I understand their hesitation, but it certainly slows down their progress and often results in social isolation. Others go out, but with blinders on, so to speak. They do their best to block out their peripheral vision to avoid noticing anyone's reactions. That's not a great idea either, since personal safety requires a heightened awareness of your surroundings. Others become hypervigilant, and overreact to perceived stares and snubs. Those who cope best with being out and about as themselves are aware of those around them but manage to develop a thick skin and a sense of humor. In other words, they don't take other people's negative reactions personally or too seriously. The more you can say to yourself "That's their problem!" the more you can let the subtle microaggressions bounce off without penetrating.

There are, of course, times for confronting persistent mistreatment. If a family member or co-worker continues to intentionally use your old name and incorrect pronouns, for example, it's time to ask for a face-to-face meeting. Politely but firmly let them know that their behavior is inappropriate and hurtful. Offer them some reading material, or the chance to ask reasonable questions. You may have to listen to their ignorance or prejudice, but you'll have the opportunity to correct any misconceptions they might have. A respectful conversation can have a powerful impact.

So what can be done to protect and/or defend yourself from harassment, discrimination and violence? You don't have to accept that you're going to be mistreated; it is not acceptable. Transgender people don't have full legal protections, unfortunately, so what you can do about it varies. We'll discuss each of the major problem areas in turn, but first I have a piece of geographical advice. If you live in the "Bible Belt" - those states in the South and Midwest that are the most religiously and politically conservative - and don't have a supportive community, consider moving. You will be fighting even more of an uphill battle if your social climate is heterosexist *and* transphobic. Come to the more liberal Northeast, or at least consider moving to a university town or a major metropolitan area.

Fighting Discrimination

I hate to say this, but the best protection against discrimination and mistreatment is presenting in a way that does not draw attention to you. Passing as best you can, dressing well, and being a gentleman or a gracious woman can make a huge difference in how people relate to you. It shouldn't matter, but it does. Gender non-conforming appearance and behavior make people uncomfortable. (If you skipped the section on gender presentation, now is the time to go back and read it, and think about what you can do and still be true to yourself.)

That isn't always possible, of course, especially in the midst of transitioning. Transitioning on the job, for example, requires you to out yourself. We'll discuss this more in Chapter 18, and focus here on what you can do about discrimination in public venues.

This may sound contradictory, but I would suggest that you always assume that discrimination is wrong and that somebody in the setting you're dealing with cares. If you are mistreated by an individual in a health care organization, shelter, school, social service agency or other public institution report it to the person's supervisor. And their supervisor's superior, if necessary. Write a letter stating what happened and why it's discriminatory. If you are discriminated against in public housing, report it to HUD. Their regulations now prohibit discrimination on the basis of sexual orientation or gender identity. The worst that could happen is that nothing changes. At best, you will help that organization change and benefit yourself as well as those who come after you.

If you live in a state, county or city where it is illegal to discriminate on the basis of perceived sexual orientation or gender presentation you can file a complaint with the local Human Rights Commission. The Human Rights Campaign, a national watchdog organization, keeps a list of the jurisdictions that include gender identity in their anti-discrimination laws. So does the National Gay and Lesbian Task Force. There is transgender-inclusive or specific legislation pending in many states at the moment, and more cities and counties every month. By the time you read this ENDA, the Employment Non-Discrimination Act, may be in full force.

If you have been discriminated against and have been harmed by it (especially financially) consider filing a civil suit against the institution. There is legal assistance available through a number of GLBT organizations. Even if transgender rights are not specifically covered, or the organization is exempt, you may end up with a financial settlement. A New Hampshire woman filed a suit against St. Anselm's College when it stated in its letter of termination that her gender transition was the reason for her dismissal. New Hampshire does not have specific protections, and as a Catholic institution St. Anselm's is exempt anyway, but she did receive financial compensation.

If your state does not have equal protection for transgender or gender non-conforming people consider getting politically involved. You can fight City Hall (or your State House) but you can't do it alone. There are groups in every state working right now to initiate or expand equal protection and anti-discrimination laws. Becoming politically active is very empowering. Many of my friends and clients have testified on behalf of transgender rights in New Hampshire, and even though the bill was deferred we made a positive impression and educated a number of legislators.

Hate Crimes

The Matthew Shepard and James Byrd, Jr. Hate Crimes Prevention Act was passed by Congress on October 22, 2009 and was signed into law by President Obama on October 28, 2009. It expands the 1969 United States federal hate crime law to include crimes motivated by a victim's actual or perceived gender, sexual orientation, gender identity or disability. If you are a victim of a hate crime report it immediately! If you don't receive fair treatment when you report it to local law enforcement, go to the media.

The same holds true for intimate partner violence. It doesn't matter what type of relationship you're in; if your partner is abusive it's a crime. Don't be afraid to admit that there's a problem, and get help. Talk to your therapist about it; it won't be used to stop you from getting hormones or surgery. Bide your time if you have to, but find your way out of any destructive relationship(s).

Personal Safety

This is tricky to write about. I don't want to give you the impression that if you are assaulted it's your fault, but there are things you can do to reduce your chances or being physically or sexually assaulted. This is new territory for those transitioning both from male-to-female and female-to-male. Those who are raised male do not always understand the vulnerability of being female, and may not even realize how often they are being perceived as female. Women grow up with an awareness of their vulnerability, however, that most men don't have. When you are perceived as female, your odds of being assaulted automatically increase. Estimates are that one out of every four women will be a victim of sexual assault at some point in her life, most likely before the age of 30. She is most likely to be raped by someone she knows, and the majority of those will go unreported.[54] Many men see women as easy targets for muggings as well as physical and sexual assault. Those who are transitioning from female to male often have a size disadvantage, and little socialization in how men posture nonverbally. They are vulnerable to being harassed when they inadvertently violate "man rules". Men are not immune to sexual assault, nor are lesbians. One out of every 10 reported rapes is a male victim. Sexual assaults against (perceived) gay men and lesbians are an all too common form of hate crime. And both transmen and transwomen are vulnerable if they are found out in a sexually charged situation.

There are plenty of courses and books on personal safety for women, and more to it than I can cover here. Here are just a few tips for avoiding potential harm:

Flying under the radar: As mentioned earlier, one way to minimize risk is to not draw attention to oneself. Fitting in as best you can to the social context, walking confidently, and behaving respectfully go a long way. Act like you belong where you are, especially in a public rest room.

Safety in numbers: It is always better to go out with others rather than alone. Even if the others aren't any more passable than you are, you're still less likely to attract unwanted attention. The best way to tackle the public bathroom dilemma is to go with a cisgendered friend.

---

[54] Catalano, Shannon M. "Criminal Victimization, 2005." Washington, DC: Bureau of Justice Statistics, 2006

Pay attention: The most important strategy of all is to pay attention to your surroundings. Keep your eyes and ears open and notice who is around you and what they are doing. Trust your gut feelings! Cross the street or stop in an open business if you think someone is following you.

Stay sober: It's a lot easier to pay attention if you're sober, for one thing. Your judgment is also not compromised. If you want to go to a club and have a drink or two, go with a friend who can stay sober. Or at the very least have someone escort you to your car when you go out. If a couple of yahoos wanted to go beat up on someone, where would they go? They would hang around outside a gay bar.

Avoid hook-ups: Do not go home, or even get in a car, with someone you've just met at a bar or club. (If you're too young to have seen the movie *Looking for Mr. Goodbar*, rent it and watch it. Or *The Matthew Shepard Story*.)

On-line dating: Be very cautious about anyone you meet on-line. There are a lot of predators out there, and they're very good at finding victims. If you do strike up a conversation with someone from an on-line forum or dating site and want to take it further, talk on the phone first. Then arrange to meet during the day in a public place. Be especially wary of Craigslist ads.

Self-defense: Taking a self-defense class is always a good idea. The best approach I've read about is "Shock, Scream and Run": do something that surprises your attacker or throws him off-balance, scream as loud as you possibly can, and run to the nearest person or business. No one can predict, however, how they will respond if attacked. Many people freeze, and anything they learned goes out the window. Do whatever you can to survive the attack, even if that means rolling into a ball and covering your face. Get immediate medical attention, and report the assault.

I hope that you will never have to face a violent situation. If you do, no matter what happens, do not beat yourself up over it. It is never your fault, no matter how you were dressed or how well you knew your attacker. Do not let anyone tell you otherwise. Women have been told for years to not fight back if they're being sexually assaulted, in order to survive, and then blamed for not resisting more. Misogyny (hatred of women) is still prevalent in our culture, but you don't need to buy into it. I also hope for you the courage and grace to fight discrimination against transgender and gender non-conforming people in any way that you can. Every time you speak up for your rights you are helping not only yourself but everyone who follows in your footsteps.

References and Resources

Human Rights Campaign: www.hrc.org

National Center for Transgender Equality: www.TransEquality.org

National Gay and Lesbian Task Force: www.thetaskforce.org

Gay, Lesbian, Bisexual and Transgendered Domestic Violence:
www.rainbowdomesticviolence.itgo.com

Leanne McCall Tigert, *Coming Out through Fire: Surviving the Trauma of Homophobia*, United Church Press, 1999

Chapter Sixteen

Wrestling with Inner Demons

You do not need to know precisely what is happening, or exactly where it is all going. What you need is to recognize the possibilities and challenges offered by the present moment, and to embrace them with courage, faith and hope.

Thomas Merton

There are plenty of external obstacles and sources of resistance to changing your gender role. For many people, however, the biggest obstacle is their own internal resistance. This too can come from many sources, but it stems primarily from our internalized messages from parents (and other family members), peers, teachers, religious institutions, and the media. These messages leave deep etchings in our psyches that are not always conscious. We can cover them over with more rational ideas, or try to drown them out with alcohol, drugs, work, and other distractions, but they don't just go away. Like inner demons, they raise their ugly heads at the most inopportune times, stopping us in our tracks. It's important to see them, name them, and put them back in their place. They belong to the past, not to your future.

The four most common inner demons I see clients wrestling with are Shame, Fear, Doubt, and Despair. They are ruthless adversaries. Fortunately, their antidotes - Pride, Courage, Faith and Hope - are also available to everyone. Looking inside oneself is like opening up Pandora's Box; the first "spirits" out of the box are the negative ones. Sometimes you have to face those first, and trust that faith, hope and courage will follow.

Shame

Shame is the most devastating inner demon. Shame is part of a constellation of related emotions that includes self-consciousness, embarrassment, regret/remorse, and guilt. Self-consciousness and embarrassment are part of being social animals; they involve an awareness of our vulnerability to being seen, and perhaps judged, by others. Guilt is a realistic assessment of having done something wrong, and regret/remorse is the wish that we hadn't done it. Shame includes all of the above. We feel exposed as a flawed human being.

John Bradshaw[55] distinguishes between healthy shame and toxic shame. Healthy shame develops in early childhood when the toddler, seeking autonomy and independence, bumps rudely into the limits imposed by caregivers. Suddenly he or she isn't so cute and endearing! Disapproving looks and words mirror back a less-than-perfect self. Shame puts down roots in that moment when we have been caught in the act and exposed.

Toxic shame is instilled by parents and others when they scold, punish, mock, insult, ridicule, tease, and humiliate in ways that convey that not only did we do something wrong, but we're somehow *bad*. Shame-based parenting leaves deep feelings of being worthless and hopelessly inadequate. Frequent humiliation by peers creates a collage of shame experiences that crystallize into shame complexes. These can shape a shame-based identity characterized by feeling fundamentally defective or deficient. We internalize the message that we are somehow sick, sinful, or unnatural. The end result is alienation from our True Self, the formation of a False

---

[55] John Bradshaw, *Healing the Shame That Binds You*, Health Communications, 1988

Self, and isolation from others. According to Bradshaw, this is the core and primary source of addictions and compulsions.

Gershen Kaufman and Lev Raphael write about the effects of shaming experiences in *Coming Out of Shame*. A *shame scene* is a traumatic memory of having been shamed in some way. "If the event is intense enough, or lasts long enough, that scene will be seared into memory. Given the tendency of negative affect to overwhelm positive, we typically remember moments of shame and fear longer than moments of joy." [56] At the moment of shaming we emotionally shut down, unable to express and discharge the emotion. The feeling of shame is stored with the memory, along with the physical sensations and visual and auditory components. Repeated shame scenes form a *shame script*. We unconsciously formulate rules for ourselves in order to avoid, escape or contain shameful feelings.

Shame scripts are learned both at home (from family rules) and in the wider world. Gender, social class, and ethnicity determine our place in society and the life scripts available to us. Kaufman and Raphael summarize the different shaming scripts for men and women. Women are shamed for expressing anger and excitement, for being "selfish", and for striving for autonomy, mastery and control. Women are also shamed for feeling proud and expressing their individuality ("Don't be a show-off!") Men, on the other hand, are shamed for showing fear and distress ("Boys don't cry!"), for seeking physical affection and affiliation, and for admitting weakness or vulnerability.

Anyone growing up gay, lesbian, bisexual or transgender in a homophobic/transphobic culture will experience some degree of shaming around feeling different. Teasing, harassment, bullying and outright humiliation for being different are rampant in our schools. Parents and teachers are no less guilty when it comes to rejecting gender-variant behavior. Many of my GLBT clients can remember vividly a time when they were subject to disapproval and ridicule. Even if a child is not the direct object of sham-

---

[56] Gershen Kaufman, PhD, and Lev Raphael, PhD, *Coming Out of Shame: Transforming Gay and Lesbian Lives*, Doubleday, 1996, p. 27

ing by others, the message is clear: straying from gender norms is something to be ashamed of and hide at all costs. This leaves a legacy of shame and low self-esteem.

Since shame is such a powerful negative feeling we all develop ways of defending ourselves against the experience. Striving for perfection is a common result of shame-based parenting; if I'm perfect no one will ever shame me again. When that fails we have to rely on other defenses. Blaming others for our mistakes is sometimes effective; this allows us to lash out at them rather than ourselves. Projecting our shortcomings onto others is another one; we keep our self-esteem intact by holding contempt for them. We might do this with humor, but it will probably come out as sarcasm or mockery, shaming others. Withdrawing inside ourselves and building walls to try to shut out feedback from the outside world is another coping mechanism, but inevitably we are own worst critic. If all else fails, we can fall back on denial - either the denial that we did something wrong or the denial that we feel bad about it.

Shame memories are like other traumatic memories; they may be repressed but they resurface in bits and pieces when triggered. The feeling of shame may be triggered by anything associated with the original scene - a sight, a sound, even a smell. Certainly a look of disapproval from a significant person, no matter how mild, can bring back waves of shame. A backlog of negative emotion can be like an underground pool that gets tapped into when we encounter new situations that evoke the same emotion. Who hasn't felt angry at someone, out of proportion with their offense, and then realized that what they did reminded you of an old injustice? We all know people who manage to "push our buttons" frequently. We have "shame buttons" as well as ones related to anger, fear and other powerful repressed emotions.

Shame is also triggered whenever our efforts at being ourselves are thwarted or discouraged. We have to take risks in order to learn new things, but failure in any area can bring up shame. Some people are so bound with shame that they rarely venture out of their narrow comfort zone. Shame can also be linked to particular needs and drives (such as affection, sex, recognition, and power) as well as emotions that are taboo in one's family or culture. Simply experiencing those needs or feelings later can be laden with shame.

Chronic anxiety and depression, eating disorders, self-loathing and self-injury, substance abuse, and other addictions and compulsions can all be rooted in shame and the avoidance of shame. It's one of the most pervasive and insidious negative influences on human behavior. There are ways, however, to lessen its impact. John Bradshaw lists fourteen ways to work on shame-reduction, based on externalizing what has been internalized.[57] I'll mention here the methods that I think are most helpful for transgender men and women:

1) "Coming out of hiding by social contact, which means honestly sharing our feelings with significant others." Sound familiar? At the risk of sounding like a broken record, I'll say again that getting support, from a therapist and/or a support group, is essential to recovering one's self-esteem.

2) "Seeing ourselves mirrored and echoed in the eyes of at least one non-shaming person who is part of our new family or affiliation." That's a large part of the job that I do with clients.

3) "Learning to recognize various split-off parts of ourselves. As we make these parts conscious (externalize them), we can embrace and integrate them." Reclaiming your masculine or feminine self and learning to value him or her is essential.

4) "Making new decisions to accept all parts of ourselves with unconditional positive regard." Learning to love all of ourselves takes a conscious decision, and practice.

5) "Externalizing old unconscious memories from the past, which form collages of shame scenes, and learning to heal them." Kaufman and

---

[57] John Bradshaw, *Healing the Shame That Binds You*, Health Communications, 1988, pp. 115-116

Raphael explore this in depth in *Coming Out of Shame*. This is best done with the help of a therapist.

6) "Externalizing the voices in our heads." You can learn to recognize the Shamer, the Judge, the Critic, and other negative self-talk and replace them with more positive messages. Kaufman and Raphael refer to these as "self-affirming scripts."[58]

7) "Learning to be aware of certain interpersonal situations most likely to trigger shame spirals." That may include avoiding certain people who are still critical and judgmental. At the very least it helps to be prepared for possible triggers and buttress your self-esteem against negative influences.

8) "Learning how to handle our mistakes, and having the courage to be imperfect." This is so important for people who are transitioning. You are not going to be able to present perfectly at first. You may have to accept yourself as an ugly duckling on the way to becoming a swan.

Both *Healing the Shame That Binds You* and *Coming Out of Shame* go into much more detail on these ways of coping with and recovering from self-loathing. They're both well worth your time. You can learn to transform your Shame into Pride. You are a Hero. As someone who has survived growing up in this culture, faced your inner demons and set sail for your True Self, you have a lot to celebrate!

Fear

Fear is another debilitating emotion experienced at some point by every transgender person I know. For some it is a constant companion, for others a frequent unexpected visitor. Every step of the way, every time you come out, fear is there, pulling you back. There is plenty to fear about being transgender. Discrimination, harassment and violence are real. Coming out as transgender can turn your world upside down. The repercussions on your family and your career are enormous and unpredictable.

---

[58] Gershen Kaufman, PhD, and Lev Raphael, PhD, <u>Coming Out of Shame: Transforming Gay and Lesbian Lives</u>, Doubleday, 1996, p. 158

In my experience, however, the fears are usually far greater than are warranted. The more you avoid something the larger the fear builds up in your mind. Most of the time the actual experience is nowhere near as difficult or as devastating as you imagined. I wish I had a dollar for every time a client has reported back, after trying something I'd been urging for months, "That wasn't that bad! I wish I'd done it sooner."

Even greater than the fear of persecution is the fear of rejection and abandonment. Human beings are social animals. We live in families, tribes, and communities. We depend on them for our survival. To be cast out of a family, tribe or community, to be shunned, was once a fate worse than death. Because of how strongly the taboos against being "queer" are imbedded in our psyche (through shaming), we assume that transgression will automatically bring rejection. Some people do experience rejection by significant others, but most are surprised at how understanding and supportive people can be.

Our biggest fear as human beings is the fear of the unknown. From the dawn of history, the unknown equaled danger, so sticking to the known and familiar evolved as a survival trait. In the middle ages, sailors used dragons to represent unknown regions on a map. All sorts of danger could lurk there, from underwater rocks that could sink a ship without any warning, to strong currents that could carry a ship so far off course that everybody on board would die once the food ran out. We still equate the unknown with danger, even when the future could hold untold good fortune. Because we can't predict the future it's impossible to be completely prepared for it. Not knowing how we're going to respond to some future action or event can still create fear and anxiety, even when we have the means to cope with most of what comes down the pike.

Internalized transphobia is another source of fear and anxiety. It's all too easy to project our own internal condemnation onto others, and assume that everyone is judging, criticizing, and disapproving. This is the basis of much of the fear of being read as trans. Being read means being exposed, and being exposed as something taboo brings shame. Many clients have said that their greatest fear was looking like "a guy in a dress". The fear of humiliation is so strong that some delay going out in public at all until they feel completely assured of passing. Since self-perception is slow to catch up to actual changes in appearance, that can take a long time!

Another common fear is that somehow someone will stop you from transitioning, or not allow you to proceed (with hormones, or surgery, or whatever your next step might be). This stems partly from the experiences that many transgender men and women have had with therapists and doctors, especially around the Standards of Care. It's unnerving to think that someone else has the power to say yea or nay to hormones or surgery. Calming that anxiety is one of the first things I try to do with clients.

So how can you deal with these fears? The first step is to acknowledge and assess your fears. Judging how realistic they are can be difficult - public attitudes are changing, but not fast enough, and not everywhere. Peer support is crucial here; hearing about their experiences from others who have come out before you can lesson your anxiety. I encourage reality-testing - slowly but surely testing out those fears, from the slightest to the greatest. I discussed some of that process in Chapter Seven, with coming out to the "easiest" people first. Venturing out in public, to safe places first, then with safe people, is a way of expanding one's comfort zone. Remember there is strength in numbers! Taking appropriate cautions and learning self-defense is an important part of managing fear.

Another method is to face those fears head on and say "OK, what if X happens? How would I deal with it?" Mara Christine Drummond believes that "the only way to successfully transition is to accept the possibility that by transitioning you may lose everything of value in your life. "[59] In other words, if you can imagine giving everything up in order to be yourself, you'll have nothing to fear. Having fall-back plans helps too. Knowing that you have money to live on while looking for another job, or a place to stay if your spouse or parents want you out of the house, makes a big difference.

---

[59] Mara Christine Drummond. *Transitions: A Guide to Transitioning For Transsexuals and Their Families,* lulupress, 2009

In the end, it all boils down to finding the courage to be yourself, and not give a damn what anyone else thinks. "Courage is not the absence of fear, but rather the judgment that something else is more important than fear."[60] You've probably already tried running away and hiding in fear. If you're reading this book, that hasn't worked very well for you. Your need to be yourself, to have your outside match your inside, is a strong force. You have already given that need great power. Like the Cowardly Lion in the Wizard of Oz you have probably already shown great bravery in spite of your fear. Embracing that will help you overcome any remaining fears.

Doubt

Where there is uncertainty, there is doubt. We can never be 100 percent certain of any decision we make. We don't know what's possible in the future, and if, how and when things will work out. Only hindsight is 20/20; at the moment of choice we are invariably working with incomplete information. If you wait until you're 100 percent sure of your decision before you move forward you'll be stuck for a long time! There will always be some questions, some lingering doubts, some "minority opinions" in your head. There is most likely a part of you that thinks doing all this is crazy. You've certainly been told that, I imagine. There's a part of you that thinks you should just accept how you were born and live with it - perhaps the same part of you that doesn't want to disappoint others. We all have different "voices" in our head giving their opinions on just about everything we do. That's normal. Getting those parts of ourselves to cooperate can be an interesting challenge.

Guilt and second-guessing your decisions can be a form of doubt. It's natural to feel some guilt about the disruption that coming out as transgender creates in a family. Excessive guilt comes from taking too much responsibility for other people's reactions. We are not responsible for other people's extreme reactions to our changes. I have a client who came in for help because she was devastated by the news that her daughter was leaving her husband because she realized she was gay. To this client, her whole

---

[60] Ambrose Hollingworth Redmoon. No Peaceful Warriors! Gnosis #21, Fall 1991.

world had just come tumbling down; she spiraled into a deep depression. After working through her grief at the loss of her dreams for her daughter's life she came to realize that she had been overly invested in her daughter's successful marriage because her own was so empty and unsatisfying. When she was able to look at her own life and her dissatisfaction with it she was able to appreciate her daughter's strength in being true to herself. Her daughter may have provoked her depression, but she wasn't responsible for *causing* it. When a client's spouse goes into a vengeful rage or deep depression I remind them that many spouses deal with the news more rationally and productively, even if they're not thrilled with the idea.

You can also expect to experience some insecurity from being in the world in a way you never have before. One client hesitantly tried to describe to me how she felt inside after changing her name. She was pleased, but still felt awkward. "This may sound strange, but I still don't feel like an adult. Maraya [her new name] is still a kid! And she's really naive." I told her it wasn't strange at all, and that a lot of people feel that way. "There's a part of you that's still stuck at age 10. When you've had to lock away a part of yourself, it's as if she's lived in a basement for 20 years (without a TV or computer). When she emerges she still has a lot of growing up to do."

Many of my clients have thought that they must be crazy because they felt like they were two people inside: their masculine (or feminine) self that they showed the world, and the feminine (or masculine) self that they hid inside. Some can remember when the two parts of themselves split. This experience doesn't mean you're crazy, or a "split personality". (In someone with Multiple Personality Disorder the different parts are not aware of each other, and different parts take control completely without the others knowing what's happening.) This internal splitting is an adaptive response to finding out that it's not OK to show your true self.

Another client describes a wall that has grown between her feminine and masculine selves. The wall keeps the feminine feelings, desires, mannerisms, etc. away from the masculine persona she learned to present to the outside world. One of the scary things about transitioning is that this wall, or whatever it is that keeps the femininity (or masculinity) hidden away, starts to break down. The inside persona becomes more insistent about being heard and expressed. The outside persona can feel very threatened by the internal pressure from the inside persona emerging. The wall needs to crumble in order to become whole as a person.

You may feel at war with yourself from time to time. You may wish you could get rid of all of your old persona. But you don't want to banish or kill off the outside persona any more than you want to suppress the emerging one. You don't want to lose all the valuable traits and skills you've developed over the years. The ultimate goal is to heal the split and integrate both parts of yourself into a dynamic whole. You can become a man who likes to cook and garden and write in a journal, or a woman who loves motorcycles and video games and Sci-Fi thrillers.

What you have to do in the meantime is learn to grow up all over again. This can be awkward! Some describe this experience as a second adolescence and attribute it to hormones (which certainly contribute to it.) Remember the self-consciousness and insecurity of adolescence? Be ready to experience some of that again as you venture out into the world "wearing" your new gender role. One of the things I've noticed is that there is often a phase of trying to dress like a teenager. If you're over 30 this will get you noticed, for better or for worse!

One of the more insidious and insistent internal voices is that of self-doubt. "Can I really do this? Will I ever be able to pass? Do I have the strength and courage to go through with it? Will my spouse/parents/therapist stop me from doing what I want and need? I'll never be able to afford surgery, so why bother? I'm not strong, smart, tall/short, thin, young/old, talented, good-looking, rich, or (fill in the blanks) enough to pull it off. I'll never be successful."

This is where Faith comes in handy. Faith in yourself, faith in your care providers, and faith in the process. I never cease to be amazed by the transformations people are capable of undergoing. The changes that take place in appearance are astounding, not to mention the blossoming of poise and confidence. I wish I had before and after pictures to show you. (You can see a variety of 'after' pictures on two web sites - one called

Successful Transsexual Women and the other Successful TransMen.) You may not be able to look as good as (insert your favorite singer, actor or actress here), but with time, determination, and help you will be able to present yourself to the world as the man or woman you were meant to be.

Affirmations are a popular and often effective way to counteract self-doubt. Our thoughts can be self-fulfilling prophecies. The more you think you're a failure the more you'll fail, and the more you think of yourself as capable the more competent you will become. Affirmations are specific forms of positive thinking, designed to focus your attitude and actions in a positive direction. Basically this involves taking negative statements, such as "I'm not strong enough", and turning them into positive ones, such as "I have the strength to accomplish my goals." It's easy to find lists of success affirmations on-line, but many of them may seem too far-fetched. Write a list for yourself that feels at least somewhat believable. (Start with something simple, such as "I can do this!") If you can't come up with anything on your own ask friends to help. Write your affirmations on sticky notes and post them on your mirror and around the house. Try looking at yourself in the mirror in the morning (yes, the dreaded mirror) and saying to yourself "I can become the man/woman I am meant to be" or even "I am becoming the man/woman I am meant to be." You'll be surprised by how much confidence that can inspire.

The process mentioned above for rooting out fears is also helpful for dealing with doubt and self-doubt. Acknowledging your fears and doubts and accepting that they're perfectly normal is the first step. It's sometimes helpful to imagine them all in one room, sitting around a big conference table. Hear them out (one at a time!), but then respond from a rational point of view. Discuss them in therapy, or in your peer support group. Find people who can be your coaches and cheerleaders, who have faith in you and/or faith in the process. Imagine them in the room when you're having a particularly hard time with fear or doubt. (My clients tell me that they ask themselves "What would Anne say?")

Despair

When shame, fear and doubt get the better of us, it's easy to end up in the land of Despair. It's not a pretty place. To despair is to lose all hope and confidence. Like shame, it is an intense negative emotional state. At that moment, there are no positive outcomes in sight. We're convinced that the light at the end of the tunnel is a train heading right toward us and there's no way out. We might as well lie down and die.

I feel like a preacher when I say "Brothers and Sisters, there is always hope." (Or Little Orphan Annie, singing "The sun will come out tomorrow.") When you're in the depths of despair those words will sound hollow, but I believe with all my being that they're true. There is always hope. There are always solutions you haven't considered yet. Even when I discourage people from holding onto too much hope that someone *else* will change I believe that *they're* still going to be all right. The human spirit is amazingly resilient. One of the more profound psychologists of the 20th century - Victor Frankl - survived a Nazi death march by imagining, in detail, how he would talk about his experience years later.[61]

The good news is that wherever there is pride, courage or faith there is Hope. Wherever there is support, there is Hope. Wherever there is determination, there is Hope. Hope is at the bottom of Pandora's Box, sometimes trapped when we shut it down in a panic after shame, fear, doubt or despair has popped out. Keep looking if you ever feel you've lost Hope. She's in there somewhere.

When people give in to despair, they sometimes consider suicide. If you ever do, please read this next section before you indulge in those thoughts any further.

---

[61] Victor Frankl, *Man's Search for Meaning*, Pocket Books, 1997

Suicide

I was interrupted one morning by a call from the state medical examiner's office on my emergency cell phone line. A former client had hung herself, and left three names for the police to contact: her sister, her ex-wife, and myself. The medical examiner was conducting a routine psychological autopsy, to confirm the death as a suicide. I had only seen her twice in the previous year, so I couldn't offer much insight. "Had she been depressed?" Who wouldn't be? How do you describe to someone not familiar with the issues how hard it is to be transgender? Yes, she was depressed when she lost her job the year before, but she had cancelled her last scheduled appointment because she had found work. Mostly she was isolated. Her wife had gone back to her parents' house, taking their son with them. It was hard for her to stay connected with him two states away. Dating was difficult because she had not been able to afford vaginoplasty. Her sister and a cousin were supportive, but her brother was not speaking to her. Somehow she must have felt that there was no one there for her, and no hope for her future. She had unfortunately stopped coming to therapy and support group, and didn't realize how many people cared about her. I cared, and I grieved her loss deeply.

The suicide statistics for the transgender population are alarming, but not as dramatic as some suggest. You'll see "50 percent higher than normal' quoted frequently, but that is not backed up by research statistics. A more accurate estimate is 20 percent higher than "normal". The national suicide rate for the United States is 11.3 per 100, 000; that would put the suicide rate for the transgender population at 13.6 per 100,000. Suicide *attempts* are more common (estimated at 30-40 percent of the transgender population), especially among GLBTQ teenagers subject to harassment and bullying. The suicide risk drops post-transition, but is still higher than one might expect. Age, gender, and race also influence suicide risk; the suicide rate for those age 65 and older is 14.3 per 100,00, the same as the rate for Native Americans.[62]

Every suicide is regrettable. Every suicide has a ripple effect, hurting not only the person's family and friends but the whole community. I'd like to say "Don't even think about it!", but I know that's not realistic. You probably have thought about it, perhaps many times, hopefully only in fleeting moments of desperation. There may have been times when you thought you'd rather die than face another day feeling the way you were feeling. Many of my clients report a pivotal moment when they were so desperate that they considered suicide, saying "Well it was either kill myself or get help, so here I am." I hope that if/when you have one of those moments you pick up the phone and call someone for help. There are suicide prevention hot-lines specifically for people dealing with issues of sexual orientation and gender identity. (See the Resources section at the end of this chapter).

Suicide is a permanent solution to a temporary problem. The way you feel when you're that far down is not going to last forever. There's a campaign currently underway to convince GLBTQ teens that "It gets better." Some people I know have a problem with it, saying you can't guarantee that. No we can't guarantee anything. But I can say with conviction that there's always hope for finding a solution that works for you. I can tell you that there are people who care, and that you matter to them and to countless other people in your life. Nobody will be better off if you end it all, no matter what someone might say in a moment of anger. I can also say with certainty that you are not alone. Someone out there knows how you feel because they've felt that way too. And that someone might just need your support, your insights, your help along the way. Whatever pain you are going through will not be in vain if you muster the courage to work through it and use what you learn for the benefit of others.

---

[62] Suicide in the U.S.: Statistics and Prevention, National Institute of Mental Health Publication, at: http://www.mentalhealth.gov/health/publications/suicide-in-the-us-statistics-and-prevention/index.shtml

References and Resources

Gershen Kaufman, PhD, and Lev Raphael, PhD, *Coming Out of Shame: Transforming Gay and Lesbian Lives*, Doubleday, 1996

John Bradshaw, *Healing the Shame That Binds You*, Health Communications, 1988

The Trevor Hotline: 1-866-488-7386

GLBT National Hotline - GLBT National Help Center: www.glnh.org

PART FOUR

TRANSFORMATION

Chapter Seventeen

Crossing the Final Threshold: Claiming Your New Identity

To be what we are, and to become what we are capable of becoming,
is the only end of life.

Robert Louis Stevenson

The third major threshold on your journey is coming out completely, and living full-time in your desired gender role. For many, this is an end in itself; for others, a step towards gender reassignment surgery. The WPATH Standards of Care reference a year of full-time real-life experience as a requirement for gender reassignment surgery. This has become known in the literature as the "real-life test". It is not a test! There are no grades, for one thing. And you don't have to prove anything to anyone. It is a period of confirmation of your gender identity and adjustment to the reality of being seen as a man or woman. If you have prepared well up to this point it is a smooth slide into full femme or full masculine presentation.

Crossing this threshold cannot be rushed! Trying to live full-time as your desired gender before you are physically ready can create more problems than it solves. Changing your name before your voice has changed, for example, creates considerable confusion, especially over the phone. If you want to pass as your desired gender, you have to wait until you're good at it. That means mastering the elements of gender presentation covered in Part Two. Clients who try to rush into the full-time experience often stall completely because they haven't prepared well. "Nicole" changed her name and transitioned at work before resolving family issues and completing electrolysis and voice training. Her career was affected, and she ended up living at home under her ex-wife's rules. She is now back on track and moving forward, but regrets the time she lost.

It's also important to time the transition to living full-time in a way that fits in with whatever else is going on in your life. If you're in the middle of a nasty divorce, or your company is downsizing, it's prudent to wait. In spite of the recent changes in the military's "Don't ask, don't tell." policy, do not attempt to come out if you're in the military. On the other hand, if you're in your last year of college, do consider changing your name before your diploma is printed.

One of the many surprises for people transitioning is just how much they can change in their appearance before it becomes obvious that they don't fit their assigned gender. You may be acutely aware of the changes, and convinced that everyone else is noticing them. Most people, however, aren't that perceptive. Because most of the physical changes are gradual, people who see you frequently adjust, seeing you as the same person. They may wonder why you've changed your hair style, but they don't pay attention to the hair on your arms or the shape of your eyebrows.

This allows people to take their time coming out to those beyond their family and friends. Take advantage of this time. Unless you know for sure that your workplace is trans-friendly, let your boss and coworkers get used to your gradual changes. Just smile when they ask about your weight loss or hairstyle, or say "I was ready for something different" and change the subject. Chances are no one is going to ask you directly if you're "getting a sex change". It's not on most people's radar.

Going "reverse stealth" at your current job affords you the time and money to do as much as possible before coming out at work. Some of my clients plan to remain closeted at work until they retire, staying on a lower level of hormones, wearing androgynous clothes during the week, and maintaining a hair style that can be worn different ways. Some live part-time in role for several years before going full-time. This can be challenging at times. Having to go back into work is hard enough some Monday mornings; having to go back into "guy mode" or "girl mode" can make it downright depressing.

There comes a time when either the changes become too noticeable or your desire to come out fully takes over. At some point it becomes hard to pass as your assigned gender. You may not be aware of this at first, but public reactions will let you know. When clients ask me "When should I change my name?" I often say "When they won't accept your ID or credit card." That's a sure sign that you can't pull off staying half in the closet. You have crossed the line in people's minds.

The next step then is fully claiming your gender identity. There are two parts to this. The first is coming out to the rest of the people in your life, including work or school. The second is changing your name and your legal gender status, to the extent possible in your state. Gender identity status is a legal quagmire. There are different requirements for different documents, and they're changing all the time. I'll try to address the issues involved in this chapter, and coming out at work in the next.

So why not hang out in the middle of the gender spectrum forever, identifying as neither male nor female, or both? Some gender variant people do just that, identifying as genderqueer, bigendered, Androgynes, or "two-spirit". Unfortunately we live in a binary gender society. Crucial identity documents identify us as either male or female. (I don't know of any yet that have room for "trans" or "other".) And there are ramifications if we don't match the gender designation on those documents. I just heard a story this week about a transwoman who tried to go through airport security with quasi-legal IDs that matched her current presentation but didn't specify gender. She ended up having to show her driver's license, with her male name, before she was allowed to board her plane. The experience was frustrating and humiliating for her.

Most transpeople are eager to claim their new gender identity and change their legal gender status. Unfortunately it's not a straightforward process. Political realities have not caught up with the complexities of gender identity. Most rules that allow changes in gender designation were written with male-to-female transsexuals in mind, and "sex-change" referred to "sex reassignment" surgery. That is beginning to change, and by the time this book is out will hopefully have changed even more. I can only describe the general process of identity change, because many of the specifics vary from state to state.

Changing Your Name

One of the first identifiers that most people want to change is their name. Unless you were blessed with a name that is used for both boys and girls your name has an implied gender associated with it. Choosing a new name is easy for some - they just know who they want to be called. Some have had friends spontaneously pick out a nickname for them, sometimes even before they come out as transgender. For others it's a more involved process. Here are a few suggestion for those who are still pondering a new name:

> One possibility is the masculine or feminine version of your given name. Michael becomes Mikayla or Michelle, Nicholas becomes Nicole, Christine becomes Christopher, etc. That requires less adjustment for the people close to you; they can often use the same nickname they've been calling you. That can be a disadvantage too, however, as they may not be able to make the changes in pronouns if they're still calling you by the same name.

> If you have a middle name that is androgynous, such as a family name, you can start using that without having to change your name legally. Susan Anderson Smith, for example, becomes S. Anderson Smith, and Michael Blair Brown becomes M. Blair Brown.

Another option is to use your initials for a period of time, if appropriate. Jane Terri Jones can become J.T. Jones, for example.

➤ Another popular option is to pick an androgynous name, especially if you plan on hanging out in the middle of the gender spectrum for a while. That allows people to see you as either male or female. (See the list of names at the end of the chapter that have been used for girls or boys.) The disadvantage here is that it may not convey strongly enough the gender you want people to perceive. It can also be hard for the people who know you to make the shift to using the appropriate pronouns later if you choose an androgynous name early in your transition.

➤ Another strategy is to research popular names for the year you were born. If you're 50 years old and pick a name that is popular among a much younger generation, it's just not going to fit as well. If you're 50+, try Beth, not Brittany, or Marianne, not Mackenzie, or Adam, not Aidan. You may feel like a teenager inside, but you probably don't look like one.

➤ If your parents are still alive, consider asking them what they would have called you if they had known you were a girl or boy. This helps them feel included in your process. (If you don't like the name, consider it as a middle name.) That will also most likely be a name that was common for your generation.

➤ You also have the option of changing your last name. Most keep it, out of respect for family connections, or out of habit or convenience. But if you don't like your last name and you don't have family ties why not pick a new one? The advantage, and disadvantage in some ways, is that it's a total break from your old name. In some situations that will require more explaining, in others less.

> ➤ There are names that I suggest people avoid if they don't want to stand out as transgender, such as very flowery names for women that sound like a stage name for a drag queen. You want a name that encourages people to take you seriously. And modern androgynous names can work against you if you're trying to make a strong impression as a trans man. A more ordinary name helps you come across as just another "average Joe (or Jane)".

You can try out your new name for a while with friends and family, and see how it feels. But even if you have an androgynous first name and want to keep it you will at some point probably want to change your middle name. Some states recognize "common-law" name changes, where you simply adopt your new name and start using it for all your legal documents. Most require a legal name change through the courts. This is not a complicated process. It varies from state to state, but it generally involves filling out a name change petition, submitting it to a lower court, paying a fee, getting a court date, and going before a judge for five minutes. Each state will have a list of what you need to provide either with the petition or at the time of your hearing. A letter from a therapist stating that this is an appropriate part of your gender transition is sometimes required, and always helpful. Dress appropriately for your hearing and be on time! The judge will ask a question or two and make a statement about not avoiding debts or other legal obligations, and it's done.

Some states require that you publish your name change in a local paper, which can be a bit daunting. There are ways to get around that requirement if it poses other risks for you. If your state has that requirement, consult an attorney or a gender specialist about it. Transgender rights groups in your state will also have more detailed information and help.

It's a good idea to take the whole day off of work when you go to court for your name change, because once you have the certificate (and 4-6 official copies) there are several places to go right away. The first is your local Social Security office, to change the name associated with your social security number. (You cannot erase your previous name, unfortunately. Credit reports and background checks will come up with both names.)

After the Social Security office, you'll need to go to your local Division of Motor Vehicles for a new driver's license. You probably won't be able to change the gender designation on your license yet (more on that later), but at least you'll have a picture ID that looks like your current presentation. After you get your new license you'll want to go to your bank and get your bank accounts changed. After that there's the ongoing process of changing your name everywhere else - the Post Office, all your bills, and then schools, libraries, agencies, clubs, magazine subscriptions, professional organizations, etc. Write a list before you change your name and work your way though it.

It's important to remember that once you have changed your name legally, no one has the right to refuse to change your name on any other document. Most places will change your name without question, or at least with a minimum of hassle. If anyone gives you a hard time, simply show them the court order and/or ask to speak with a supervisor. Be polite and patient, but persistent.

The other essential part of changing your name is truly owning it. That means asking everyone to use it, and to use the correct pronouns. You may have to explain to them that calling you by your old name and/or using the wrong pronouns in public will out you, and that's just not OK. Reinforce your new name by not responding to your old one, and gently reminding anyone who slips. Doing this with humor is more effective than getting angry. If John forgets and calls you Sue, respond with "Yes Jane?" Even your best friends will slip from time to time. The longer someone has known you the deeper your name is ingrained in their consciousness. If someone deliberately refuses to use your new name or the correct pronouns, however, reconsider that relationship. At the very least, avoid going out in public with him or her.

Using Gendered Bathrooms

Speaking of going out in public, an essential part of owning your new identity is being able to use a public restroom appropriate to your avowed gender. This is not always easy. Clients have spent many sessions working on getting up the courage to use the appropriate bathroom. Fears of being called out, harassed, even arrested, run rampant. These fears are not totally irrational, especially for those transitioning from male to female. Conservative groups were able to derail a transgender rights bill in New Hampshire in 2009 by dubbing it the "bathroom bill". The fears that the political strategists preyed on are primarily women's fears of encountering a man disguised as a woman spying on them in a woman-only space. The "crossdresser as perverted predator" media image was used to obscure the issue completely.

The truth, of course, is that gender non-conforming people are far more likely to be molested or harassed in a public restroom than anyone else. Some avoid public restrooms altogether, which can be restrictive and unhealthy. Eventually, however, there comes a time when necessity calls and demands bravery. While there is no way to guarantee that you won't be called out for using a bathroom that doesn't match your assigned gender, there are some ways to minimize the risk. Here are some suggestions:

> Wait until you pass reasonably well! The best time to go is when you're dressed nicely and appropriately for the setting and don't stand out.

> Wait, if you can, until the restroom is less crowded. Wait for women with young children to exit before using a women's room. Children are curious and speak their mind, and mothers can be very protective.

> Go with a buddy, possibly a cisgendered friend. This way you'll have someone to look out for you and will blend in more. Women are more likely to use the restroom in pairs; men less so.

> Learn the gender norms for behavior in public restrooms. Men go in, do their business, and leave. They don't chat much and they do *not* make eye contact. Women are friendlier; they are more likely to

smile and make chit-chat. And women almost always wash their hands and check their hair or make-up in the mirror. Do not spend a lot of time doing so, however, as that may draw attention to you.

➤ If you are a transman, don't worry about using the stall and sitting on the toilet; plenty of men do. If there's a man in the stall next to yours you can just sit for a minute after you pee, as if you have further business. If you are a transwoman, please *do* sit on the toilet to urinate.

➤ Act as if you belong there! Walk in with confidence. You have every right to be there. You are there for a legitimate reason, just like everyone else.

➤ If someone does call you out, pretend you made a mistake and apologize. Look at the signs and say "Oh my gosh! Sorry!" It's not the time or place to make an issue out of bathroom access. People can be very forgiving; almost everyone has gone into the "wrong" bathroom at one time or another.

Using the appropriate bathroom would not be so problematic if it was easier to change the gender marker on your ID. Then you would know that if you were questioned by security anywhere you could simply pull out your license and say "But I am female (or male)." If you haven't been able to change your gender marker, a letter from your therapist can be helpful.[63] I know it's demeaning; it's like being in high school and needing a hall pass, but it works.

---

[63] This is called a "carry letter" or letter of passage. There's an example in Gianna Israel, and Donald Tarver, II, *Transgender Care*, Temple University Press, 1997. p.163

Gender Markers

Gender markers are those ubiquitous Ms or Fs on documents that identify you as male or female. In an ideal world, they wouldn't be there at all, because they really aren't necessary. In a just world, you'd be able to change the designation when your gender presentation changes. In the real world, there are different documents with different rules about how to change the gender marker that vary from state to state. Not only that, but the rules are applied differently, or not at all, depending on who you happen to talk to and how much they know or care about rules and regulations!

The major documents that have gender markers are 1) your driver's license or state non-driver ID, 2) your birth certificate, 3) your Social Security account, and 4) your passport. Of these, your driver's license is probably the most important, because it is the most common form of ID. With the gender marker changed there, you can get most school, medical and other records changed.

Driver's License: Each state has its own rules and regulations about changing the gender marker on a driver's license or non-driver ID. Most states require proof of complete sex reassignment surgery, which makes it difficult for anyone who doesn't want or can't afford surgery. Some of those states regulate what qualifies as SRS; others do not. Many states have recently eliminated or modified that requirement, and more will soon. In these states, a letter from a therapist or physician stating that you are living full-time as your desired gender is all that is required. Check with transgender groups in your area to find out what your state's rules are, and how they're applied. Looking up 'gender marker change' on-line may be helpful, but many sites have not kept up with recent changes in different state regulations. Calling your DMV/RMV is a last resort, since the person who answers the phone probably won't know.

Even in states with stricter regulations, there are ways to get around them. Chest surgery can be described as sex reassignment surgery in a physician's letter. Some of my clients have had success in New Hampshire with a letter stating that the person has been living full-time as a man/woman for a period of time and has had irreversible changes due to hormone treatment. I've heard of people applying for a replacement for a "lost" license, checking off M or F as desired, and getting a new license with a new marker. (That only works if you pass well.) Dallas Denny suggests going to a more rural licensing office, where perhaps they are not as familiar with the regulations.[64] If you don't get cooperation at one office, try another. You don't know what will work until you try!

Birth Certificate: You will have to contact the state in which you were born to see about changing your birth certificate. It isn't easy. State regulations vary, with some states issuing new birth certificates in your new name and gender, others modifying the original, and still others prohibiting gender changes. Almost all require an original letter from a surgeon, and some require a court order specifying a change of gender. If you can change your birth certificate, all the better, because it can help you change the other documents, but it isn't essential if you can change your license.

Social Security Administration: Since your Social Security number is issued by a federal rather than state agency, there is only one rule to consider. Unfortunately, it's a strict rule. The regulations state clearly that a letter from a surgeon must say that SRS has been *completed*. It does not define what "completed" means, however, so it's possible that "top" surgery will suffice. The application for a new Social Security card can be found on-line, or at your local SS office.

Internal Revenue Service: The IRS uses your Social Security number as the primary means of identifying you, so any dealings with them must use the name associated with it. After your change your name with Social Security, the next time you file your taxes use your new name and put "formerly known as" (or FKA) your old name . Attach a copy of your name change certificate for good measure. The IRS doesn't care about your gender, but they can be suspicious about name changes.

---

[64] Dallas Denny, MA, *Identity Management in Transsexualism*, Creative Design Services, 1994

Selective Service: There's a great deal of confusion about whether transmen have to register for the draft or not. That's because the answer is yes and no. The law requires that anyone assigned male at birth register with the Selective Service within 30 days of their 18th birthday. Those assigned female at birth are exempt. If you are between the ages of 18 and 26, have transitioned completely and have changed the gender status on federal documents such as Social Security card and passport, you can and probably should register. If you apply for student financial aid or other government benefits and your gender comes up male and you have not registered you will have to prove that you are exempt. The best way to prove that is a birth certificate that still lists you as female. Transwomen should register as well, unless you can change the gender marker on your birth certificate and federal IDs before you turn 18. The draft hasn't been used since the Vietnam War, and you wouldn't be expected to serve, so there's little risk of actually being called for military duty.

Insurance and Medical Records: This is another area full of Catch-22s. There is a discussion currently on the WPATH list-serve about the problems with gender markers in electronic medical records. Insurance and medical records presently cannot accommodate female-bodied men or male-bodied women. Changing your gender marker on your insurance forms or medical records can end up with unintended consequences. There are certain medications and procedures that are covered by insurance (or not) depending on whether you are listed as male or female. Some doctor's offices manage this by switching the gender marker back and forth for different medications or procedures, but not all places can be that flexible and accommodating. Since insurance companies look for any reason to deny claims, you may have to either do battle with them over denials or pay out-of-pocket.

Criminal Justice System: From all reports, there is no justice for transgender people in the criminal justice system. Jails and prisons are sex-segregated, based on birth sex, and will use the name assigned at birth.[65] They often refuse hormone treatment and "inappropriate" toiletries. There

---

[65] "Rights of Transgender Prisoners", National Center for Lesbian Rights 6/2006 at: www.nclrights.org

is a recent ruling by a Federal court stating that withholding hormone treatment is unconstitutional, but it may take a while before the issue is settled.[66] There is no crueler environment than a men's prison, especially for a transsexual. Transwomen are subject to physical and sexual abuse by other inmates and even guards. Whatever you do to earn a living and survive, stay out of trouble!

Passport: And now for the good news! Here is a recent announcement from the State Department:

Office of the Spokesman Washington, DC June 9, 2010

The U.S. Department of State is pleased to use the occasion of Lesbian, Gay, Bisexual, Transgender Pride Month to announce its new policy guidelines regarding gender change in passports and Consular Reports of Birth Abroad.

Beginning June 10, when a passport applicant presents a certification from an attending medical physician that the applicant has undergone appropriate clinical treatment for gender transition, the passport will reflect the new gender. The guidelines include detailed information about what information the certification must include. It is also possible to obtain a limited-validity passport if the physician's statement shows the applicant is in the process of gender transition. No additional medical records are required. Sexual reassignment surgery is no longer a prerequisite for passport issuance. A Consular Report of Birth Abroad can also be amended with the new gender.

As with all passport applicants, passport issuing officers at embassies and consulates abroad and domestic passport agencies and

---

[66] "Federal Court Upholds Transgender People's Right to Access Medical Treatment in Prison", at: www.aclu.org/lgbt-rights/federal-court-upholds-transgender-peoples-right-access-medical-treatment-prison

centers will only ask appropriate questions to obtain information necessary to determine citizenship and identity.

The new policy and procedures are based on standards and recommendations of the World Professional Association for Transgender Health (WPATH), recognized by the American Medical Association as the authority in this field.[67]

Not everyone needs a passport, of course, but consider getting one even if you don't have foreign travel plans. You can use it if you travel by air domestically as well, and avoid some airport security hassles. Just ask your physician to write a letter that meets the criteria listed in the State Department's regulations and take it to your nearest passport agency (usually your local Post Office) along with your other identity documents and passport size photos. Smile for the camera!

It takes a lot of time and energy, and often patience and persistence, to change your identity documents. It is important to do so, however, to the extent possible in your state. No one wants to get funny looks every time they have to show their license. It can get tricky applying for a job and then having to show them a driver's license with a gender marker that doesn't match your name and/or appearance.

On the other hand, if you can't change your gender marker on your license, it's not the end of the world. Most people don't look at it closely enough to notice the discrepancy, or if they do they'll assume it's a mistake. If your name matches your appearance, they'll take you at face value.

What should be clear from all of this is that it's just not possible to erase your assigned name and gender. In this age of electronic information, your old name and gender will always be out there somewhere. Be prepared to live your new life as a transman or transwoman, with the possibility that employers, medical personnel, police officers and various officials can find your original identity.

---

[67] http://www.state.gov/r/pa/prs/ps/2010/06/142922.htm

It's also a good idea to ask your therapist for a 'carry letter' or 'letter of passage' that can be used if you are stopped by police looking very different from your driver's license photo. This is a letter that states that you are under the care of a health professional for "Gender Identity Disorder", and are required to dress as a woman/man as part of your treatment. I know, the language is obnoxious, but it's effective. I end my letter with "I trust that you will treat (name) with the same courtesy and respect you would offer any other man or woman." This is meant to appeal to the police officer's professionalism, at least. Clients have reported being stopped by a police officer *en femme* on the way to support group meetings, with and without such letters. In both cases they were treated professionally, without so much as a raised eyebrow. (What was said later at the police station is anyone's guess.) Courteous treatment is not always the case, unfortunately. Be prepared to respectfully explain the difference in your presentation, no matter how rude the officer might be.

Resources and References

Dallas Denny, MA, *Identity Management in Transsexualism,* Creative Design Services, 1994

Spencer Bergstedt, Esq, *Translegalities: A Legal Guide for FTMs*, and *Translegalities: A Legal Guide for MTFs.* Bergstedt 1997

National Center for Transgender Equality: www.transequality.org

Transgender Legal Issues:
        www.glad.org/uploads/docs/publications/ trans-legal-issues.pdf

Transgender Law Center: www.transgenderlawcenter.org

Androgynous names

Aaron/Erin, Abbie, Addison, Ainsley, Andy/Andi, Alex, Andre(e), Ashton, Aubrey, Avery , Bailey

Cameron, Campbell, Carmen, Carson, Cary/Kerry, Casey, Chris, Clare, Cy, Corey

Dakota, Dale, Darrel/Darryl, Dana, Darrin, Devin, Diamond, Drew Dylan

Evan , Fern, Francis/Frances, Fran, Frankie

Gale, Gene/Jean, Georgie, Gerry, Hayden, Harper, Hunter

Jackie, Jamie, Jan, Jayne, Jesse/Jessie, Jo/Joe, Jordan, Jude, Jules, Jaiden/Jayden, Justice

Kai, Kelly, Kerry/Carrie, Kendall, Kennedy, Kim, Kit

Lane, Lauren/Lorne, Laurie, Lee/Leigh, Leslie, Lindsey, Logan, Lou, Lynn

Mackenzie, Madison, March, Marion, Martie/Marty, Mel (Melissa or Melvin), Michelle/ Michel, Meredith, Michael, Micah, Mo, Morgan

Nat (Natalie/Nathan/Nathaniel), Nikki/Nicky, Noel/le

 Parker, Pat, Perry, Peyton, Piper, Quinn

Rene(e), Robin/Robyn, Reagan, Reese, Riley, Rowan, Ryan

Sam, Sandy, Sasha, Sean/Shawn/Shaun/Sian, Shane, Stacy, St. Clair (pronounced Sinclair), Stevie, Sydney

Taylor, Terry, Tony/Toni, Tracy, Tristan, Vic

Chapter Eighteen

OJT: On the Job Transitions

So many of our dreams at first seem impossible, then they seem improbable, and then when we summon the will, they soon become inevitable.

Christopher Reeve

In the last chapter I mentioned that some transpeople I know choose to live part-time in their new gender role. They lead two separate lives. Monday morning they put on their work clothes and name tag and their male or female persona for their 40+ hours of work. No one at work knows who they are the rest of the time. This works as long as there are no obvious signs of hormonal changes. Some choose to stay on low levels of hormones, or to delay hormones altogether. They do this often out of a strong sense of commitment to their family and/or their career. It is not an easy or comfortable solution, but it can work for a period of time.

There are others I know who have already completed their transition and changed all of their identity documents, including their resumes and school transcripts. They may have completed their transition during school, and/or moved to a new community. They are now living "stealth";

only their family and a few friends know their former identity. They have learned how to fudge their personal history in conversations, being careful to avoid references to gender-related activities. They will disclose their former gender identify on a need-to-know basis, but consider that most people don't need to know. Reasons for going stealth are varied, and will be discussed more in Chapter 20.

If you are early in your transition or post-transition you have that choice. There are risks and benefits to coming out as transgender at your workplace to consider. The benefits include:

> Being able to be more open and authentic. The value of being able to be yourself 24/7 is often underestimated until you experience it. Being "out and proud" builds confidence and self-esteem.

> Reducing the stress and anxiety of having to hide your "other" identity. I've seen clients become almost housebound out of fear that someone they know from work will see them out and about when they are dressed as themselves. If you live in the town where you work, you'd have to go several towns away just to do your grocery shopping.

> Having closer relationships with co-workers, because you don't have to watch what you say all the time. One of the things that often isolates gays and lesbians who hide their sexual orientation is trying to answer simple questions such as "What did you do on vacation" without referencing the gender of their partner.

> Being more productive at work because of the reduced stress, higher self-esteem, and better relationships with co-workers. A recent study reports that out LGBT workers have higher rates of promotion that those who are closeted.[68]

---

[68] Sylvia Ann Hewlett and Karen Sumberg, "For LGBT Workers, Being "Out" Brings Advantages", Harvard Business Review, July–August 2011

> Not having to stay quiet when people make homophobic or transphobic jokes or comments. Several of my clients are especially frustrated by this; they know that once they come out they'll be able to say something about it, but they don't dare now. Some feel pressured to participate in sexist and homophobic conversations.

> Being able to have a positive impact on people's understanding of transgender issues. It isn't fair, but everyone who comes out as gay or transgender becomes an ambassador for the LGBT community. You are in a position to educate people and open their minds to diversity. How you interact with others at work (and elsewhere) can create a favorable impression that overrides ignorance and prejudice. Coming out at work paves the way for those who follow behind you.

> Being able to be a role model for others. I remember a client who knew that there was someone else where she worked who was struggling with her gender identity, but she didn't feel she could say anything to her out of fear of outing herself. Once you come out and transition successfully at work others can look to you for guidance.

There are risks associated with coming out at work. Ignorance, sexual prejudice and transphobia are still prevalent in many parts of the country. Not everyone understands, or wants to understand, the transgender experience. Coworkers may be shocked, confused, or even hostile, especially at first. Your relationships with people at work will change as you transition. You can expect to see some amount of microaggression (described in Chapter 15). You will need a thick skin and a sense of humor to cope with some of the comments and looks, and especially the silence, when you enter a room.

The greatest fear, of course, is losing your job. There are some states and municipalities that explicitly prohibit discrimination based on gender identity or expression, but there is no federal anti-discrimination law at this time. Religious organizations and small companies are often exempt from local employment statutes. And if a company wants to get rid of you, they can usually find a way. You may find yourself written up for behavior that was acceptable before, or given assignments that set you up to fail, or have your hours decreased, or you end up in the next round of layoffs. A quarter of the transgender people in one survey reported losing a job because of their gender identity.[69]

I've seen only a few instances of outright transgender discrimination; one was by an exempt religious organization. I have seen a handful of people lose their jobs after coming out at work, ostensibly for other reasons. Some of them made errors in judgment that led to their dismissal. Most of my clients, however, have been quite surprised at the positive responses to their transition plans at work. After putting off coming out at work for fear of getting fired, many were blown away by the support they received from their employers and coworkers.

Unfortunately, there's no sure way of predicting how your employer or coworkers will respond. The good news is that the number of companies that have explicit diversity-friendly policies is growing steadily. The Human Rights Campaign maintains a Corporate Equality Index, measuring LGBT-friendly policies and practices in major companies. [70] The vast majority of Fortune 500 companies and many law firms and academic institutions are represented on their list. Hospitals, medical practices and social service agencies are also more likely to be LGBT-friendly. Many companies now strive to achieve a 100 percent rating on the Corporate Equality Index. Enlightened companies realize that it's good business to attract and maintain the best workforce possible.

---

[69] Jaime M Grant, Lisa A. Mottet, Justin Tanis, Jack Harrison, Jody L. Herman, and Mara Keisling. *Injustice at Every Turn: A Report of the National Transgender Discrimination Survey*. Washington: National Center for Transgender Equality and National Gay and Lesbian Task Force, 2011.
[70] The Human Rights Campaign, "Corporate Equality Index: Rating American Workplaces on Lesbian, Gay, Bisexual and Transgender Equality", 2011. (http://www.hrc.org/cei2011/index.html)

If you work for one of the companies, firms, or academic institutions on the list, there should already be a transition policy in place. At the very least, Human Resources will have some familiarity with the issues involved. Go to them as soon as you feel ready to initiate coming out at work, but certainly before people notice major changes. Work with them to draw up a transition plan - who to tell, when and how, when to begin coming in "dressed", etc. These companies also often have an Employee Resource Group or Diversity Committee. They will be your biggest allies during your on-the-job transition.

Most of you, however, will be in the position of not knowing how your employer will respond to your gender change. There is no way to guarantee a positive reception to your news, but in my experience there are some things you can do ahead of time to maximize their acceptance.

> Be a "Boy Scout" at work. Remember the boy scout motto? It's a pledge to be Trustworthy, Loyal, Helpful, Friendly, Courteous, Kind, Obedient, Cheerful, Thrifty, Brave, Clean, and Reverent. It's hard to be cheerful and outgoing when you can't be yourself, or are afraid of showing your true self, but keeping to yourself at work can work against you. Let yourself be likeable!

> Do not, however, come out to co-workers before management, even to the ones who seem open or curious about any changes you're going through. You just never know when someone could use that against you. Loyalties shift easily in work relationships. If you are promoted over someone who holds your secret they could out you before you're ready.

> Stay out of trouble! Come to work on time, don't argue with your boss or co-workers, and do what's asked of you. Do what you can to get good performance reviews, with no black marks on your record. Don't give management any excuses to let you go. I've seen

several clients sabotage themselves at work, perhaps assuming that they're going to get fired. It becomes a self-fulfilling prophecy.

➤ Become as indispensable as possible. Take on a job that no one else can do, get specialized training, do favors for your boss or co-workers. Limit any job-hopping for advancement; seniority and being a long-time employee may be your saving grace.

Your objective is to build up what I call "social capital". The more people like you and value your work, the more likely they are to respect your decision to come out and transition on the job.

When?

The first question clients usually have about coming out at work is usually "When is a good time?" That will of course vary with your situation, but there are a few things to consider:

➤ Go as far along in your physical changes as you can. For one thing, it helps people adjust to your changes in appearance gradually. And if you lose your job, you'll be able to look for another one as your new identity. You may have to hide some of the physical changes for a period of time.

➤ Consider the seasons or cycles at work and pick a time when it's least busy. Tell your accounting firm after April 15, for example. If you pick a date or even have a meeting scheduled and there's a crisis at work, delay it until the crisis is resolved. You don't want to become yet another problem.

➤ Give your employer time to prepare for your on-the-job transition. Your gender change at work is best done at the same time as your name change, so tell your boss or HR representative 6 - 8 weeks before then.

> That said, if you suspect that someone has outed you, or is about to, go to management or Human Resources immediately. It's far better for them to hear it from you.

Who?

The next question is usually "Who do I tell first?" If you have an actual Human Resources Department (more than someone who sets up your benefits every year), that is the first place to start. If not, it all depends on the size of your company and how much the owner is involved. In most places, it's best to go to the top first. If you work in a small place that's part of a larger organization you may want to start with your local manager. If your immediate supervisor is your mentor and can be an advocate for you, you should probably start there. Sometime it's better to set up a meeting with the owner or top manager, someone from HR, and your immediate supervisor. Take a look at your organization and figure out who the key players are. In any case, management should be informed before you let the word out among your coworkers. Above all, respect the chain of command.

How?

The next question is "How do I tell him/her/them?" Here is the sequence of steps to take::

1) Be prepared! Research different transition policies and procedures developed by other companies (Available from the Human Rights Campaign at www.hrc.org). Find out if your state or municipality has any laws that protect you from discrimination. Print out Transgender 101 or FAQs for anyone you suspect doesn't know much about the issues. Put together a packet with everything they need to know. Most companies want to abide by the law and/or standards in the industry and will welcome the information you provide.

2) Set up a private meeting, after hours if necessary, with enough time to answer questions. A minimum of an hour is suggested. If you have support from a diversity group one of their representatives may be able to come with you. If you've already talked to Human Resources, they should set up the meeting with your superiors and be there with you.

3) Write out your coming out letter. This helps you prepare what you're going to say, and gives you something to leave with them. Keep it short and sweet! Give a brief history of your gender issues (without too much personal information), where you are in your transition, and what you'd like to accomplish. Present coming out at work as simple and straightforward. Tell them about resources available on-line or in your community for managing the transition. A letter from your therapist may be helpful as well.

4) In your letter and in person, emphasize how much you value your job, and mention how hard you've been working to maintain a high level of performance throughout your transition. Reassure them that you intend to keep up your work performance and keep any personal problems out of the workplace. Be understanding about their concerns, and let them know you want to help make this as smooth as possible for everyone involved. Be flexible about the timing of your transition, but definite about your desire to do so at your current job.

5) Address your employer's concerns. One of the most common ones is about mode of dress. If you are transitioning from male to female, people have some pretty bizarre ideas about what you're going to look like when you transition. Reassure them that you are not going to come to work in a short skirt and fishnet stockings! (Unless of course you work at a seaside bar.) Take note of what

others in your work position wear, and be prepared to dress accordingly.

One of the first issues raised will be which bathroom you'll be using once you transition. You have every right to use the bathroom appropriate to your gender presentation. If you have been doing this without problem when you're out and about, tell them so. But also let them know that you are flexible, and can give people at work time to adjust. Be willing to consider using a single-stall or gender-neutral bathroom, if available, for a specified period of time. A federal court has ruled that employers may let a transgender employee use the bathroom that matches their gender presentation without violating other coworkers' rights. If another employee complains, the company should provide the one who complains with alternatives.[71] OSHA regulations state that employers must provide toilet facilities and may not restrict an employee's use of them. [72]

Then what?

Once you have come out to management they or you can either designate one person or set up a team to work with you on transitioning at work. The next step is to formulate a Transition Plan. This should include:

A Transition Timetable: There are typical steps involved in transitioning at work - notifying managers, then coworkers, then picking a date to change your name and return as your new identity. It is suggested that there be at least a week and no more than a month between coming out to your work group and starting your new gender role.

How coworkers will be informed. Some organizations will want to hold a meeting with your work group without you, so that they can answer questions and address coworkers' concerns. It is best in a large organization

---

[71] United States Court of Appeals, Eighth Circuit, CRUZAN v. SPECIAL SCHOOL DISTRICT, June 20, 2002
[72] United States Department of Labor, Occupational Safety & Health Administration Memorandum, April 6, 1998

for the word to come from the top. A manager or department head should call the meeting, and cover the company's policy, your rights and theirs, and what's expected of them. They should be told that when you come to work in your new role they are to use your new name and the appropriate pronouns.

If your employer really wants to be supportive, it's helpful to have your therapist or someone from the outside present a Transgender 101 training. PFLAG and local trans groups may be able to help with this.

Some places, however, will leave all that up to you. One transwoman I know wrote a very sincere, straightforward and humorous e-mail to everyone in the company while she was out changing her name. One transman simply told people as he encountered them at the different work sites he visited. Others have told key coworkers, knowing that the news would spread from them quickly enough.

How and when your name will be changed on your paycheck, ID, name tags, email address, health insurance, and any other places your name appears. It will most likely take time to straighten this out, but the goal is to have as much changed by your new start date as possible. That's another reason that people often take a few days off between the announcement and their return date.

What, if any, accommodations are needed. If you are transitioning from male to female in a physically-demanding job, for example, you may have to set some limits on how much you can lift. Uniforms may need to be altered. You or your employer may want to shift you to a less public position while your voice changes and beard grows.

Any leave requests for surgery. Try to be flexible about this, and not ask for time off during their busy season. If you don't have enough earned time available, you may have to file for FMLA (Family Medical Leave Act). Discuss any temporary accommodations that you may need following surgery, and if it's possible to return part-time until you are able to handle your full workload.

And then?

Once you have a transition plan in place, preferably in writing, do your part to keep it running smoothly. Maintain your exemplary job performance and keep your plans under wraps until the announcement. Think about your wardrobe changes - skirts or slacks, tie or no tie? Schedule your name change, if you haven't already. And then prepare yourself for the day when you get to walk in as yourself. This will be one of the most terrifying and exhilarating events of your transition. It can also seem anticlimactic when it happens.

If management has been supportive that day will be like any other day in most respects. Do not expect a lot of comments at first. Coworkers may be hesitant around you, afraid of doing or saying the wrong thing. Let them know that you're willing to answer questions (within limits). Show them that you're still the same person, still like the same music and food and jokes, etc. Having a sense of humor and being open will help put them at ease.

Vanessa Sheridan writes about the importance of setting the tone through your own attitude about your transition. "By behaving in a dignified yet personable and friendly manner, as though you assume your transgender situation is normal (which it is, at least for you), you also silently demand and serve notice that you expect to be treated respectfully by others."[73] Show your pride and self-respect and others will mirror that back.

Be very sensitive, however, to other people's boundaries and limits, as well as your own. Do not give out more information than is asked for or more than you're comfortable disclosing. What's under your clothes is no one else's business. If someone asks "Are those (your breasts) real?", for example, you can just say "A real woman doesn't answer that!" There may be questions about your sexual orientation; answer those only if you're comfortable doing so. Above all, remember what's appropriate at work.

---

[73] Vanessa Sheridan, *The Complete Guide to Transgender in the Workplace*, Praeger, 2009, p.89

Showing off your chest scars or new bra or hidden tattoo is never acceptable.

One of the mistakes I've seen clients make is assuming that they were automatically "one of the guys" or "one of the girls" now. That takes time to earn. Behavior that should be appropriate for your new gender role may not go over well yet. Being too friendly with other women, for example, can get you into trouble at work if they still see you as a man. Transmen can expect some sort of hazing or test of their masculinity before being accepted.

Your transition plan, and your transition, will be unique to you and your work place. Even if all does not go as planned (and what event ever does?) chances are you will have a positive experience. If you have the support of management and encounter problems with co-workers, be sure to bring those to their attention. Other people are entitled to their own beliefs and opinions, but disrespectful behavior should not be tolerated. You and they are there to do your jobs, not act out their own agenda. Any verbal or physical harassment should be reported immediately. If management is not responsive, consider filing a grievance through your union or other regulatory board.

In this uncertain economic climate, with so many people being laid off, clients are often hesitant to take a leap of faith and transition. Here is a story of how it worked out for one of my clients (in his own words):

> After years of introspection coming to understand myself as transgender, and months of counseling coming to understand that I need to be recognized as male in order to live an authentic life, I began a medical transition. I was undecided about hormone therapy but my breasts had always made me extremely embarrassed so in December of 2010, I scheduled what was for me scary and expensive chest surgery. A month later, I found myself in my supervisor's office being told that the non-profit agency where I had worked very happily for eleven years had just lost an important contract. I, along with thirteen others, would be permanently laid off in June.

For the next six months I rode a rollercoaster of emotion where on a random Friday I would be confident that I had such a good professional reputation no one would care about my emerging trans status, and then on the next random Wednesday I would be convinced that no one would ever hire me again. To make a long story short, I decided not to cancel the surgery; it had taken me too long to find the courage to schedule it, and from a practical viewpoint, what better time to use a stockpile of sick leave than when you have limited time to use it! March 17th came fast and the surgery went incredibly well. After three weeks of recovery, I went back to work and also started job searching.

As soon as I began sending out resumés, it occurred to me that I would need to make a fairly quick decision about how to present myself. In fact, this decision felt all-consuming . An employer could call any day and I hadn't decided whether to present myself as a boyish lesbian, which was incorrect but was generally how I thought people perceived me. Or, should I take the "clean slate" approach and present as male, which seemed exciting but risky as I feared I would look like a woman in a tie and be off-putting to interviewers meeting me for the first time. With the help of my therapist, an encouraging partner, supportive friends and co-workers, and some inspirational books, I realized that the only direction to go was forward. In a whirlwind (or at least in a style much faster than my usual deliberation), I started taking testosterone, asked people to switch pronouns, changed all of my legal documents to male, and bought a new interview suit.

As I write this, I have been at my new job for about two months. Here's what happened.

In May, a colleague from another office told me about an opening where she worked. She mentioned that the supervisor of this position was a woman I had worked with before. It happened to be someone I liked who I thought liked me, and someone I remembered as quite open-minded. My application materials made it through the screening of the HR department, which meant that I would interview with the woman I knew. When she called to schedule the interview, I wanted to let her know to expect my appearance to be different than she may have remembered. I said something like, "Did you hear that I changed my name...and my gender?" (She had.) "I just didn't want you to be surprised when I show up in a suit and tie." She thanked me for being candid and trusting her with personal information. Most importantly, she assured me that this would not be an issue. Her positive response enabled me to interview with confidence because I knew that at least she would not be confused by my appearance. I was able to answer the questions as calmly as possible without worrying (too much) that my voice was giving away a secret...because there was no secret to give away. I was not a woman. I was not trying to "pass" as a man. I was a transman and it was okay.

So far, my experience in my new position has been more validating than I could have imagined. My chest is flat but my backside is still wider than a typical guy's. My facial features are androgynous but I still don't have one lick of facial hair. Still, most of the time, people get the pronouns right. Sometimes female coworkers even refer to me as "new guy" or dare I say, flirt a little bit. And occasionally on a random day standing at the copy machine, something like this happens:

Coworker: "If my husband's 1965 Corvette and I were both rolling off a cliff, he would save the car first."

Me: "Well, they've been together longer, right?"

Coworker: "That's exactly what my husband said! *Not to lump all you guys together*, but that's just what he said...geesh."

I'm pretty sure I have never smiled that much at a copy machine.

References and Resources

Vanessa Sheridan, *The Complete Guide to Transgender in the Workplace*, Praeger, 2009

Janis Walworth, *Transsexual Workers: An Employer's Guide*, Center for Gender Sanity, 1998

Workplace Gender Transition Guidelines For Transgender Employees, Managers and Human Resource Professionals, the Human Rights Campaign Foundation, 2006

Transgender at Work: www.tgender.net/taw

LGB *and* T: Transgender at Chevron, Chevron, 2005-2008, at: https://www.hrc.org/documents/workplace-Chevron_Corp-Transition_Guidelines-Rev_2008.pdf

The Center for Gender Sanity: www.gendersanity.com

Jillian T. Weiss J.D., Ph.D, *Transgender Workplace Diversity*, BookSurge Publishing, 2007

Chapter Nineteen

The Final Ordeal:
Gender Realignment Surgery

Even while you strive to improve your life, part of you is whole, well,
and perfect right where you stand.

Alan Cohen

In every hero's journey, there is a final ordeal - a battle or task that transforms the hero forever. For a transsexual, that ultimate task is typically gender reassignment surgery (GRS). This usually refers to genital reconstruction surgery, reflecting the cultural norm of defining sex (gender) by the shape of one's genitals. Once referred to as "sex reassignment surgery" or a "sex change", the preferred term now is gender reassignment surgery. I prefer the word "realignment" - surgery that puts mind and body back in alignment.

The first complete male-to-female sex reassignment surgeries were performed in Germany in the early 1930s. Dr. Magnus Hirschfeld, a pioneer of transsexualism, began working with surgeons in the 1920s to develop the procedures. The first surgeries were crude at best, consisting of castration, penectomy and then construction of an artificial vagina. Progress was halted by the Nazi raid on Dr. Hirschfeld's Institute, but medical advances in World War II made refinements to the procedures possible. The introduction of Premarin in 1941 made hormone therapy for male-to-female transsexuals possible.

Transsexualism came to the United States officially in 1952, when Christine Jorgensen returned from Copenhagen after her SRS. Dr. Harry Benjamin began treating transsexuals with hormone therapy in the 1950s, and SRS clinics opened in Europe and Mexico. In 1956, in Casablanca, Morocco, a surgeon named Georges Burou, working on his own, developed the penile inversion form of vaginoplasty. Surgeons in the United States, however, were reluctant to perform SRS, fearing criminal or civil complaints against them. The first reported SRS performed in the United States was at the University of California in Los Angeles in 1958.

Also in 1958 the first complete phalloplasty for sex reassignment was performed in Russia. The technique had been developed primarily for amputees during WWII. The first attempt at female-to-male SRS was in 1949. This was performed by Sir Harold Gillies, who played a pioneering wartime role in Britain developing pedicle flap surgery. Gillies also performed surgery on the United Kingdom's first male-to-female transsexual in 1951.

SRS took hold in the United States in large part due to the efforts of Reed Erickson, a wealthy female-to-male transsexual. He founded the Erickson Educational Foundation and generously supported the treatment of transsexualism. In the mid-1960s Johns Hopkins University opened the first Gender Identity Clinic, followed by Stanford University, UCLA, Northwestern University, the University of Minnesota, and dozens of others. Dr. Stanley Biber, working from the Johns Hopkins team's drawings, became the first private physician to offer SRS, starting in Trinidad Colorado in 1969.

During the 1970s, however, the university clinics began to fold, under pressure from psychiatry and from both feminist and conservative groups. The Harry Benjamin International Gender Dysphoria Association was formed in 1979 to bring together all health and mental health practitioners who treated transsexuals. In 1980 they published the famous Standards of Care. Also in 1980, the American Psychiatric Association listed transsexualism as a psychological disorder in the DSM-III. (This was later changed to Gender Identity Disorder in the DSM-IV.)[74]

Since then, a growing number of surgeons here and abroad have refined the techniques for both vaginoplasty and phalloplasty, as well as other procedures for transgender men and women. It's amazing what can be done, along with hormone therapy, to physically transform a person into their opposite-gender "twin". (If you have any doubt, check out the web sites called Transsexual Women's Successes and Successful TransMen.)[75] These surgeries are expensive, however, and can only do so much. The decision to pursue GRS needs to be explored thoroughly.

The reasons for having GRS may seem obvious. It does give a sense of completion to the process of transitioning from one gender to the other. It can correct what feels wrong or incomplete about the body you were born into. It qualifies you in all states for a change of legal gender status. It gives you some status in the LGBTQ community as a post-op transsexual. Genital reconstruction surgery can allow you to experience sexuality in a way that fits more closely with your true gender. For some transmen chest reconstruction surgery is essential in order to pass. Facial surgery can help you look more attractive as well as more feminine (or more masculine).

But GRS is not a cure-all. It will not solve all your emotional, social or sexual problems. Are you seeing surgery as the way to become a "real" man or woman? Gender reassignment surgery does not make you into a man or a woman. It can only finish the process of realigning your body with your

---

[74]"A Brief History of Transsexuality" at: http://www.cinematter.com/tshistory.html
[75] http://ai.eecs.umich.edu/people/conway/TSsuccesses/TransMen.html and http://ai.eecs.umich.edu/people/conway/TSsuccesses/TSsuccesses.html

gender identity. Are you thinking that once you have surgery then you'll be a desirable man or woman and can find a partner? There's certainly no guarantee of that. Are you hoping that the right surgery will give you the sexual experience you've been longing for? There's unfortunately no guarantee there either. Are you hoping that facial surgery or body contouring will transform you into a beautiful woman or totally handsome dude? Or that it will give you instant confidence? Attractiveness and confidence have to come from within. I have seen some radiant transwomen who are very attractive in person, but objectively, in a photo, they're far from gorgeous. And I've seen transmen whose confidence creates a masculine presence far taller than their body frame. I've also seen transwomen with all the right clothes and facial surgery who are so awkward and ungraceful that they stand out like a sore thumb.

It's important to know your goals and how GRS would help you achieve them. A. J. Simpson and Joshua Mira Goldberg list eight questions to ask yourself before you decide on surgery.[76]

1. Do you have a clear mental picture of what you want to look like after SRS? How do you think you might feel if the results don't match that mental picture?

2. Are you hoping SRS will fix anything, and if so, what?

3. What parts of your life might change after SRS? What do you hope might change, and what do you fear might change?

4. Do you think your hopes for SRS are realistic? How can you tell if they are or not?

5. How much do you know about the options for SRS? What more do you need to know to be able to make a fully informed decision?

---

[76] A. J. Simpson and Joshua Mira Goldberg, *Surgery: A Guide for MTFs*, Vancouver Coastal Health, Transcend Transgender Support & Education Society and Canadian Rainbow Health Coalition, February 2006

6. Are the parts of your body that will be changed by SRS connected to your sexuality? What will happen if you lose that part of your sexuality?

7. Who else in your life will be affected by your decision? How do you think they will feel about you having SRS? How will their reactions impact you?

8. What do you think is a "wrong reason" to have SRS? What do you think are the "right reasons"?

Many of my clients will never be able to afford surgery, and others have decided it's just not necessary or important. That doesn't stop them from living successful lives as transgender men and women. Some are out and obvious, some are not. Some have chosen to preserve some male sexual functioning or parts of their female anatomy for their partner's sake. They are able to be the man or woman they *have always been inside* without surgery. For others, some surgery feels absolutely necessary. There are transwomen who see breast augmentation as more important than genital reconstruction, and certainly plenty of transmen for whom chest reconstruction is essential. The point is that they have all examined their options and their resources and decided for themselves what is important and what is not. They, and you, don't have to accept one road map as the only way to go.

Your decision about gender realignment surgery will be based on the results you wish to achieve and the resources you have available. It is important to do your own research, and not just follow what someone else you know did. Your body is unique to you, and your results will be different from everyone else's. Start your search by defining your geographic region. Some people have no problem going halfway across the country, or even to another country, to find the surgery they want at the best price. Others prefer to stay close to home. Either way, consider your support system and how far they're willing or able to travel.

Within that region, check out *all* the surgeons who perform the type of surgery you want. There are several web sites that list surgeons by region. Do a background check for each one, and check some of the sites listed at the end of the chapter for reviews. Talk to others who've been there if you can. Don't rely completely on before and after pictures posted on-line; no one publicizes the less-than-stellar results. Read the surgeon's requirements for surgery, to make sure you're a good candidate.

Once you have narrowed your search to a few you'd be comfortable with, consider the cost of the surgery plus any related expenses (travel and lodging, time out of work, etc.). Your top choice might not be financially feasible, but your second or third choice may be just as adequate. Then you're ready to contact the surgeons directly to find out more about their requirements, how far out they're scheduling, etc. Don't be shy about asking questions. Email is usually the best way to reach a surgeon, but be patient; surgeons are busy! Once you have your initial questions answered, call or make an appointment for a consultation. There is no substitute for that consultation. The surgeon needs to know exactly what he or she will be working with, and you need to know if you're comfortable with what he or she recommends. [77]

When you have all the information, sit down with your therapist and/or partner and review your options. The Standards of Care have different requirements for different types of surgery, but your therapist will need to know that you have done your homework and are making a truly informed decision for any surgery. Here is a summary of the requirements for surgery:

Criteria for breast or chest surgery: One letter of referral from a qualified mental health professional is required for breast augmentation or chest reconstruction. The following must be documented:

- persistent gender dysphoria,

---

[77] "How to Choose a Surgeon for GRS" (http://gay-lesbian.helium.com/how-to/8551-how-to-choose-a-surgeon-for-grs)

- capacity for fully informed consent,
- age of majority, and
- adequate control of any medical or mental health issues.

Hormone therapy is not a prerequisite for breast/chest surgery. It is recommended, however, that MtF patients have at least one year of feminizing hormone therapy, for best results.

Criteria for hysterectomy/ovariectomy in FtM patients and orchiectomy in MtF patients. Two letters of referral from qualified mental health professionals are required - one from a treating MHP and another from a consulting MHP. These must document:

- persistent gender dysphoria,
- capacity for fully informed consent,
- age of majority,
- adequate control of any medical or mental health issues, and
- 12 months of hormone therapy (unless contraindicated).

Criteria for metoidoplasty or phalloplasty in FtM patients and vaginoplasty in MtF patients. Two letters of referral from qualified mental health professionals are required - one from a treating MHP and another from a consulting MHP. These must document:

- persistent gender dysphoria,
- capacity for fully informed consent,
- age of majority,
- adequate control of any medical or mental health issues,
- 12 months of hormone therapy (unless contraindicated), and
- 12 months of living in the gender role consistent with their gender identity.

It is not an absolute requirement, but it is recommended that patients have ongoing counseling with a qualified mental health professional. Patients with severe psychiatric issues must be stabilized with psychotherapy and/or medication before referral for surgery, and reassessed prior to surgery.

I will review here the surgeries most commonly sought by trans men and women. You will find more details about specific procedures on the websites for the surgeons listed at the end of the chapter.

Surgeries for the Female-to-Male Transition

Chest surgery

One of the biggest obstacles to passing for transmen is the size of their chests. There are plenty of biological males with gynecomastia ("man boobs"), but large breasts are unmistakably female. Binding is painful, restrictive, not healthy for skin and breast tissue, and not always effective. Plus, for someone who identifies as male, breasts just don't belong there. They're a continual reminder of how "wrong" their female body is. For these reasons, chest or "top" surgery is a high priority for transmen. For many it is the only surgery they pursue. The WPATH Standards of Care recognizes this, and recommends that the same criteria for starting hormones be applied to chest surgery. Thus there is no requirement to be on hormones or live in the new gender role for a specified period of time. Most surgeons require one letter of recommendation from your primary therapist or a gender specialist.

There are two types of surgeries available for changing the size of your chest:

Reduction mammaplasty, or breast reduction: A breast reduction is the same procedure used by women whose large breasts are a problem for them. Several incisions are made in order to removes excess breast fat, glandular tissue and skin. The nipples remain attached to their blood supply and nerve endings, thus preserving sensation and reducing the risk of losing them. You can get a breast reduction down to an AA cup, which will resemble a man's chest under clothing. The advantage is that if you have large breasts that are causing back pain you may qualify for insurance coverage. The disadvantage is that it may not look like a man's chest enough to go shirtless in public. Once you have had a breast reduction, it affects your options for chest reconstruction, so it is recommended that you choose one or the other.

Chest reconstruction, or chest contouring: The goal of chest reconstruction/contouring is to create a more masculine-looking chest. There are three common methods for doing this: keyhole, peri-areolar (also called drawstring or pursestring), and double incision. Which one you'll need depends on the size and shape of your breasts.

The keyhole method is used for small breasts. The incision (and scar) runs along the bottom or the areola, and breast tissue is removed without resizing or repositioning the nipples. In the **peri-areola procedure**, the incision and scar goes around the areola, and skin as well as breast tissue is removed. This allows for some resizing and repositioning of the nipple and areola without detaching it completely from its nerve and blood supply. This method can often be used for up to B cup size breasts. The advantages of the keyhole and peri-areola methods are minimal scarring, less trauma, and better retention of sensation. The disadvantages include less than ideal nipple placement, possible puckering around the scar, possible lumpiness, and a need for revisions.

The double incision method is a bilateral mastectomy with nipple grafts. It is the only method suitable for larger or sagging breasts. Horizontal or U-shaped incisions are made across each breast, and fat and breast tissue removed. Different surgeons have different methods for resizing and repositioning the nipples and areola; some are better at maintaining sensation and minimizing risk of losing the nipples. Usually, the original nipples and areola are completely removed, trimmed to a smaller size, and are then grafted onto the chest in a higher, more aesthetically-male location. The advantage is that the result is usually a more masculine-looking chest. The disadvantage is that the scars will be more noticeable.

All of these methods require general anesthesia, but can usually be done on an outpatient basis. You will, however, have to have someone drive you home or to a motel nearby. You will probably have drainage tubes left in place and bandages that need to be checked daily. Each surgeon will have his or her own follow-up procedures. Proper after-care is extremely important, in order to reduce the chance of infection and other complications. (See the end of the chapter for a list of possible complications.) Do not expect to see the results you are looking for right away. It will take time for bruising and swelling to go down. You also need to realize that your results will be unique to you, and may not resemble the ones posted on-line. If you are not happy with your results after 6 to 8 weeks, talk to your surgeon about revisions. Many surgeons include revisions in their fee.

You will need to take time off from work or school for recovery. Full healing takes time! Depending on your physical condition and the types of surgery, it will take 6-8 weeks before you can do any heavy lifting or working out.

The cost of chest surgery varies from surgeon to surgeon. The current range for reputable surgeons is between $5000 and $10,000. Many surgeons do not have a set fee. They need to evaluate your body and physical condition in order to give you their estimate. You will either need to have an initial consultation in person or send them pictures. They will also ask for a medical history and pre-op physical. As with any surgery, you need to be healthy. It really is important to quit smoking, lose weight, and get in good physical shape before chest surgery.

Hysterectomy and Oophorectomy

Removal of your uterus (hysterectomy) and ovaries (oophorectomy) are not necessary steps for transitioning from female to male. Many transmen chose to do so, however, for a number of reasons. For some, having female organs at all is too dysphoric. For them it is traumatic to undergo pelvic exams and Pap smears. Removing the uterus and ovaries eliminates the risk of uterine, cervical or ovarian diseases. For those who choose not to start testosterone, having menstrual periods is a periodic reminder of those female organs. There are procedures and medications to stop periods, but a hysterectomy will do so for sure. Removing the ovaries not only stops menstrual cycles it also allows for a lower effective dose of testosterone. A hysterectomy and/or oophorectomy is often recommended for those who have cysts, endometriosis, abnormal bleeding or other gynecological problems, and those who are at risk for uterine, cervical, or ovarian cancer. Also, in some states a hysterectomy is required before the gender marker can be changed on a birth certificate.

A hysterectomy and/or oophorectomy can be done along with genital reconstruction surgery, or they can be done on their own, by a competent gynecologist. If you have an acceptable medical reason for a hysterectomy it might be covered by your health insurance. Some gynecologists will not perform the procedures without an acceptable medical reason, especially on a young person. Those who do will most likely require a letter from your therapist.

Hysterectomy: There are several different methods for removing the uterus. A Total Abdominal Hysterectomy (TAH), with incisions across or down the abdomen, is the most invasive. It may be necessary, however, if there are any disease conditions such as endometriosis or cancer. A Laparoscopically Assisted Vaginal Hysterectomy (LAVH) uses smaller incisions in the abdomen to insert a laparoscope (a tiny telescopic camera) and other small surgical instruments. The uterus and cervix are removed mostly thorough the vaginal canal. A Total Vaginal Hysterectomy (TVH) removes the uterus though an incision in the vagina. This procedure can only be done, however, if the vagina is wide enough and flexible enough and the uterus is free and clear. A **Total Laparoscopic Hysterectomy (TLH)** is done through small slits in the abdomen. This procedure can be done with a small or atrophied vagina, which is more likely the case for someone without a history of vaginal sexual activity, and/or after several years on testosterone.

A **Bilateral Salpingo Oophorectomy (BSO)** is usually done at the same time as a hysterectomy. Both ovaries and Fallopian tubes are removed to prevent the possibility of ovarian cancer. Hormone replacement therapy is recommended after removing the ovaries. If you are already on testosterone, your dose should be lowered.

All of these procedures require general anesthesia, a hospital stay, and 4-8 weeks of recovery time. Which one your surgeon chooses will depend on your body and medical conditions. This is not really negotiable, so don't waste your time trying to figure out which procedure you'd prefer. You should, however, discuss your options with at least two gynecologists if possible.

As with any surgery, there are risks involved. In addition to the general risk of reactions to the anesthesia, blood clots, cardiac and pulmonary problems, infection, bleeding, pain and adhesions and scarring, there are risks specific to these procedures:

- accidental damage to the bladder, rectum, or other internal organs, resulting in problems with bladder or bowel control
- bladder or urinary tract infections
- sinking of the top of the vagina (vaginal vault prolapse) which would need surgical repair
- changes in sexual sensation and/or decreased intensity of orgasm
- pain and menstrual bleeding if ovaries are removed inadequately (ovarian remnant syndrome)
- menopausal symptoms and loss of bone density if ovaries are removed without some form of hormone replacement

Genital Reconstruction Surgeries

The biggest limitation of the female to male transition is the difficulty creating a penis. At this point in time, in 2011, a fully functioning, normal-sized penis cannot be recreated. There are two procedures, however, that offer something more than testosterone alone can provide.

Metaidoioplasty (sometimes spelled metaidiopasty or metoidioplasty), or **clitoral release,** is a procedure that capitalizes on the growth of the clitoris from testosterone therapy. Hence it can only be done after a year or more on hormones, when the clitoris has grown sufficiently. The ligaments that hold it in place are cut, and some of the surrounding tissue is removed to free up the enlarged clitoris. This creates a small sexually responsive penis. A **urethral extension** and **colpectomy** (vaginal removal) or **colpocleisis** (vaginal closing) can be done at the same time. This allows you to urinate through the small penis. With the Centurion method, a scrotal sac is also formed, for **testicular implants**.

The advantage to the metaidoioplasty is that it is a less complicated (and less expensive, ranging from $2,000 to 20,000) procedure than phalloplasty, with minimal scarring. It also retains sexual responsiveness, becoming erect when excited and capable of orgasm. The disadvantage is that it will always be a small penis, not really capable of penetration. It won't fill up the bulge you want in your pants, or anyone's orifice. A metaidoioplasty can be done first, and a phalloplasty can still be done later.

Phalloplasty is a more complicated procedure. There are a variety of methods, depending on the surgeon, but basically it involves taking a flap of skin, blood vessels and nerves from one part of the body, rolling it into a tube, and attaching it right above the clitoris. In a more recent development a **pedicle flap** is released from the abdomen to create the tube. It is then sculpted to look like a penis. The vagina is closed and the urethra is lengthened to flow through the new penis. It may take more than one surgery to complete the whole procedure. After the new phallus has healed, a rod or pump can be implanted to provide erectile capabilities.

The advantage to the phalloplasty is that the result can be a natural-looking full sized penis. It can be used for vaginal penetration with the pump or rod. The disadvantage is that it will not be a fully-functioning penis. Although there is a chance of some sensation, it will not respond to stimulation, and orgasm and ejaculation are not possible.

A **scrotoplasty** (construction of a scrotum) can be done along with either of these procedures, or later. Vaginal removal or closure is done first, and the outer labia are used to create two pouches joined in the middle. Once the sacs are stable, silicone implants are inserted to resemble testicles. Sometimes the sacs are stretched first and testicular implants added later.

As you can imagine, all these surgeries are expensive. They can cost from $50,000 to $150,000, and are usually not covered by health insurance. Hospital stays range from 1 to 14 days, depending on the procedure(s), and the recovery process is lengthy and complicated. In addition to the usual complications of involved surgeries, such as reactions to the anesthesia, blood clots, cardiac and pulmonary problems, infection, bleeding, pain and adhesions and scarring, there are complications specific to each type of procedure. Revisions are often needed, and the satisfaction rates are not as high as they are for genital surgery for the male to female transition.

Cosmetic Surgery

There are other surgical procedures that transmen may wish to explore in order to have their body more closely fit their gender identity. Facial masculinization surgery can include chin implants, rhinoplasty, and other modifications. Liposuction can be used for body contouring - to bring hips and shoulders more in proportion, for example. These are available through qualified plastic surgeons, and do not generally involve letters of recommendation.

Surgeries for the Male to Female Transition

There are three main areas that male-to-female transsexuals seek to alter through surgery: their facial structure, the size of their breasts, and their genitals. These can be pursued separately or together. As mentioned before, your needs and priorities are unique to you. All surgery has risks and benefits; it's important to be realistic about both.

Facial Feminization Surgery (FFS)

Facial Feminization Surgery is available from a few qualified plastic surgeons in the United States and abroad. FFS is based on analysis of the differences between men and women's facial structures. (The same science that is used in forensics to tell the difference between a male and a female skull.) In Chapter 10 we reviewed these in reference to creating the illusion of a more feminine face with make-up. These differences are:

Men	Women
Wide high foreheads, receding hairline	Curved, contoured fore-heads, framed with hair
High and thick brows, protuding brow bones	Arching brows, no visible brow bones
Straighter noses, or curved outward	Softer, more curved noses
Low, flat and rectangular cheek bones	Curved cheek bones, fuller-looking face
Wider, larger, more muscular jaw	Narrower jaws and softer, rounder jaw line
Wider, protuding chin	Gently pointed or curved chins
Straighter, thinner and longer lips	Plump, puckered lips, more open mouth

Using these differences, FFS surgeons have developed techniques for physically modifying a male face to make it look more feminine. Douglas K. Ousterhout, a maxillofacial surgeon in San Francisco, pioneered facial feminization surgery as part of male to female surgery in the 1980s and

'90s. There is a long list of possible surgeries that can be performed for this purpose:

Forehead:

- Brow shave
- Brow lift
- Forehead implant
- Forehead reconstruction
- Scalp advancement

Chin and Jaws:

- removing bone from the back of the jaw
- reshaping the chin
- chin implants
- surgical rotation of the jaw
- liposuction under the chin

Nose (rhinoplasty):

- reducing the bone from the bridge of the nose
- reducing the width
- shortening the nose
- narrowing the nostrils

Cheek augmentation and/or implants

Lip augmentation

In addition, some transwomen have a tracheal shave (thyroid chondroplasty) to reduce the size and prominence of the laryngeal prominence (Adam's Apple).

Each FFS surgeon has his own particular techniques and style. Only a consultation with one of them can tell you what would work best for you, and what results you can expect. Dr Jeffrey Spiegel in Boston bases his recommendations on the science of facial recognition. We compare each face we see to a cognitive "template" to distinguish between a man and a woman. Some cues, such as the eyebrows, are more important than others in making that differentiation. Studies show that we have a perceptual bias towards seeing an ambiguous face as male. Thus transwomen have to work harder than transmen to be seen as their true gender. It is also interesting to note that younger-looking faces are more likely to be read as female. A general "face lift" by a competent plastic surgeon, designed to make you look younger, may be all you need to look more feminine.

Jennifer Seeley cautions against getting carried away with facial feminization surgery. She's seen transwomen do so much surgery that they look like a caricature of a woman.[78] I've seen transwomen assume that FFS will be needed before even beginning their physical transition. See how your face looks after 1-2 years on hormones, and once you have a hairstyle that flatters your face.

There are of course risks associated with facial surgery. In addition to the general risks of surgery (reactions to anesthesia, excessive bleeding, etc.) you may experience:

- numbness, pain, or problems with facial muscle control from nerve damage
- problems with implants, screws, wires: infection, reabsorption and/or misplacement
- damage to the voice from the tracheal shave
- thick, red, or obvious scars
- difficulty adjusting to the change in your appearance, or disappointment with the results

---

[78] Jennifer Seeley, *The Transgender Companion*, 2007

Breast Augmentation Surgery (Augmentation Mammaplasty)

Transwomen seek breast augmentation surgery for the same reasons as other women do - they're not happy with the size and/or shape of their breasts. Feminizing hormone therapy stimulates the growth of female-looking breasts, and most are happy with what develops. Some transwomen are unable to take hormones, however, or decide not to. Others are not happy with the results of hormone therapy. After two years of continuous hormone treatment, you've got what you're going to get for breast size. Only then should you consider breast enlargement or enhancement.

Saline vs. Silicone? Breasts can be enlarged with the use of silicone or saline implants. Small incisions are made and the desired implant is placed under the breast tissue (or, in some cases, under the muscle). A saline implant is a silicone shell filled with a sterile salt water solution. Silicone implants are filled with a silicone gel. They are reportedly softer and have a more natural feel than saline. Saline implants, however, are less expensive and require a smaller incision.

Both types of implants are considered safe by the FDA. There has been concern about silicone implants, however. If a saline implant ruptures, it drains and the solution is absorbed by the body. The breast goes flat and is noticeable right away. A silicone implant leaks slowly when ruptured, and since it is not a natural substance it is not easily absorbed by the body. There were reports in the 1990s of silicone implants causing serious health problems in some women. Although these claims were not backed up by research, the concerns were enough to halt their use in the United States in 1992. They were put back on the market in 2006, with the condition that the recipients have them checked via MRI periodically.

It is interesting to note, however, that the FDA cited "frequent complications and adverse reactions" in a recent statement.[79] And the research that claimed to disprove the association between implants and serious health risks was funded by two of the top manufacturers of implants.

---

[79] Jennifer Corbett Dooren, "FDA: Sees Frequent Complications With Silicone Breast Implants" Dow Jones Newswires, June 22, 2011

Breast implants are not guaranteed to last forever, and need to replaced or adjusted as you get older. The "life expectancy" of the silicone implants is estimated at 10 years - the longer they are in the more likely they are to rupture or leak. Between 20 and 40 percent of the women who received silicone implants in those studies had to have them removed or redone within 10 years.

The possible risks of breast augmentation and complications after breast implants include:

- Unfavorable scarring
- Bleeding (hematoma)
- Infection
- Poor healing of incisions
- Changes in nipple or breast sensation, which may be temporary or permanent
- Capsular contracture (formation of firm scar tissue around the implant)
- Implant leakage or rupture
- Wrinkling of the skin over the implant
- Anesthesia risks
- Fluid accumulation
- Blood clots
- Pain, which may persist
- Deep vein thrombosis, cardiac and pulmonary complications
- Possibility of revisional surgery

Breast augmentation, therefore, is not a decision to be made lightly. Consider the risks and benefits for you in your life. There are plenty of women with small breasts; you don't have to have large ones to look and feel like a woman. The right bra, padded if necessary, can do wonders for your figure without the expense and risk of surgery.

Finding a surgeon who will do breast augmentation on a transwoman can be a challenge as well. It is best to see a surgeon who is familiar with the unique challenges of breast augmentation in a male chest. Many plastic surgeons offer breast enhancement and reconstruction for women, but not all are trans-friendly. "Nancy" lived for years as a woman, without hormones. She decided when she retired to pursue breast augmentation. One surgeon told her flat out, "We don't do that for your kind." Another wanted to give her DDs, for an outrageous fee. She did finally find someone who was very supportive and performed successful breast enlargement at a reasonable price. To find a qualified plastic surgeon, check forums online, and ask those who have had positive results. Most of the surgeons who offer genital reconstruction do breast enhancement as well.

Genital Reconstruction Surgery for Transwomen

This is the Holy Grail for many transwomen. Modern surgical techniques can create a realistic-looking functional vagina. The basic components are vaginoplasty (creation of a vaginal vault), orchiectomy (removal of the testicles) and labiaplasty (construction of minor and major labia). There are different procedure for accomplishing this; each surgeon has his or her own techniques. Here are some brief descriptions of a few of the more popular ones:

Dr. Pierre Brassard, in Montreal, Canada, uses a one-stage penile inversion method, with a flap of the glans (the sensitive head of the penis) for the clitoris. The orchiectimy, vaginoplasty and labiaplasty are accomplished in one surgery. This results in natural-looking labia and a hooded clitoris with good sensation.

Dr. Toby Meltzer, in Scottsdale, Arizona, uses a two-stage penile inversion method. The testicles and erectile tissue of the penis are removed, and a vaginal space created below the urethra. The penile skin is used to line the new vagina, a clitoris is formed from the glans of the penis, and a small portion of scrotum is used for the labia. (If the penis is shorter than the desired depth of the vagina, skin grafts may be used.) The second stage is an optional labiaplasty, and requires a separate operation at least three months later. This involves further refinement of the labia and hooding the clitoris.

Dr. Marci Bowers, who trained with Dr. Stanely Biber in Trinidad, Colorado, is now practicing in San Mateo, California. Hers is a refined one-step procedure, but she also offers second-stage labiaplasty. She also offers further repairs/refinements from previous vaginoplasties.

Dr. Gary Alter, in Beverly Hills, California, performs vaginoplasty using portions of the rectosigmoid colon (colovaginoplasty), as well as the penile skin inversion technique. The advantage to using part of the colon is that the vagina is then self-lubricating and can be made deeper than the length of a penis. The disadvantage is that this is a more complicated procedure, with greater risk of infection.

Dr. Suporn Watanyusakul, (known as Dr. Suporn) in Thailand has developed a combined vaginoplasty/labiaplasty technique which does not use penile inversion. The clitoris and vestibule of the vagina are made from the glans penis, with sensory nerves intact. The labia are made from penile skin and scrotal skin, and the vaginal wall is made from scrotal skin and groin skin if necessary.

Each surgeon I have read about has his or her fans, and occasional dissatisfied customers. Most of them take great pride in their work, and provide excellent before and after care. They all provide excellent information on their web-sites, including their requirements for surgery. These must be followed!

Before Surgery: Many of the surgeons who perform penile inversion require or recommend hair removal from the scrotal area. If this is the area that will be used to line the vagina, you really don't want any hair growing there. Existing hair can be removed at the time of surgery, but that does not guarantee that it won't regrow. Laser and/or electrolysis will remove unwanted hair.

Every surgeon will have weight limits as well as other health requirements. GRS is a long and complex surgery, and complications are common. It is imperative that you be in your best physical condition. You have done everything else to prepare for this final passage; use the same determination to lose weight and get in better shape.

Most surgeons will require you to stop smoking for some period of time (often at least two months) before surgery. Smoking delays healing and increases the risk of cardiac and pulmonary problems. If you haven't done so for hormones, please quit now. Withdrawal before and during recovery is not pleasant! It takes up to three months for your body to clear the effects of cigarette smoking.

You will also need to stop taking your estrogen and other medications two weeks prior to surgery, especially anything that effects blood-clotting. This may not be pleasant, but do follow your surgeon's advice - it could save your life.

After surgery: You will be in recovery, under your surgeon's care, for up to 2 weeks, either in housing provided or nearby. Every surgeon will also have detailed instructions for follow-up care. Follow them religiously! You will be sore, bruised and swollen for quite some time. You will also be tired. Your body will need rest in order to heal. Plan to take 2-3 months off from work. You will not have time to get bored. The first month will be spent taking care of your new vagina - sitz baths, dilating, etc. There is an excellent article on-line called "Zen and the Art of Post-operative Maintenance", which details the procedures involved.[80] Basically, you will be using what are called stents (in progressive sizes) to expand the vaginal opening, and keep it open. Failure to keep up with dilation can cause the new vaginal opening to shrink or close. Using the stents improperly can cause serious damage.

Genital reconstruction is major surgery, and the list of possible complications is long. It's important to make sure you keep in touch with your physician and report any problems. This is not the time to "tough it out".

---

[80] Zen and the Art of Post-operative Maintenance" http://www.intelleng.com/zen.html

Your new genitals may need revision(s)! If you are unhappy with the results, return to your surgeon to discuss your options. Most transwomen are happy with their surgery, but sometimes things don't come out exactly as planned. One common problem is a change in the urinary stream; as things heal, scar tissue may form and push the urethra in directions that are not helpful for urinating sitting down. Your surgeon should fix that for you as part of his or her fee.

It is important to remember that any type of vaginal penetration will require lubrication (unless you have had the colovaginoplasty). Once you have healed, you can't just fall into bed with someone and expect to have a wonderful sexual experience. It will take open communication, slow, gradual steps, and some trial and error, to learn how to enjoy your new genitals. Rushing the process can be not only painful but discouraging for you and your partner. Experiment on your own first in order to get to know your new sexual response. Some transwomen have good sensation and wonderful orgasms after surgery, and some do not. Not all natal women are orgasmic, so you're not alone if you have difficulty achieving orgasm. Focusing on the totality of the sensual/sexual experience with your partner rather than the end result will make it more enjoyable for you.

Orchiectomy (also called orchidectomy or castration): Contrary to popular impression, castration refers to an orchiectomy, not a penectomy (removal of the penis). In an orchiectomy, small incisions are made and the testicles are removed, leaving the scrotal sac intact. This can be done separate from a vaginoplasty, by a qualified urologist. Some transwomen opt to do this instead of the full GRS, some before. The advantage to the removal of the testicles is that the production of testosterone stops. Thus you don't need to take an anti-androgen (such as spironolactone, and you need less estrogen for feminizing effects. [81] The disadvantage to doing it before vaginoplasty is that with time the scrotal sac will shrink, thus

[81] Reid, R., (1996), *Orchidectomy As A First Stage Towards Gender Reassignment: A Positive Option.*, GENDYS '96, The Fourth International Gender Dysphoria Conference, Manchester England. London: Gendys Conferences.

providing less tissue to line the vaginal vault. You would then need a skin graft to achieve normal depth to the vagina. Some surgeons will not perform a vaginoplasty after an orchiectomy.

There are also potentially serious side effects of an orchiectomy without some form of hormone replacement. The first is depression and lethargy. Testosterone is a mood-enhancer. If you take it away without adding estrogen, you'll notice the mood difference. I've seen what happens when testosterone is lowered too much before estrogen levels are adequate. Clients feel "flat", "blah", "like a non-entity". The other side-effect of long-term hormone insufficiency is lower bone density and osteoporosis. Another client of mine has a pronounced "dowager's hump" from osteoporosis.

It's also important to find a competent Board-certified urologist, or one of the GRS surgeons. As with any surgery, there's a risk of infection and other complications if an orchiectomy is not performed correctly, in sterile conditions. This is not a do-it-yourself job!

Surgeries to Avoid:

As mentioned in Chapter 12, surgery for voice modification has little to recommend it. The chances of complications and unsatisfactory results are too high. **Injections of liquid silicone** (also called free silicone) to the breasts, buttocks, hips, cheeks, lips or anywhere else is not advised! It is extremely dangerous and illegal in the United States and Canada. The risks include permanent disfigurement, lung disease, brain damage, and death.

References and Resources

A. J. Simpson and Joshua Mira Goldberg**, Surgery: A Guide for MTFs**, Vancouver Coastal Health, Transcend Transgender Support & Education Society and Canadian Rainbow Health Coalition, 2006

Facial Feminization Surgery (FFS) at www.facialfeminizationsurgery.inf

A. J. Simpson and Joshua Mira Goldberg, **Surgery: A Guide for FTMs,** Vancouver Coastal Health, Transcend Transgender Support & Education Society and Canadian Rainbow Health Coalition, 2006

Dr. Anne Lawrence, "Sex Reassignment Surgery (SRS)", at http://www.annelawrence.com/srsindex.html

Joanne Meyerowitz, *How Sex Changed: A History of Transsexuality in the United States,* Harvard University Press, 2004

Lynn Conway, "Vaginoplasty: Male to Female Sex Reassignment Surgery Historical notes, descriptions, photos, references and links", 2000-2006, at ai.eecs.umich.edu/people/conway/TS/SRSlink.html

"Zen and the Art of Post-operative Maintenance", Intelligence Engineering, LLC, 2000 www.intelleng.com/zen.html

Here is a selection of surgeons who provide services to transsexuals (in alphabetical order):[82]

Gary Alter, MD - Hollywood, CA: www.altermd.com

Joel B. Beck, M.D., F.A.C.S. - San Mateo, CA (FFS): www.feminizationsurgery.com

Marci L. Bowers M.D. - San Mateo, CA: marcibowers.com/grs/gender

Pierre Brassard, MD - Montreal, Canada: www.grsmontreal.com

Michael Brownstein, MD - San Francisco, CA: www.brownsteinmd.com

Charles Garramone, MD - Sunrise, FL: www.transgenderflorida.com

---

[82] This is not an exhaustive list and does not constitute an endorsement of any of these surgeons.

Sherman Leis, MD - Philadelphia, PA: www.drshermanleis.com

Christine Mcginn, MD - New Hope, PA: www.drchristinemcginn.com

Harold Reed, MD - Miami, FL: www.srsmiami.com

Jeffrey Spiegel, MD, FACS - Boston, MA (FFS): www.drspiegel.com

A. Neal Wilson - Detroit Michigan: nealwilsongendersurgery.com

Mark Zukowski, MD - Wilmette, IL (FFS): www.mlzukowski.com

Possible Complications of Chest Reconstruction Surgery

- Infection, poor wound healing (especially if you are a smoker)
- Anesthesia risks (allergic reactions, etc.)
- Bleeding (hematoma)
- Blood clots
- Chest contour and shape irregularities, chest asymmetry
- Skin discoloration, permanent pigmentation changes, swelling and bruising
- Changes in nipple or breast sensation
- Damage to deeper structures - such as nerves, blood vessels, muscles, and lungs - may be temporary or permanent
- Fluid accumulation
- Unfavorable scarring (red, raised or thick)
- Excessive firmness of the breast
- Potential, partial or total loss of nipple and areola
- Deep vein thrombosis, cardiac and pulmonary complications
- Pain or numbness, which may persist
- Allergies to tape, suture materials and glues, blood products, topical preparations or injections
- Fatty tissue deep in the skin could die (fat necrosis)
- Nipple size/appearance or placement may be uneven or not aesthetically pleasing
- The appearance of "dog ears" under the armpits
- Appearance of puckering along the scars
- Areas of numbness in the armpits due to liposuction in that area
- Possibility of revisional surgery

Possible Complications of Genital Reconstruction Surgery (MtF)

Bleeding (hemorrhage or hematoma)is rare (less than 0.5%) but can be life-threatening.

Blood clots can lead to heart attack or stroke. Stop all drugs and hormones at the time recommended by the surgeon. Stop smoking!

Infection is rare but would require a course of antibiotics to resolve.

Irregularity or asymmetry of the labia may result from excessive swelling or a disruption of stitches. This may require revision surgery.

 Hypertrophic or Keloid scarring is rare but if it does occur it may require specific injection therapy or possibly revision surgery.

Bowel injury is a very rare but serious complication; an injury to the bowel could result in a fistula (leak) into the vagina.

Penile bulb enlargement may develop months or even years later, due to sexual activity stretching the tissue covering the bulb.

Narrowing of the external meatus (urinary opening) is a post-operative problem that can cause spraying of the urine or difficulty in passing urine.

Necrosis or death of tissue can be caused by infection, tissue rejection, or loss of blood supply to tissue.

Vaginal collapse can occur, which may lead to reconstruction or removal.

Numbness or hypersensitivity can result, due to nerve damage. **Loss of sexual sensation** can occur, with inability to experience orgasm.

Insufficient depth or width can make intercourse difficult and/or painful.

Aesthetically unsatisfactory results can occur. Your vulva and labia may not look exactly like the pictures on-line! Remember that there is variability among natal women as well.

Chapter Twenty

The Return

And so the Hero's Journey ends, or at least rests for a while, for the journey of life and the adventure of story never really end.

Christopher Vogler

Mythic stories don't end with the final ordeal, or even with the attainment of the ultimate goal. The Return to the Ordinary World is a subplot all its own. In a hero's journey story there is often a refusal to return, or a perilous trip back with demons on the hero's heels, or a dramatic rescue by another benevolent ally. There is almost always a symbolic threshold to cross to return to ordinary living, and challenges readjusting to it. The new-found wisdom and transformation is not always appreciated by those who were left behind when the hero began his or her journey. The hero often finds a new task ahead - sharing his or her story with the people of the ordinary world in order to give them a glimpse of the possibilities of human growth and potential. In any case, all that the hero has gained on his or her adventures must be lived out in the ordinary world.

A key element of the final chapters of the mythic journey is the integration of two worlds - the one experienced before the journey and the one recently travelled. Through this integration, the hero achieves "at-one-ment" - a whole self that is greater than the sum of the parts. This integration of old and new selves, and the ability to pass between the two worlds, gives the hero the freedom to live his or her new life authentically. Living in two genders gives transgender people a unique perspective on life and valuable insights into their culture. This is why "two-spirit" people are revered in some cultures. They have transcended the limitations of living in one gender. Some of the successfully-transitioned people I know consider their "gender identity disorder" to be a gift. They recognize the uniqueness of their experience, and value the courage, strength and wisdom they have gained from it.

One of the challenges that some people face when transitioning is how much of their old self to keep and how much to leave behind. Some changes happen naturally, due to hormones and the personal growth that comes from no longer denying and hiding one's true self. Old defenses often melt away when they're no longer necessary. But there are still choices to be made about interests and activities that may be gender-based. Some choose totally new interests, taking up more feminine or masculine pursuits. "Suzanne" was thrilled to start sewing classes and dance lessons; she enjoyed all things "girlie". "Judy" didn't want to give up some of her former pursuits, but some of those interest groups didn't accept her as a woman; we worked on finding similar co-ed activities. Some of my clients reported feeling that they were "supposed to" give up their former interests for more gender-appropriate ones. What's the point of transitioning if you go from one straitjacket to another? You can keep all your interests and activities (unless you can't do them physically anymore or are banned from them now), AND explore new ones. You can be a tomboy who prefers jeans over dresses, or a sensitive artistic transman. You can be a transman or transwoman who knits and cooks and bikes and loves to fix things. There's no need to limit yourself to gender-typed activities and interests.

Personality integration is another task of the hero's journey. As discussed earlier, those who had to separate their inner (boy or girl) self from their outer persona often feel a split inside. As the inner self emerges it can crowd out the other half and take over. If the masculine and feminine selves are kept separate, you can end up with parts of yourself hidden once again. Sometimes those are parts that are simply no longer needed or wanted, such as a critical competitive male persona or a flirtatious female persona. On the other hand, the outer persona you developed to adapt to your expected gender role has some valuable coping skills. You don't need to throw the baby out with the bath water! Ideally, the walls that separate your masculine and feminine selves dissolve, and you have a full range of feelings and behaviors available to you. You can be tough when you need to be and soft and tender when that's more appropriate. Through his/her journey the hero returns healed and whole.

Returning to the Ordinary World can be a letdown for any hero. The transgender hero is no exception. There is a great deal of concern among professionals about the possibility of a post-surgery or post-transition depression. It is a real, fairly common experience, but not necessarily a negative outcome, as some would suggest. It's another phase in the journey. There are several common experiences that can result in some depression. The first is simply the letdown that occurs after someone has put so much time, energy, and focus into attaining a goal. (I remember the first year after I finished graduate school I spent a lot of time lying on the couch looking out the window, not knowing what to do with myself.) The gender transition requires a great deal of time, energy and determination, and has been or will be your primary focus for several years. You get to the finish line, exhausted, and wonder "What's next?" Then you realize that the real work is still ahead, - what's next is (or at least was for me) the "real world" of getting a job, finding a place to live, and getting on with one's life.

Another possible reason for some post-transition depression is the awareness of the limitations of what you can change about your appearance. A crucial time for everyone transitioning is that moment when they look in the mirror and see reflected back someone of their true gender. It can take a long time to see that. Self-perception changes more slowly than appearance. For some people, who they see reflected back is never quite right. They may struggle through years of working on themselves and end up profoundly disappointed. It's difficult enough, for example, to be "sirred" or "ma'amed" inappropriately during the middle stages of transition; it can be devastating after doing everything you can to pass. Some transitioning people encounter problems with surgery that leave them with less-than-satisfactory results. This can precipitate a depressive episode. One of my clients went into a tailspin after a botched chest reconstruction surgery. It was more awful to him than having breasts. (Fortunately, the surgeon was willing and able to fix the problem, with good results.)

Even if all goes well, and there's a feeling of pride and satisfaction with the results of your transition, there's another possible source of depression. That is the fact that the ordinary world still has its share of ups and downs. Going into a gender transition many people believe that it will solve all their problems - all their social anxiety will disappear, there will be no more spells of depression, and nothing will bother them again. Well, guess what? It doesn't happen that way. All the problems you went into your journey with are still there. Any personal issues that you shelved while you transitioned will come back up again. Now that your gender dysphoria is reduced you may be better able to deal with them, but it doesn't happen automatically. You still have to build up the confidence to overcome social anxiety, or the courage to end a bad relationship or find a better one. And all the everyday problems - making ends meet, kids becoming teenagers, cars breaking down, dead-end jobs or job layoffs, aging parents - keep on coming. Some of those problems may have worsened while you were busy with your hero's journey. You come home ready to put up your sword and shield and find there are more battles to fight. That can be disheartening.

Another reality that hits home post-transition is the sense of loss that accompanies such a major change.[83] Not only the all-too-common losses of family, friends or jobs that can happen when you come out as transgender, but also the loss of your old self. Even when change is sought after and appreciated, there is a loss of what is familiar. Even unwanted body parts require some grieving. The loss of fertility may become an issue long after

---

[83] Stephanie Budge, "Well-being in the Transition Process: The Role of Loss, Community and Coping", Division 44 Newsletter, American Psychological Association, Spring 2011

the decision to start hormones or undergo surgery has been made. There may be some regrets. Any time you make a life choice that takes you in one direction you close doors to other options. It's normal to wonder about the roads not taken. Some of the changes that come with transitioning from one gender role to the other are unexpected, and not all are appreciated.

So if you have some depression following surgery, or when you reach your end goal, don't be alarmed. It does not mean you made a mistake. Continue to see your therapist and work on coming to terms with whatever is on your plate now. What you thought of as your final destination is really just the beginning of life in your new gender. If you do have regrets, face them squarely. You've made some tough choices and you've done the best you can. It's just not possible to predict and control the outcome of any life change. (Just ask any divorced person who really thought they were marrying for life.) You can have regrets about the way things have turned out without regretting for a moment having made the decision to embark on this journey.

Occasionally - very occasionally, according to most sources - someone goes through a full transition and decides that it was not the right path for them. A few - some of them highly publicized - have chosen to go back to their assigned gender. It may be because of the losses involved, or the difficulty adjusting in their new role, or perhaps too hasty a transition. As Joanne Herman writes, most don't stop being transgender, they just give up on transitioning.[84] And once you have come out publicly, you can't really go back into the closet. This makes "retro-transitioning" difficult. It certainly took its toll on the sportswriter Mike Penner/Christine Daniels.[85]

The vast majority of post-operative transsexuals, however, are very satisfied with their transition. When their gender dysphoria is reduced they go on to lead happy productive lives. Depression and anxiety are reduced, and self-confidence and social engagement increase. Suicide rates drop from 20

---

[84] Joanne Herman, **Transgender Explained**, Authorhouse, 2009
[85] http://latimesblogs.latimes.com/lanow/2009/11/veteran-times-sportswriter-mike-penner-dead.html

percent to no more than two percent, way below national averages.[86] The clients I have worked with through a full transition, whether they have had genital reconstruction surgery or not, have no regrets about their decision. They are more relaxed about life, and have an inner strength that is enviable. They have been through the belly of the whale, and lived to tell about it.

In my experience, the only real danger I have seen post-transition is social isolation. The other post-transition issues are surmountable as long as you have support. Facing them alone carries the greatest risk of all. Social isolation is a silent killer, rivaling high blood pressure and diabetes in its negative health effects. People who have fewer contacts with friends, family and other social supports have higher rates of physical and mental health problems, and higher mortality rates.[87] Transgender people who have kept to themselves for years to hide their true selves, have little contact with other transgender people during their transition, and are socially ostracized when they come out, are at high risk. If their primary supports are their therapist and other transition-related professionals, what happens when they no longer have contact with them?

So once again I will stress the importance of finding social supports, whether it's an LGBT-related group or not. Even if you "graduate" from a transgender support group when you've reached your goal, stay in touch. Remember, it helps those coming along behind you as well. And don't quit therapy right after surgery, just because you don't need any more letters. Reid Vanderburgh's book is called *Transition and Beyond* for a reason. He has valuable insights into the issues faced by transgender people as they begin life in their new gender role. He cautions those transitioning from female to male not to adopt the "lone wolf" position, and those becoming women to leave behind their male socialization and learn to ask for help.[88]

---

[86] A. Michel, M. Ansseau, J.J. Legros, W. Pitchot, and C. Mormont "The transsexual: what about the future?" in Eur Psychiatry 2002; 17: 353-62

[87] James S. House and Karl R. Landis, "Social Relationships and Health", *Science*, New Series, Vol. 241, No. 4865

[88] Reid Vanderburgh, *Transition and Beyond*, Q-Press, 2007

Changing Social Relationships

Once you are presenting consistently in your new gender role you are in
for some real surprises. You have probably underestimated the ways in
which men and women are treated differently in American society. Some
of it obviously comes from sexism and the disparate assumptions about
what men and women are capable of. But the role expectations of men are
not all that kind either. Here are some (humorous but true) examples of
what you may encounter:

> ➤ If you are now presenting as female, you will be treated as if you
> know very little about cars, construction, sports, home mainten-
> ance, computers and all things mechanical or electronic. Your opi-
> nions in these areas will be disregarded.

> ➤ If you pass as male, your opinions on all things electronic and me-
> chanical will be solicited. You will be expected to know how to fix
> things.

> ➤ If you pass as female and are under the age of 40, your eyes will
> now be located chest high - at least that's where men will be look-
> ing. Get used to being seen as a sex object.

> ➤ If you are now male and are under 5'4", attractive women will
> probably ignore you. Do not expect to get a phone number from a
> woman taller than you.

> ➤ If you pass as female, you will be assumed incapable of lifting heavy
> objects, even if you are 5'10" and weigh 200 pounds. Get used to
> letting people help you. It makes them feel better.

> ➤ If you are now presenting as male, you will be expected to lift heavy objects and carry several bags of groceries at once, even if you are 5'2" and weigh 102. And please remember to hold the door open for everyone - they will get hurt if you don't because they won't expect it to swing back at them.

> ➤ If you present as female, women will tell you all about their love life, menstrual periods, favorite foods and recipes, and all the best places to shop. Take mental notes!

> ➤ If you present as male, men will talk about your local sports teams. If you live in Massachusetts, New Hampshire or Rhode Island, for example, you will have to follow the Red Sox, Patriots and Celtics. Read the sports section of the newspaper to stay informed.

> ➤ If you are now living as a woman, you are subject to an automatic salary decrease if you apply for a new job. That is, if you can get an interview for your previous job level.

> ➤ If you are now living as a man, you may be asked to train as a manager before equally-qualified female peers, who will no longer speak to you. Women at work will stop talking when you enter the room.

> ➤ If you pass as a woman, and act like one, you are more likely to get a warning than a speeding ticket when pulled over by a police officer.

> ➤ If you pass as a man and act like one you will not only get a speeding ticket, you might be asked to step out of the car and searched. This is practically guaranteed if you are non-white.

> ➤ If you pass as a woman, you can expect men and women to notice what you are wearing. Both will look you up and down, but for dif-

ferent reasons. If a woman says "Nice dress!" it could have any of a half dozen different meanings, from "You look ridiculous" to "I hate you for looking that good in it". If a man says "Nice dress", it could mean he's thinking about what's underneath it.

➢ If you are now passing as a man, be prepared to have the server hand you the check at a restaurant. You will also be handed the "beefier" meal, and any female companions will get the diet beverages.

➢ If you present as a woman, you will be scrutinized by everyone if you order more than a salad and a diet drink. You can have a dessert after your salad and diet drink, especially if it's chocolate, but you must offer a bite to everyone at the table.

➢ If you are now living as a woman, you will be expected to remember birthdays, anniversaries, the names of your coworkers' children and other formerly irrelevant details. You will also be expected to find the right card and the right gift for every occasion.

These experiences are not universal, of course, but they are pervasive. It can be quite a shock to be treated so differently, knowing that you haven't changed inside. It takes time to get used to these changes, especially if you still aren't convinced that you pass. You may be thrilled at first to realize you are being seen as a man or a woman, but over time some of these changes may become troublesome.

Transitioning from female to male has particular challenges. There will be a growing gap between you and women, including female friends. They will hug you less frequently, and perhaps confide in you less. They will perceive your anger differently, and will be more easily threatened by your behavior. Your lower voice triggers different reactions than your prior female voice, and your masculine attitude on testosterone may be offensive or intimidating. You may find that women cross the street at night to avoid passing you, just because you are now seen as a man.

Men will also respond differently to your new "aura". They will slap or pat you on the back, sometimes hard, to demonstrate affection. You will be included in crude conversations that you may find thoroughly offensive. It can be difficult to not give yourself away if you respond with any feminist sensibility. You will also elicit more aggressive responses from men, especially if you inadvertently intrude on their territory in some way. And that girl from class that you're chatting up at a party may be some guy's "territory".

Many transmen find the masculine social role very restrictive. The limitations to the expression of emotion can be hard to get used to. You may want to jump for joy when you get a new job, but remember the beating in the press that Tom Cruise got for doing just that? You'll have to balance being authentically you and fitting in as a guy, especially if you don't want to be perceived as a gay guy.

Another surprise may be the responses you get from gay men, who may mistake your lingering feminine attributes for the signs of being gay. You might encounter some awkward situations if you misread their cues. If you've been used to being seen as butch and ignored by men, being hit on by a gay man can come as a total shock. Of course, if you're interested in gay men, that's not a problem!

There are particular challenges for those transitioning from male to female as well. They don't usually realize how much they have taken their male privilege for granted until they lose it. Male (or white, or heterosexual) privilege refers to the status and accommodations granted by society based on simply being male (or white or heterosexual). Because these are part of the fabric of society they are just seen as normal, just "the way things are". It seems like everyone has those rights and privileges until you are in the non-privileged shoes. Those transitioning from male to female are often used to dominating conversations, having their opinions respected, being hired or promoted because they deserve the job, being able to walk down the street at night alone without fear, having their needs accommodated in relationships, and being supported in their endeavors.

So it can be quite a shock to have their opinions dismissed, be treated like a "dumb blonde", get propositioned or harassed at work, or be passed over for a deserved promotion. Formerly acceptable language and behavior may now be seen as shocking and/or offensive to others. You may encounter discrimination not necessarily because you're transgender, but because you are now in the second class category of female. It can be a humbling, or even humiliating, experience. Any vestiges of male ego will be challenged, if not crushed.

How you are now seen and related to by men in personal relationships will also be an eye-opener. To be pursued by a man may be flattering at first, but when you realize that he may be pursuing only one thing it can be disappointing, if not infuriating. Having a man take charge and order for you at a restaurant may seem romantic, but having your needs and wishes disregarded is not. You may not be prepared for his expectations at the end of the evening.

The other part of the experience of being a woman that some are not prepared for is the very real threat of being sexually assaulted by a man. Those raised male are not used to the idea that how they dress or how they walk or even just smiling at a man can be seen as an invitation for further intimacy. Walk boldly down the street at night alone dressed up as a man and people will assume you're going somewhere. Walk like you own the street as a woman dressed to the nines and people will think you're a hooker.

Changing Sexual Relationships

For most transgender men and women, their sexual orientation does not change after they complete the physical aspects of their transition. Their sexual behavior may change, however, especially if they have genital reconstruction surgery. In Chapter 13 we discussed the impact of coming out as transgender on the person's spouse or partner. One of the changes addressed is the impact on their sexual relationship. The true test of sexual compatibility may not come until after surgery. The wife of someone transitioning from male to female, for example, may still be in some degree of denial until then. Only after her husband's penis is gone and her now wife has a new vagina will she need to make a complete adjustment in her sexual behavior. She may not be comfortable being the active partner her wife now needs. The same dynamic could apply for a gay male couple. Creativity and open communication are necessary for a couple to adapt.

For some transsexuals genital reconstruction surgery opens up possibilities for sexual activity that may alter their sexual orientation. Transwomen who had previously denied and/or suppressed attraction to men may find that they are now free to indulge those feelings and fantasies. Or they may simply be curious now that they have a new vagina. It seems that the experience of gender fluidity that occurs with transitioning often leads to greater flexibility in sexual exploration as well. I've also seen a shift from focusing on sexual attraction as the driving force in partner selection to affection and affiliation as the primary interest. It may be partly for this reason that transgender people often date or become involved with other transgender people.

These new fantasies and attractions may be hard to accept if you've always thought of yourself as gay or straight. You may find yourself attracted to people you didn't even think you liked. New sexual interests may be threatening to your primary relationship. Try to accept these as a byproduct of changing hormones and physical possibilities. You don't have to act on every new attraction. After careful reflection, if you realize your sexual orientation really has changed from what you thought it was, be honest with yourself and your partner. You know by now that living a lie just doesn't work.

Transmen and women who stay in a committed relationship may experience some shift in their sexual interests after surgery, but their behavior may not change. For those who have left their primary relationship (or been left) and waited until after surgery to begin seeking new relationships, the field is wide open. They have to factor in, however, not only who they are attracted to but also who's attracted to them (and available). They also have the dilemma of how much to share with a prospective partner and when. If your completed transition hasn't changed your genitals, then obviously you will need to disclose before any sexual activity occurs. In order to be fair to yourself and the other person, I recommend disclosure as soon as it's clear that he or she is interested in a sexual or romantic relationship. You may be disappointed if the person isn't interested in continuing, but the risk of hurt feelings and/or violent reactions is lower.

Annie Richards discusses the difficulties with hiding one's transgender status from a lover in her article "The Stealthy Transsexual Woman".[89] Even if you have the perfect anatomy after surgery, your lack of experience as a woman can make someone wonder about you. If you are outed once you are in an intimate relationship, it's not likely to end well. You may be eager to get into a relationship and experience your new body, but it's not going to immediately live up to your fantasies. You'll need a patient, understanding lover; you'll be a newly minted virgin, after all!

This leads us into our next discussion: how out/open to be after you've transitioned.

"Stealth" or "Out and Proud"?

Once you have transitioned to the point of passing successfully you have options about how public you want to be about your transition. There are some definite and differing opinions about this in the transgender community. Many transsexuals feel that the ability to slip inconspicuously into society as someone of their true gender is the ultimate goal. They want to be seen and known exclusively as their true self. Others feel it is important to be out publicly about being a transman or transwoman, for themselves and for the transgender community. They are proud of their transgender status and want to promote understanding and acceptance of it.

---

[89] Annie Richards " A Stealthy Transsexual Woman", 2009, at: http://www.secondtype.info/stealth.htm

In reality, this doesn't have to be a black-or-white, either-or decision. It can be seen as a continuum, and your place on that continuum can change over time or in different situations. We'll discuss the two extremes first, and then how to find what's comfortable for you.

"Stealth" is the term for hiding one's transgender status after transitioning. Someone who "goes stealth" will live and work in a community as a man or woman, not as a transman or transwoman. Only a handful of close people will know his or her history. "Deep stealth" refers to living completely in your new gender, with no one knowing your former identity. Deep stealth is very difficult to achieve. It requires erasing all documentation and cutting all ties of your former life and starting over with a new identity, similar to being in a witness protection program. You have to create a new life story with a different history, and be vigilant about slips that might give you away. That can be as stressful and alienating as being closeted was before transition.

You should only consider total stealth if you are willing and able to:

- pass and blend in completely and convincingly 99 percent of the time, and believe it,
- cut off all family ties - parents, siblings, spouse(s), children - and friendships,
- change all your documentation, including transcripts, resume, references, etc.,
- get a new job in a new city and state, possibly a new career,
- resign from all groups and organizations, especially any transgender groups, and
- rewrite your history and learn your new "cover story", or simply not talk about it.

This is easier if you are young and attractive, have few long-term relationships, and have had limited exposure on the Internet. I have one client who has a chance of going deep stealth, if she can scrape up the money for surgery in the next few years.

Even if it is possible for you to consider total stealth, it's important to realize that it can really take a toll on your mental health. The anxiety about being read or outed can be overwhelming. The grief and loss and social isolation that comes from starting over without a past can lead to depression. Donna Rose writes eloquently about the problems she encountered with a stealth life.[90] She found that hiding her past life left her unable to share anything important with people she met and develop close friendships. Eventually she opened up and started talking about her transition, and felt liberated.

The other extreme is being very public about your transition and becoming a transgender rights activist or educator. There are several noted authors who have done so - Leslie Feinberg, Kate Bornstein, Jennifer Finney Boylan, and Chaz Bono, to name a few. Their writings have done a great deal to both educate and inspire others. By the time you read this, we will know the outcome of Chaz's appearance on the Dancing With the Stars TV show. He has already used his celebrity status to raise the public's awareness of transgender issues. It has been said that the 2010s is the decade of the transsexual, which is the media's way of saying that people are fascinated by transgender stories. Every major talk show has done a segment or two on transgender children. Newspaper articles about couples staying together after one transitions, or a prominent local figure losing his or her job, or keeping his or her job, are popping up everywhere. Every article or TV show means that someone has agreed to go public and be interviewed, or has written about their experience themselves.

Vanessa Sheridan and Virginia Ramey Mollenkott write about the reasons for coming out and staying out in their book *Transgender Journeys*. They see it as an act of faith, self-acceptance, integrity and empowerment. "Any person who cares about integrity longs to operate from a place of truth, a place of comfort and internal peace. Continuing to keep a masquerade going on in our lives, especially about something as important as our

---

[90] Donna Rose, "A Stealth life: The View from the Passing Lane", at www.donnarose.com/Stealth.htm

gender orientation, is debilitating and dehumanizing."[91] They add this is important for the community as well as the individual. "Our own empowerment is essential if we are to develop a strong sense of individual and community transgender identity."[92]

As liberating as it is, there is a cost to going public and staying out, for the individual and for their family. There is first and foremost the risk of discrimination and even violence. There are some communities that just won't tolerate a transgender doctor, minister or teacher. Sometimes starting over stealth at a new job is a necessity. Concern for one's spouse and/or children is another reason that some people choose stealth as much as possible. It's one thing to be out yourself, but when it results in kids being harassed in school or a spouse losing his or her job, that's another story. Your family may still be struggling with acceptance and fear of being shamed in the community.

How public to be is a very personal decision, one that only you can make. You may decide, once you've transitioned, that you're tired of having to explain yourself. You'll want to meet people as their co-worker or neighbor or tennis partner, not as "Joe (or Jane), the transsexual". You certainly don't need to introduce yourself that way. You can tell people on a need-to-know basis, and most people don't need to know. I've heard some people say that telling only some friends and not others may put a burden on them, but I don't agree. There are different degrees of intimacy in friendships. A woman might tell only one or two friends that she once had an abortion, or gave a child up for adoption. There is always the possibility that one of them would broadcast that, but it's reasonable to expect that a good friend can and should keep a secret.

In any case, if this is indeed the "decade of the transsexual", being outed is not the end of the world. You have a unique story to tell, the story of your hero's journey. There is no need to be afraid or ashamed of telling it.

---

[91] Virginia Ramey Mollenkott and Vanessa Sheridan, *Transgender Journeys*, Resource Publications, 2003: p.128

[92] Virginia Ramey Mollenkott and Vanessa Sheridan, *Transgender Journeys*, Resource Publications, 2003: p.129

You've come a long way, surmounting many obstacles. You have slain the dragons and battled demons to claim your true identity. You have every right to be proud of your accomplishment. You are a hero/ine.

In the mythic story, the hero brings back something of value (called the elixir) from his or her journey. This elixir must be shared. "If the hero doesn't bring back something to share, he's not a hero, he's a heel, selfish and unenlightened. He hasn't learned his lesson. He hasn't grown. Returning with the Elixir is the last test of the hero, which shows he's mature enough to share the fruits of his quest."[93] The elixir is so powerful that it changes not only the hero, but those around him or her. The elixir can be a renewed capacity for love and intimacy, a sense of responsibility in the world, or the profound wisdom that comes from surviving adversity.

It's up to you how you share the fruits of your journey. For some it will be simply being themselves, happy and whole, with their family and friends. Becoming a better partner, parent and friend are noble outcomes. For others, sharing their experience with others becomes important. In addition to the more famous authors there are several transsexuals who have written and self-published their stories, and many more who share their journey via a blog or YouTube series.

For some, sharing their story is just the beginning. Many seek empowerment through organizing and leading others for support, education and political action. Many of the web sites listed throughout the book represent organizations by and for transgender people. Most of them were started by one person or a small group of people. Margaret Mead, the famous anthropologist, is often quoted: "Never underestimate the power of a small group of dedicated people to change the world. Indeed it's the only thing that ever has." It can be liberating, empowering and rewarding to be part of one of those small groups of dedicated people.

Whatever your decision, I wish you the best on your journey. May you be blessed with courage, faith, hope, and wonderful allies.

---

[93] Christopher Vogler, *The Writer's Journey*, p. 221

References and Resources

Jennifer Finney Boylan, *She's Not There: A Life in Two Genders*, Broadway, 2003

Reid Vanderburgh, *Transition and Beyond*, Q-Press, 2007

Chaz Bono, *Transition: The Story of How I Became a Man*, Dutton Adult, 2011

Donna Rose, *Wrapped In Blue: A Journey of Discovery*, Living Legacy Press, 2003

Virginia Ramey Mollenkott and Vanessa Sheridan, *Transgender Journeys*, Resource Publications, 2003

Epilogue

Just when I thought I was finished writing this book the new WPATH Standards of Care (Version 7) came out. They are most excellent! There are significant changes in the language and emphasis in the new SOC. This version is clearly trans-affirmative, and makes strong statements about the rights of all transgender, transsexual, and gender nonconforming children, adolescents and adults to adequate treatment for gender dysphoria. As a gender specialist who believes in the value of psychotherapy I was actually pleased to see that therapy is not an absolute requirement for the initiation of hormone therapy. This allows for more flexibility in the timing of key transition pieces and a more individualized approach, which I have advocated for all along. It also means (hopefully) that clients can be more honest with their therapists.

So I went back to the drawing board, and revised the chapters of the book affected by the new Standards. I also wrote the summary you'll find in Appendix B. I noticed some other areas where I need to highlight changes recently in the news:

The Social Security Administration announced that it will no longer send out letters to employers notifying them of a mismatch between the gender a new employee has listed and the gender associated with his or her Social Security number. Mara Keisling and the National Center for Transgender Equality were instrumental in getting this changed. This makes it easier for transgender employees to use the appropriate designation on their employment forms even if they have not been able to change their gender marker with Social Security. According to NCTE, there were 711,488 gender no-match letters sent in 2010 alone.

The State Department has made additional changes to its policy regarding gender markers on U.S. passports. "The changes make clear that any physician who has treated or evaluated a passport applicant may certify that he or she has had appropriate treatment for gender transition. The revised policy also clarifies language and procedures to ensure that individuals with intersex condition can obtain documents with the correct gender."[94]

The U. S. Bureau of Prisons announced last week that it has revised its policies regarding medical treatment of transgender inmates. Previously an inmate's treatment was "frozen" at the time of his/herincarceration at a federal facility; those who were on hormones could stay on them, but others who were eligible but had not started them were not allowed to start. Now all inmates can receive transgender care as needed according to the standards of care set by WPATH. Training will be made available to staff, but treatment will not be limited to what is currently available inside the walls of the federal penitentiaries.[95]

In an update to the Maryland beating of a transgender woman, an 18-year-old woman pled guilty and was sentenced to ten years in jail, with five years suspended. A 14-year-old was also charged in juvenile court. Because the attack was caught on video, prosecutors had no trouble charging them both with a hate crime. Attacks on transgender people continue to make the news, bringing frequently national attention to the problem.

And Chaz Bono is still Dancing with the Stars!

October 15, 2011

---

[94] Advancing Transgender Equality, NCTE blog:
http://transgenderequality.wordpress.com/2011/01/28/victory-state-department-makes-additional-changes/

[95] http://www.washingtonpost.com/national/health-science/feds-revise-transgender-inmate-rules-to-permit-previously-disallowed-prison-treatments/2011/10/03/gIQAuablIL_story.html

APPENDIX A:

A Brief Transgender Glossary

Androgyny, androgynous: Expressing both masculine and feminine characteristics, either in obvious contrast or as part of an integrated whole. **Androgyne:** A person who presents and identifies as neither man nor woman, masculine nor feminine. This can be done with a gender neutral presentation, or by combining elements of both.

Assigned sex/gender: The gender someone is considered to be at birth, generally based on genitalia. Also referred to as biological sex.

Bigendered: Those who feel they have both a male and a female side to their personalities. They may have two modes of gender expression, with different personas, or they may present androgynously. May identify as **Two Spirit**.

Bind, binding: To tape one's breasts to hide their presence.

Butch: Masculine-appearing person. Masculine or macho dress and behavior. Often used to refer to masculine-appearing women who identify as lesbian.

Cross-dresser (CD) Someone who enjoys dressing part of the time as other than their assigned gender. This can be associated with transitioning, sexual fetish or simply to relieve stress. This term is preferable to "transvestite".

Cisgendered or Cissexual: Someone whose biological sex/assigned gender is consistent with their gender identity. Opposite of transsexual.

Coming out: The process of telling people that one is transgender (or gay, lesbian or bisexual). Being **outed** is having someone else tell people.

Detransition: To return to living as a member of one's biological sex after an extended full-time period of living as one's target gender.

Drag: Originally used in Shakespeare's Globe Theatre to mean DRessed As a Girl, referring to male actors playing female roles. Now mainly used by gender benders and cross-dressers of both directions to mean "in women's clothes". Less frequently used, **Drab** means DRessed As a Boy.

Drag King: Often an FTM cross-dresser, dramatically using masculine dialogue, mannerisms and voice. Could also be a drag performer.

Drag Queen:. Gay man who from time to time wears women's clothes, generally without trying to be convincing. Also can refer to a female impersonator.

Female or male impersonator: A person who cross-dresses for professional entertainment. Also called drag performers.

Femme: Feminine-appearing person. May be used to describe a feminine-appearing woman who identifies as lesbian, or dressing in a feminine manner ("en femme").

FtM: Female-to-male transsexual. A person assigned as female at birth who identifies as a boy or man and wishes to change his external appearance to match his gender identity. Biological sex is female, gender identity is male. More accurately, refers to transitioning from assigned gender (female) to true gender identity (male).

Gender: Sex is a set of biological differences between people – male, female or intersexed. Gender is the designation for the role of man, woman or "other".

Gender Dysphoria: Profound and persistent discontent with one's biological sex and/or one's assigned gender. Often includes **anatomical dysphoria,** the discomfort with one's primary and/or secondary sex characteristics.

Gender Expression: Physical manifestation of one's gender identity, often expressed through clothing, hairstyle, accessories, mannerisms, and chosen name. **Gender attribution or perception** is how someone else sees your gender.

Gender Identity: A person's innate, internal sense of him or herself as a boy or girl, man or woman, or other.

Gender roles and norms: Culturally determined behaviors, interests, relationship patterns and other characteristics typically associated with being male or female. Also called sex-role stereotypes. **Gender variant** refers to not fitting these norms.

Genderqueer or gender-nonconforming: People who think of themselves as falling completely outside the gender binary. **Gender-crossing:** Temporary forays into the other gender role, adopting the characteristics, dress and mannerisms of another gender. **Gender-bending:** Testing the limits of societal norms by expressing aspects of the opposite gender without attempting to pass as that gender.

Hermaphrodite: A person biologically intermediate between male and female. A true hermaphrodite is a person with both ovarian and testicular tissue, i.e. a person with ambiguous gonads. A "pseudohermaphrodite" is a person with two ovaries or two testes, but ambiguous genitals. The term 'intersexual' or "intersexed" is now preferred.

Heteronormative : heterosexual and cisgendered. **Heteronormativity** refers to a set of norms that hold that people fall into distinct and complementary genders (male and female) with natural roles in life. It also holds that heterosexuality is the normal sexual orientation. A **heteronormative bias** is one that assumes and/or promotes alignment of biological sex, gender identity, and gender roles.

Hormone Therapy: Hormones taken to change ones secondary sex characteristics. This includes feminizing hormones (estrogen and androgen blockers) for MtF , and masculinizing hormones (testosterone) for FtM transsexuals.

Intersexual, or Intersexed: A person biologically intermediate between male and female. Born with one of over 100 conditions resulting in having both male and female anatomical characteristics, including in varying degrees reproductive organs and secondary sexual characteristics.

Living in role, or "real-life test": Living full-time in the preferred gender image, opposite to one's assigned gender; a prerequisite for gender reassignment surgery.

MtF or Male-to-female transsexual: A person assigned as male at birth who identifies as a woman and wishes to change her physical characteristics to match her gender identity.

Packing: Wearing a penile prosthesis, called a packer. Some can be used to urinate standing. There are other devices as well that can be used to urinate standing.

Pass, or passing: To be seen as one's true gender identity. The opposite is to be 'read' or 'clocked' as someone presenting as the 'opposite sex'.

Primary sex characteristics: Reproductive/sexual anatomy present at birth: the male penis, prostate and testicles, and the female clitoris, vagina, uterus and ovaries.

Read: The opposite of passing; to be seen as a man dressed as a woman or vice versa.

Secondary sex characteristics: The biological differences between males and females that begin to develop at puberty. Includes breasts, facial and body hair, voice deepening, and changes in body mass and fat distribution.

Sex: A classification based on primary sex characteristics. Preferably, an erotic physical activity between two (or more) people.

Sexual Orientation: Which gender one finds emotionally and erotically attractive: opposite (heterosexual or straight), same (homosexual or gay/Lesbian), both (bisexual), all/any (pansexual, omnisexual) or neither (asexual).

She-male: A male with breasts and a penis. This is considered a derogatory term by many, especially since it's often used in the sex industry.

SRS (or GRS): Sex (or Gender) Reassignment Surgery. This is the preferred term for what is colloquially referred to as a 'sex change operation'. This can includes vaginoplasty, tracheal shave, facial feminization, orchiectomy and breast augmentation for MtF. and chest reconstruction, hysterectomy and/or oophorectomy, phalloplasty or metoidaplasty for FtM.

Stealth: Living in one's preferred gender role without being noticed.

Transgender (TG): Transgendered originally referred to a pre-operative transsexual who has no desire to have the SRS. It later became an umbrella term for transsexuals, transvestites, female and male impersonators, drag queens/kings, intersexuals, gender dysphorics, and those that do not fit any gender label. Now used as an identification for anyone who is gender-variant. The term **"trans"** is also common.

Transgenderists live as members of the other sex, but without the need or desire to modify their bodies shown by transsexuals. Some live as members of the "opposite sex", while others stake out third gender status. Transgenderists may take hormones, but do not have genital reconstruction.

Transition, transitioning: The process of changing one's appearance and social role to match a gender identity different from the one assigned at birth.

Transfeminine: A person whose femininity or female identity is not universally considered valid. Often used to talk about a wider range of how a person might identify her gender and would cover a spectrum of transwomen, as well as genderqueers, and people with non-binary genders.

Transmasculine : A person whose masculinity or male identity is not universally considered valid. Often used to talk about a wider range of how a person might identify his gender and would cover a spectrum of transmen, as well as genderqueers, and people with non-binary genders.

Transphobia: The fear and hatred of all gender-variant people and behavior, resulting in denial of rights and needs, harassment, and at times violence.

Transsexual (TS): someone who is extremely unhappy in the gender to which he or she was assigned and wishes to change gender roles and bodies in order to live as the 'other' sex. **A "pre-op" transsexual** is someone who has not had surgery. This covers people who have just begun to identify as transsexual to those who are very close to the actual surgery. **A post-operative transsexual** is someone who has had gender reassignment surgery. **A "non-op" transsexual** is a person who has had all the hormonal/surgical treatments except the genital surgery, and who either has no desire to proceed with surgery, or who cannot proceed due to financial or other constraints.

Appendix B

Summary of the WPATH Standards of Care for the Health of
Transsexual, Transgender, and Gender Nonconforming People

September 2011

Introduction

The Harry Benjamin International Gender Dysphoria Association was
established in 1979, after challenges to the legitimacy of the hormone
and surgical treatment of transsexuals developed in the 1960s and
1970s. To provide its members with a consistent standard for treatment of transgender issues, the HBIGDA adopted a group of guidelines called the Standards of Care. The SOC have been revised six
times since (previously in January 1980, March 1981, January 1990,
June 1998, and February 2001). These guidelines outlined a blueprint
for those transitioning from one gender role to the other and were
referred to as the "Harry Benjamin Standards". Even though the SOC
were meant as guidelines, not hard and fast rules, they drew heavy
criticism from the transgender community. In 2006 the HBIGDA
changed its name to the World Professional Association for Transgender Health and began working on revisions to the Standards of
Care. Through a lengthy peer-reviewed process new standards were
written, with substantial changes in some areas. The new document
(Version 7) is available on-line at www.wpath.org. Since it's over 100
pages long I'm providing a summary here.

Version 7 is from the very beginning a trans-affirmative approach to
health care. The emphasis is on providing guidance for the many
health professionals who provide services to TG/TS/GNC (transgender,
transsexual and gender nonconforming) people. It represents a shift
away from telling transgender people what they must do to educating
providers about how to help. It reiterates that the Standards of Care
are guidelines, to be applied within the provider's and client's social
and political context. The Standards aim to balance the goal of the

highest quality of care with the reality of at times limited resources and the need for harm reduction strategies. The emphasis is on informed decision-making as well as measures to promote successful outcomes. This shifts the power more to the consumer of transition-related services.

The underlying principles of the new Standards for all health care providers are as follows:

1) Show respect for all nonconforming gender identities and expression; do not pathologize.

2) Provide care that affirms the individual's gender identity and lessens gender dysphoria.

3) Become knowledgeable about and sensitive to the specific health care needs of TG/TS/NGC individuals , including the risks and benefits of various treatment options.

4) Match the treatment to the individual's specific needs, goals and desired gender expression.

5) Seek fully-informed consent before providing treatment.

6) Facilitate access to appropriate treatments not provided by the particular care provider.

7) Offer continuity of care and coordinate treatment with other providers.

8) Be prepared to provide support and advocacy for TG/TS/GNC patients within their families and communities.

One of the first issues addressed is the question of diagnosis, and whether gender nonconformity is a mental illness. In 2010 WPATH went on record stating that "the expression of gender characteristics, including identities, that are not stereotypically associated with one's assigned sex at birth is a common and culturally-diverse human phenomenon [that] should not be judged as inherently pathological or negative."[96] SOC Version 7 goes on to explain that because gender nonconforming is so stigmatized in many countries and TG/TS/GNC people are subject to so much harassment and discrimination, many suffer from minority stress and develop socially-induced anxiety and depression. The SOC also differentiates gender nonconformity from gender dysphoria, which presents as at times acute discomfort and distress. Gender dysphoria may rise to the level of a "disorder" as described by the DSM (Diagnostic Statistical Manual of Mental Disorders) and ICD (International Classification of Diseases). It emphasizes that a disorder is a cluster of symptoms, not an attribute of a person. "A disorder is a description of something with which a person might struggle, not a description of the person or the person's identity."[97]

The next section describes some of the history and advancements in the treatment of gender dysphoria. It acknowledges that in the beginning the emphasis of the SOC was on identifying those TG/TS patients who were appropriate candidates for hormonal and surgical gender reassignment. The current Standards take into consideration a wider range of options for alleviating gender dysphoria. What that means is that the "cookie-cutter" approach to transitioning has been discarded and treatment has become more individualized. Gender-variant people who seek gender expression in a variety of ways are affirmed and supported by the new SOC. With that comes a new definition of the role of health professionals: "Health professionals can assist gender dysphoric individuals with affirming their gender identity, exploring different options for expression of that identity,

---

[96] The World Professional Association for Transgender Health: *Standards of Care for the Health of Transsexual, Transgender, and Gender Nonconforming People,* September 2011, p.4
[97] p5.

and making decisions about medical treatment options for alleviating gender dysphoria."[98]

These options include:

- ➢ changes in gender role expression (full or part-time),
- ➢ feminizing or masculinizing hormone therapy,
- ➢ surgery to change primary and/or secondary sex characteristics,
- ➢ psychotherapy (individual, family, couple, or group) to explore gender identity and expression, address the negative impact of growing up gender-variant, develop stronger social supports, improve body image and promote positive coping skills,
- ➢ on-line and off-line peer support for TG/TS/GNC individuals and their families and friends,
- ➢ voice and communication therapy,
- ➢ hair removal,
- ➢ breast binding or padding and/or genital tucking or prostheses, and
- ➢ changes in name and gender marker on identity documents.

Children and Adolescents

The SOC Version 7 covers in more detail the treatment options for children and adolescents who present with gender dysphoria. Because of the nature of child development, gender ideas and presentations are fluid and changeable before adolescence. Children may be gender-nonconforming without gender dysphoria. The existing research finds that many gender-variant children "outgrow" the desire to be a different gender, becoming either gay or lesbian as adults, or simply gender-variant heterosexuals, happy with their assigned gender. When gender dysphoria appears in adolescence it is

---

3. p. 9

more likely to be both enduring and acutely distressing. For this reason, there are greater cautions and more extensive protocols for treating gender-variant children.

The SOC outlines the competency requirements for mental health professionals who work with gender-variant children and adolescents. In addition to the requirements for working with adults, a child and adolescent gender specialist must have a background in developmental psychology and psychopathology. The SOC cautions inexperienced clinicians not to assume that children who present with unique ideas about their gender are confused or delusional. It also outlines the various roles of the mental health professional who works with children and adolescents with gender dysphoria, including direct assessment, child and family counseling, assessment and treatment of other co-existing mental health issues, referral of adolescents for medical treatments to alleviate gender dysphoria, and education, advocacy, and peer support as needed.

The guidelines for the psychological assessment of children and adolescents are quite clear and directive. "Mental health professionals should not dismiss or express a negative attitude towards nonconforming gender identities or indications of gender dysphoria."[99] Acceptance and exploration of gender identity is recommended, along with a thorough assessment of individual and family functioning, peer relationships, emotional and cognitive development, etc. The assessment phase should also include information about the treatment options available and their risks and benefits. The adolescent client should be involved in all such discussions.

The Standards also very clear that any treatment that tries to change a client's gender identity and expression to match their assigned sex is not only ineffective but unethical. The goals of treatment should be to:

---

[99] p.15

- help families (and communities, where possible) develop an accepting and supportive response to the child's gender dysphoria,
- help families manage the anxiety and uncertainty about the outcome of their child's gender nonconformity (and not push for resolution of their gender identity),
- give the child or adolescent room to explore different ways of expressing their gender, without imposing a binary gender paradigm,
- support the child or adolescent and his/her family in making difficult decisions about how the child's gender presentation plays out in their extended family, school, church, and/or community,
- help families of younger children make decisions about the timing and nature of social transitioning,
- help educate the wider community as necessary and advocate for the child/adolescent's freedom of gender expression,
- maintain a supportive therapeutic relationship with the child or adolescent and family throughout their social changes and/or physical interventions.

There are no physical interventions available for prepubertal children, but they can transition socially, assuming a new name and their preferred gender identity full-time. Because there isn't enough research yet on the outcomes of children who transition early, the SOC does not take a stand on whether children should or should not be allowed to socially transition. It encourages mental health professionals to work with families to evaluate the pros and cons and communicate their decisions sensitively to their children.

There are physical interventions available for adolescents, beginning in puberty. These have been divided into:

Fully reversible interventions: GnRH analogues (and at times other medications) are used to suppress estrogen or testosterone production and thus delay the development of secondary sex characteristics. The SOC describes the pros and cons of such treatment, and how it should be monitored. These treatments are initiated after puberty has started, and after a thorough assessment determines that the adolescent meets the criteria and will benefit from them. This allows the adolescent time to explore more thoroughly their gender identity and expression. Stopping these interventions allows puberty to proceed as genetically programmed.

Partially reversible interventions: Adolescents are eligible for cross-gender hormone therapy at the age of majority or with parental consent. This will initiate the development of the desired secondary sex characteristics and continue to suppress unwanted development. The typical masculinizing and feminizing treatment regimens are modified to take into consideration the physical and emotional development of the adolescent. If these are discontinued later in adolescence or in young adulthood normal pubertal development will resume.

Irreversible interventions: Chest surgery for adolescents wishing a masculine presentation can be done after sufficient time living in role and/or one year of testosterone treatment, with parental consent and recommendation by a mental health professional. It is recommended that adolescents attempt their social transition before chest surgery. Genital surgery cannot be approved until the person has reached the age of majority and met the other requirements (such as living in role for a year).

These medical interventions are recommended as harm-reduction strategies, given the degree of abuse and harassment that gender nonconforming adolescents endure and its effect on their mental health.

Mental Health

The next section of the SOC is written for mental health professionals (MHP) who work with TG/TS/NGC (primarily adult) clients. It begins with setting the minimum requirements for those qualified to do so:

> ➢ A Master's degree in a mental health field from an accredited institution, appropriately credentialed in their state.
> ➢ Competence in mental health diagnosis, using the DSM and ICD and the ability to distinguish between gender dysphoria and other mental health issues.
> ➢ Documented supervised training in counseling or psychotherapy.
> ➢ An understanding of gender nonconforming identities and expressions as well as the assessment and treatment of gender dysphoria.
> ➢ Continuing education in the assessment and treatment of gender dysphoria.

The SOC also recommends ongoing development of "cultural competence", which involves familiarity with the TG/TS/GNC community and awareness of public policy and current events. Knowledge of sexuality and sexual health concerns and disorders is also recommended.

The new Standards devote another 10 pages to the various roles and tasks that at a mental health professional can undertake with TG/TS/GNC clients. The clear message from these is that services must be "consumer-driven". The first task of the MHP is to ascertain what the client is looking for and how he or she can help. It states "mental health professionals may serve as a psychotherapist, counselor, or family therapist, or as a diagnostician/assessor, advocate, or educator."[100]

---

[100] p. 23

The following guidelines are listed for the different tasks of the mental health professional:

Assessment of gender dysphoria: An evaluation should include an assessment of gender identity and dysphoria, a history of the gender-related concerns, the impact of "minority stress", and the availability of support from others.

Education: Any assessment or intervention should include information about the diversity of gender identity and presentations as well as various treatment options for gender dysphoria. These options can then by explored, along with their short and long-term consequences.

Assessment and treatment of co-existing mental health concerns: The MHP should screen for the difficulties common among TG/TS/GNC clients, as well as other disorders, and present treatment options for those. The presence of other mental health disorders does not necessarily prevent further treatment for gender dysphoria, but should be addressed first. Appropriate medication can be prescribed or recommended and referrals made if necessary.

Assess eligibility, prepare, and refer for hormone therapy: The new Standards make it clear that decision-making regarding hormone therapy is a collaborative process, and provide guidelines for helping clients prepare, as well as making the appropriate referrals.

Assess eligibility, prepare and refer for surgery: Again, decision-making for breast or chest surgery and genital surgery is considered a collaborative process. Guidelines for preparing clients and writing the appropriate letters are covered.

These tasks are best done by a qualified mental health professional, but other trained health professionals may provide assessment, education and referral, particularly within a multidisciplinary team that provides other treatments for TG/TS/GNC clients/patients.

Psychotherapy: One of the major changes in Version 7 is that while psychotherapy is highly recommended, it makes it clear that it is not a requirement for hormone therapy and surgery. There is no minimum time or number of sessions set for the assessment and referral process. This is intended to not only reduce the obstacles to further treatment but also to open up the psychotherapy process to genuine exploration of all concerns. The goals of psychotherapy and ways that MHP can help clients are covered, including clarifying and exploring gender identity and expression, coping with minority stress, and facilitating the coming out process. For those planning a gender transition, the MHP can help the client develop an individualized transition plan. Psychotherapy can be individual, couple, family or group, as needed. Support for family members and peer support groups are encouraged. Caution is advised in providing on-line or long-distance counseling.

Other tasks of the mental health professional: MHPs are encouraged to educate and advocate on behalf of TG/TS/GNC clients, consult with community members when necessary, provide documentation for changes in legal documents, and remain knowledgeable about the needs of the TG/TS/GNC community. Understanding cultural differences in their communities is also expected.

Ethical guidelines: In addition to the ethical principles of their mental health profession, the following guidelines apply: 1) treatment aimed at changing a client's gender identity is unethical, and 2) if an MHP is uncomfortable or unfamiliar with TG/TS/GNC clients he or she must either refer to a competent provider or seek expert supervision/consultation.

These new guidelines make it clear that the therapist is no longer a gate-keeper, but a valuable guide and ally in the transition process.

Hormone Therapy

This sections begins by emphasizing that hormone therapy is a medical necessity for many TG/TS/GNC people with gender dysphoria. It also states that hormone treatment is not just for those who wish complete gender reassignment, and must be individualized to the person's goals, medical issues and social context.

Criteria for hormone therapy: Hormone therapy can start after the psychosocial assessment and informed consent process have been completed. A referral letter from the MHP who conducted the assessment is required, unless the assessment was done by a specially qualified health professional who prescribes hormones. The minimum criteria are:

- persistent, well-documented gender dysphoria,
- capacity for fully-informed consent,
- age of majority or with parental consent, and
- adequate control of any significant physical or mental health conditions.

Physical effects of hormone therapy: The SOC provides charts for the timing of the different effects that can be expected of masculinizing and feminizing hormones. For masculinizing hormones this includes: deepening voice, clitoral enlargement, growth of facial and body hair, cessation of menstruation, increased libido, skin changes, increased muscle mass and strength, and body fat redistribution. For feminizing hormone treatment this includes: breast growth, decreased libido and changes in sexual functioning, redistribution of body fat, skin softening, decreased muscle mass and strength, and changes in hair growth. It emphasizes that the amount and timing of physical changes varies depending on dose, particular medications, and method of administration. It states that results cannot be predicted based on age, body type, ethnicity, or family appearance. No particular medications or method of administration is recommended over any other.

Risks of hormone therapy: The medical risks of hormone therapy are also listed, and rated according to current research. Details are provided in Appendices. The most likely risks are blood clots, gallstones, elevated liver enzymes, weight gain and elevated triglycerides with feminizing hormones and polycythemia, weight gain, acne, sleep apnea and balding for masculinizing hormones.

Information for Physicians: The next ten pages go into more detail for the physicians who prescribe hormones. They outline competency requirements, responsibilities of prescribers, different clinical situations they may encounter, risk assessment for MHT and FHT, hormone regimens, clinical monitoring for safety and effectiveness of the treatment regimens, and the use of bioidentical hormones.

Reproductive Health: The Standards of Care cover the reproductive options for TG/TS patients and urge all health care professional to discuss them with their patients. A review of the options should take place before hormone treatment or surgery. MtF patients should be informed about sperm preservation and encouraged to bank their sperm before hormone therapy. FtM patients should be counseled regarding egg or embryo freezing and the chances of fertility returning if testosterone therapy is stopped for a period of time. Reproductive options should not be refused to TG/TS/GNC patients.

Voice and Communication Therapy

The SOC outlines competency requirements for voice and communication specialists who work with TG/TS/GNC clients. Specialized training and continuing education is required, as well as an understanding of transgender health. Respect for the individual's goals is considered essential. "Individuals should not be counseled to adopt behaviors with which they are not comfortable or which do not feel authentic."[101] Vocal health should be emphasized, especially after voice feminization surgery. This is a new section of the Standards of Care, and an important one for those seeking voice feminization.

---

[101] p. 53

Surgery

This section begins by stating that sex reassignment surgery is not only overwhelmingly beneficial but often medically necessary. It goes into the ethical considerations that many surgeons have about removing or altering otherwise healthy body parts and explains the joint responsibility of the surgeon, patient and mental health professional. Competency requirements for surgeons who perform the various surgeries are specified. Appropriate surgeons are encouraged to learn more about gender dysphoria and how and when SRS becomes a medical necessity. Collaboration with mental health and other professionals is encouraged, to ensure continuity of care and appropriate after-care.

The requirements for surgeries have not changed substantially in Version 7, but there is a greater responsibility placed on the surgeon in the informed consent process. Surgeons are responsible for discussing with TG/TS/GNC patients:

- the different surgical techniques available,
- the advantages and disadvantages of each technique,
- the limitations of their procedures (with realistic before and after pictures), and
- the risks and complications of various techniques, and the frequency of those in their practices.

The surgeon is responsible for providing enough information that the patient has realistic expectations and can make a truly informed decision. (In other words, they need to do more than just try to sell you on their services.)

The surgical procedures discussed in the Standards of Care include:

> breast surgery (augmentation mammoplasty), genital surgery (penectomy, orchiectomy, vaginoplasty, clitoroplasty, vulvoplasty), and aesthetic procedures (facial feminization, liposuction, tracheal shave, hair reconstruction, etc.) for the male-to-female patient,

> chest surgery (mastectomy, chest contouring), genital surgery (hysterectomy and/or ovariectomy, reconstruction of the urethra, metoidioplasty, phalloplasty, vaginectomy, scrotoplasty, and implantation of erection and/or testicular prostheses) and aesthetic procedures (liposuction, pectoral implants, etc.) for the female-to-male patient.

Criteria for breast or chest surgery: One letter of referral from a qualified mental health professional is required for breast augmentation or chest reconstruction. The following must be documented:

- persistent gender dysphoria,
- capacity for fully informed consent,
- age of majority, and
- adequate control of any medical or mental health issues.

Hormone therapy is not a prerequisite for breast /chest surgery. It is recommended, however, that MtF patients have at least one year of feminizing hormone therapy, for best results.

Criteria for hysterectomy/ovariectomy in FtM patients and orchiectomy in MtF patients. Two letters of referral from qualified mental health professionals are required - one from a treating MHP and another from a consulting MHP. These must document:

- persistent gender dysphoria,
- capacity for fully informed consent,
- age of majority,
- adequate control of any medical or mental health issues, and
- 12 months of hormone therapy (unless contraindicated).

Criteria for metoidoplasty or phalloplasty in FtM patients and vaginoplasty in MtF patients. Two letters of referral from qualified mental health professionals are required - one from a treating MHP and another from a consulting MHP. These must document:

- persistent gender dysphoria,
- capacity for fully informed consent,
- age of majority,
- adequate control of any medical or mental health issues,
- 12 months of hormone therapy (unless contraindicated), and
- 12 months of living in the gender role consistent with their gender identity.

It is not an absolute requirement, but it is recommended that patients have ongoing counseling with a qualified mental health professional. Patients with severe psychiatric issues must be stabilized with psychotherapy and/or medication before referral for surgery, and reassessed prior to surgery.

The SOC explains the rationale for a full year of living in an identity-congruent gender role. "The duration of 12 months allows for a range of different life experiences and events that may occur throughout the year (e.g., family events, holidays, vacations, season-specific work or school experiences). During this time, patients should present consistently, on a day-to-day basis and across all settings of life, in their desired gender role. This includes coming out to partners, family, friends, and community members (e.g., at school, work, other settings)."[102]

A brief overview of the techniques and complications of various surgeries is provided, with recommendations for post-operative and follow-up care. This leads into:

Lifelong Preventive and Primary Care

The SOC stress the importance of ongoing medical care throughout the lives of TG/TS/GNC people, especially after any medical treatment for gender dysphoria. This section provides information for primary care physicians to better provide ongoing transgender health care. Specific references are listed for guidelines for primary care. In addition to routine health screenings, the following areas are discussed:

Cancer screenings: The challenges of cancer screenings of reproductive organs include the risk of over-screening due to lack of relevant research, under-screening and missing treatable cancers, and the reluctance of many TG/TS/GNC patients to undergo certain procedures.

Urogenital Care: Gynecological care is recommended for (pre-op and non-op) FtM patients and post-operative MtF patients. MtF patients need follow-up care and counseling regarding their new genitalia, especially around sexual health concerns. They may also need care for urinary tract problems, due to the mechanics of genital reconstruction. FtM patients who retain their vagina may experience changes that make examinations difficult, but lack of treatment can make those changes worse. FtM patients are likely to be very conflicted about internal exams and need to be counseled sensitively.

---

[102] p. 61

The Standards of Care concludes with two sections about applications in special circumstances:

Applicability of the Standards of Care to People Living in Institutional Environments

The SOC makes a point of saying that all of these guidelines can and should be applied to all TG/TS/GNC individuals, regardless of their living situation. This is meant to apply to prisons as well as other settings such as long-term health care facilities. Residents of those facilities should not be denied care, and outside consultation should be provided if in-house staff are not qualified. More specifically, people who have begun masculinizing or feminizing hormone treatment should not be denied access to them, and those who are appropriate to begin hormone treatment should be allowed to do so. Accommodations need to be made to protect the dignity and safety of all TG/TS/GNC residents. "Institutions where transsexual, transgender, and gender nonconforming people reside and receive health care should monitor for a tolerant and positive climate to ensure that residents are not under attack by staff or other residents."[103]

Applicability of the Standards of Care to People with Disorders of Sexual Development

The term "disorders of sexual development" (DSD) refers to physical conditions of the reproductive tract resulting from atypical development. This includes many intersex conditions. It is still a controversial term, but is included in the SOC because it is current medical terminology. Traditionally (in the DSM IV) a diagnosis of a DSD disqualified someone from a diagnosis of Gender Identity Disorder. This will hopefully be rectified in DSM V, with a change to Gender Dysphoria rather than Gender Identity Disorder. Those with both a DSD and

---

[103] p. 68

gender dysphoria would be considered a subset of that diagnosis. They present with unique physical and psychological concerns.

Deviations of sexual development are often diagnosed at birth, or in utero via ultrasound. They are typically treated surgically at birth, or soon after, and a birth sex assigned, after consultation with the family and medical specialists. Other DSDs don't show up until puberty, with the development (or lack of development) of secondary sex characteristics. Rarely, the DSD diagnosis is made in adulthood as part of the assessment of gender dysphoria. Most people with a DSD do not develop gender dysphoria, but some do. The Standards of Care are relevant in treating those individuals, but need to be applied in the context of the existing medical condition. Any change in gender role assignment should occur only after a thorough assessment. It is suggested that six months of consistent gender dysphoria and gender variance be observed before implementing the SOC guidelines.

It is clear from the wording of this section that there is still controversy in this area, and perhaps conflicts between pediatric specialists (endocrinologists and urologists) and gender specialists. The SOC defers to the guidelines developed by those pediatric specialists. This is an area that should see some changes in the next edition, with more input from the transgender and intersex community.

About the Author

Anne L. Boedecker, PhD is a licensed psychologist and senior gender specialist. She obtained her PhD in Human Development from The Pennsylvania State University, and completed her internship at the Counseling/Psychological Services Center at the University of Texas at Austin. She has been in private practice in central New Hampshire since 1981, proudly serving the GLBTQI community. She has taught at several area colleges, and presented many workshops and talks. She is also a trained SoulCollage® Facilitator, and leads workshops in spirituality and expressive art. When she is not working she enjoys horseback riding, cooking, gardening, shopping and making art.